FOR A BETTER WORLD

FOR A BETTER WORLD

Reading and Writing
for Social Action

RANDY BOMER & KATHERINE BOMER

HEINEMANN • PORTSMOUTH, NH

Heinemann
A division of Reed Elsevier Inc.
361 Hanover Street
Portsmouth, NH 03801–3912
www.heinemann.com

Offices and agents throughout the world

The authors and publisher wish to thank those who have generously given permission to reprint borrowed material:

"If We Sing Together" lyrics by Anita Hollander. Copyright © 1998 by Anita Hollander. Reprinted by permission. All rights reserved.

Library of Congress Cataloging-in-Publication Data
Bomer, Randy.
   For a better world : reading and writing for social action / Randy Bomer and Katherine Bomer.
      p. cm.
   Includes bibliographical references and index.
   ISBN 0-325-00263-0 (alk. paper)
   1. Language arts—Social aspects—United States.   2. English language—Composition and exercises—Study and teaching—United States.   3. Critical pedagogy—United States.
   4. Social justice—Study and teaching—United States.   I. Bomer, Katherine.   II. Title.

LB1576 .B516 2001
302.2′244—dc21

                                                                              2001039312

Editor: William Varner
Production: Vicki Kasabian
Cover design: Jenny Jensen Greenleaf
Authors' photo: Rob Kling
Manufacturing: Louise Richardson

Printed in the United States of America on acid-free paper

08   07   06   05   04   VP   5   6   7   8

*Dedicated to every educator who spends
part of her teaching day
turned against the current.*

CONTENTS

ACKNOWLEDGMENTS

One of the guiding principals of this book is that people do not read and write alone but in communities, and we have been blessed with a series of wonderfully helpful communities as we have worked on this project. We are speaking in echoes from many previous conversations, and since those talks were the best part of the work, we need to name our partners here.

Some of the work we describe began when we both worked at the Teachers College Reading and Writing Project in New York City, where we met brilliant teachers, administrators, and teacher educators. Over our years there, conversations with Donna Santman, Kate Montgomery, Carl Anderson, Kathy Collins, Isoke Nia, Kathleen Tolan, Grace Chough, Terry Moore, Shirley McPhillips, Kathryn Meyer Doyle, Brenda Wallace, and Georgia Heard were especially nourishing to the thinking in this book. We both owe our careers, not to mention many of the habits of our thinking, to Lucy McCormick Calkins, our teacher, mentor, colleague, and friend.

Many of Katherine's teaching colleagues have helped grow these ideas. Anne Powers provided a model for the fourth and fifth graders of someone who lives a life of social action and also introduced the biography study of freedom fighters to the classroom. Kate Abell and Alva Buxenbaum brought rich experience with social activism and education to the collaboration early on. Brenda Steele, a passionate and intelligent administrator, gave the gift of her trust that our social action study was the best teaching we could be doing in the classroom. Cindi Byun and Natalie Louis were student teachers in Katherine's New York class while we conducted the research, and their input and conferences with children were immensely helpful. Most important, we are grateful to the students in Katherine's classrooms who gave their energy and caring so fully to making the world better. It was in their spirit of hope that we saw the title, *For a Better World*.

Conversations with Randy's partners at Queens College—Doug Dixon, David Gerwin, Phil Anderson, Rikki Asher, and Jack Zevin—occurred at crucial junctures in our inquiry, and our thinking was richer as a result. At Indiana University, collaborations with Beth Berghoff, Amy Seely Flint, Jerome Harste, Mary Beth Hines, Chris Leland, and Mitzi Lewison have helped us to mature our initial ideas by laying them out alongside the advanced thinking of others.

Bill Varner has been as patient, supportive, and wise an editor as anyone could ever hope for. The referees for the manuscript were generous and helpful, and we are grateful to them; we can thank two of them by name, Patrick Shannon and Maureen Barbieri.

It should not go without saying that the conversational turn we take here comes late in a dialogue that has been ongoing for a long time. We were brought into the conversation about education for social justice initially by our teacher Maxine Greene and later by our friends Carole Edelsky, Patrick Shannon, and Bess Altwerger. We are grateful to all the voices resonating through the decades, to all who have kept alive the intention that education should be about more than reproducing the most thoughtless and unjust elements of our society. We hope our contribution here can help bring more people into that discussion.

INTRODUCTION
Questioning Our Teaching and Making It Better

Like many teachers, we have talked with colleagues at times about just closing our classroom doors and teaching according to our beliefs. Sometimes, that strategy has served us and our students pretty well. But if we really lived within our own classroom walls, isolated in our own little teaching worlds, we might never have been troubled by what was so obviously missing from our students' writing and reading. We had developed an image of what good writing and reading could be, and we valued our students' progress in that direction. We could see the significance in what our students were doing. But, because we had such a definite image of quality literacy, we could not see what was left out by that vision.

What we did not see was that student readers and writers were rarely reaching consciously for socially significant ideas in their language and thinking. Though they wrote about things that were privately important to them, they usually did not go the extra step toward connecting their interests to socially significant themes. This blind spot in our teaching slowly became illuminated by insistent critiques from others in the larger conversation about literacy education.

Criticisms of our teaching are not new to us. Teaching writing and reading as social processes is a big break from education as usual. Educational conservatives (think E. D. Hirsch or William Bennett), who want to maintain a centralized, controlled culture, naturally object to the kind of pedagogy in which students study their own lived experience and teachers honor the language of students' everyday lives. That's neither surprising nor upsetting.

But what about the criticisms of those speaking up for the marginalized and arguing for social change, those interested in empowering students to participate in that change? Many of these people complain that writing process and whole language teachers work in ways not all that different from the practice we worked so hard to change. Much of our teaching focuses on the individual (to the exclusion of collective social knowledge and action) and ends up reproducing the same old dominant culture and social divisions. We don't provide explicit instruction in the forms of writing that help get people power in society (Christie 1989; Cope and Kalantzis 1993; Lemke 1995; Walton 1996). We emphasize artistic and personal writing at the expense of more politically engaged, socially transforming kinds of writing (Power 1995). We advocate a weak or transparent teacher presence that invites the inequities of the wider world to fill the vacuum (Bernstein 1990; Gilbert 1989; Lensmire 1994). We employ the language and values of middle-class capitalism (take the word *ownership,* for example) (Dudley-Marling and Searle 1995; Kamberelis 1993). We don't question the cultural ideology out of which students write and read (Gilbert 1994; McCormick 1994). Overall, writing process and whole language have been described as politically naïve at best and, at worst, as a means for the white middle class to keep the oppressed busy playing with toys and sucking on pacifiers while that same white middle class reaps all of society's benefits.

If that is what we're doing, we want to stop it.

The Political Importance of Unheard Voices

We want to preserve an observing, listening, researching stance in teaching, to honor what students are saying about their lives and learning. The default assumption about education is that the teacher's attention is primarily on the material to be taught and the most effective means for delivering that material to students. This is what Freire (1970) called "the banking model of education." This assumption is undemocratic because it takes the process of change out of the hands of the people directly affected by the change. It remains undemocratic even when the content is intended to be emancipatory—that is, to convey understanding that helps people liberate themselves from oppression.

Progressive literacy pedagogies have developed strategies that allow students' language and thinking to be respected. Miscue analysis (Goodman 1973; Goodman, Watson, and Burke 1987) assumes that readers' mistakes show not their ignorance but rather their knowledge of language systems. The same is true for error analysis of student writing (Shaughnessy 1977). Retrospective miscue analysis (Goodman and Marek 1996) assumes that readers are equipped, by virtue of their own linguistic competence, to recognize, reflect on, and learn from their miscues. Bilingual and multicultural education (Edelsky 1986; Nieto 1999) and the various sociolinguistic approaches to multiple dialects in classrooms (Heath 1983; Perry and Delpit 1998; Smitherman-Donaldson 2000) respect and accept the everyday language of students and their families and friends. Pedagogical perspectives like these say to students and the general public, "Your language is competent, intelligent, coherent, and good enough for your learning." They dismiss assumptions of deficit in favor of respect.

Writing process pedagogies (Atwell 1986; Calkins 1994; Graves 1982; Murray 1985) assume that not only is student language good enough for school, but so are their life experiences and interests. The stories, views, and expertise of ordinary people, even ordinary little children, are as significant as those of powerful adults. A democracy depends on public attention to the concerns of its members. A conversation aimed at bringing more social justice into a culture must, in part, stem from individual life stories. Furthermore, learning to speak out in the world about what previously seemed domestic and walled in is a step toward political efficacy. When we write, we are always doing something with and to others; writing in school should also address real audiences for real purposes. Only by participating in communities where others are waiting to hear from us, where a group believes our words and thoughts are significant, can we develop a habit of speaking out about things we care about.

Language is the medium of democracy. Unless everyone's ways with words are accepted into the great conversation, any conception of public dialogue and mutual decision making is, at best, partial and, at worst, illegitimate and unstable. Unless people can speak to others about what their lives are like—and be heard—there is no mechanism for the political system to work for all its constituents. Failing to ask people to tell their stories is not only rude and uncivil but also a functional failure of a democratic public. If voices of the vulnerable are silent, there is no hope of renewal and justice.

The Political Importance of Choice and Freedom

We cannot imagine teaching in a way that overrides students' decisions about what they read and write. First, any teaching that does not harness itself to the energy of students' interests, motives, wills, and intentions is pushing itself uphill. Furthermore, acculturating students to becoming active, involved, purposeful, deliberative citizens requires that they be allowed to make decisions about what they are learning and what they are doing as their identities evolve.

Too often, people think the idea of letting students choose their own topic or text comes from the romantic notion that adults shouldn't interfere with children's development, that it should be allowed to unfold naturally. Letting kids "do what they want" sometimes strikes observers as quaintly soft-headed and naïve. This may be because some teachers express the principle of choice as a negative: "In writing workshop, you don't assign the topic. Kids get to choose their own." But the value of choice is part of something larger and more important in literacy education: intention and initiative in using language. This is not about letting things happen "naturally." Learning to use literacy to obtain or accomplish something is a cultural norm and a political predisposition, one that adults must pass on to children.

A literacy event is what it is largely because of what the participants intend. Writing to an assigned topic, no matter how "good" the teacher thinks the assignment, is, from the writer's perspective, largely if not entirely an act of compliance rather than a linguistic *doing* meant to affect the world. Asking writers to come up with a topic, to formulate a purpose with respect to readers, to design the content and form of their piece, to pay enough attention to their own dialogue with the world that they can identify trails of thought they would like to develop through writing—this is more than a different route to the same goal. *It is a different literacy.* True, some elements of craft in writing (design, diction, grammar, spelling) can be taught in the context of drafting and revising regardless of whether or not the topic and purpose came from the writer; however, the essence of craft lies in what the writer is trying to *do*. If the writer's task is compliance, the craft of written expression easily becomes identified in the writer's mind with pleasing authority—"doing it right."

The only way to be free is to act freely. In a study of Americans' perceptions of their freedoms, James Gibson (1993) found that a surprisingly large percentage of the citizens he surveyed thought that the government would prevent them from publishing pamphlets, making speeches criticizing the government, or organizing protest marches and public meetings. However, those who had been politically active in the past were significantly more likely to perceive of themselves as free to act. Gibson concludes that "to the extent that citizens confidently assert freedom, it seems to be available to them" (131). Likewise, the experience of coming up with something to say, developing intention and purpose, invoking an audience, and speaking out in the world *gives* one a sense of having important things to say and the language with which to say them. *Efficacy,* the sense that one can act politically on purpose, arises from experience. Such a promise confirms the importance of student initiative and intention while pointing up the need for explicitly political work in literacy education.

The Political Importance of Art

Art encodes what is important to people in the border between the personal and the public. On momentous social occasions, it is more likely that a poem, a song, or a story, not rhetoric, will linger in public memory. More people remember Maya Angelou's reading at Clinton's first inauguration than the then new President's speech. Poetry is better able than an editorial, a letter to the mayor, even a legal brief, to change hearts and minds. Only poetry has the grace to reside at funerals and weddings, to mark the transformations in peoples' lives, to say what cannot be said.

Looking in on most writing workshops, we usually see students working in literary genres: poetry, memoir, short stories, feature articles, personal essays. The historical reasons for the persistent centrality of these kinds of texts in writing process classrooms are complex, but there are functional reasons as well. To differing degrees, these genres are found in children's literature, so kids are more likely to experience them as authentic—the kinds of texts real writers make rather than school assignments. Students learn to craft their writing by emulating writers they like. It is more difficult to accomplish the same ends with nonliterary forms such as petitions, newsletters, status reports, research memos, letters of complaint, grant proposals, and city ordinances.

Furthermore, nonliterary genres emerge out of a need felt by a writer, or more commonly a group of writers, living in a community and interacting with other community members in ways that raise problems writing can help solve. You don't just sit down to write a letter of complaint; the need arises in life, and the genre is always and only tied to that need. The letter has no life apart from its social context; that is its power and its limitation. Pieces of literature, on the other hand, are relatively detachable from the contexts in which they are made. That is, anyone can pick them up and read them at any time, and they are still interesting. They appeal to a more general audience. A writer can say *I think I'll make a poem* without necessarily having experienced a social situation that *requires* a poem. Art can live independent of its specific location and the interactions that provoke it; it is, as Ezra Pound said, "news that stays news."

For teachers, this means that a student's poem can be published on a bulletin board, in a class magazine, in a collection of other poems, or on the Internet, and people—kids and adults—can read it, like it, respond to it. The student has as real a relationship with the audience as any professional writer does. A whole class can investigate the genre of poetry, all the kids can write poems, and everyone can *still* have a real audience in mind and receive a real response from that audience. In contrast, if we do a genre study of petitions, it will be inauthentic from the start, since it's not likely that every student's life has led him or her to petition someone at the same time. Most of the students will pretend to petition someone, and that quality of practice writing, of writing in order to learn how to write instead of writing in real interaction with real readers, is inauthentic (Edelsky 1992).

Inauthentic writing experiences are disempowering because they keep student writers *students*, dependent on the authority of the teacher instead of engaged in linguistic action. When a writer writes a petition because she has to for class, she isn't petitioning, she's obeying authority. Whenever a writer isn't really *plugged in* to the world outside the classroom, to an audience wider than the teacher, he is politically less powerful, regardless of the genre, than he would be if he wrote a poem that would be read by real readers. Chapters 7 and 8 introduce strategies for supporting student writing for social action that circumvent this difficulty.

Some of the critique of writing process is really a critique of art. Many educators ignore the fact that poems, stories (even personal stories), and plays are legitimate and potent ways of responding to social realities and of acting on them. They are not cute, fluffy middle-class genres fit only as diversions for people with ample leisure time. The history of literature is full of socially engaged artists—from Aristophanes to Jonathan Swift to Victor Hugo, from Dickens to Gorky to Neruda to Havel to Vargas-Llosa—whose works, through an appeal to the imagination and through passionate craft, contributed to social critique and social change. In contemporary America, our poets are at least as likely as anyone else, through their art, to be voices for the powerless: Amiri Baraka, Adrienne Rich, Jimmy Santiago Baca, Carolyn Forché, Sapphire. Writers currently in jail around the world would be surprised to hear of the political irrelevance of artistic genres, and so would the governments that imprison them. If children's writing in writing workshops bears no resemblance to these writers' work, the reason may be our failure to help them think about social issues during their years in school, not some flaw in the genres or processes of writing. (Of course, all art does not need to take up explicitly political topics; there would be something neo-Stalinist in asserting that literature must advance the cause of the proletariat or else be censored as a bourgeois instrument of oppression.)

Almost all varieties of aesthetic knowing—visual arts, manual arts, music, dance, drama—are marginalized in schools when they aren't absent altogether. Only literature remains central in most schools' curricula. What is lost in general is tremendous, and what is lost in terms of educating for social justice is also huge. Creating freedom, for oneself or for others, is always an act of imagination, of envisioning, of creating a new world (Greene 1995). If we expect people to vote for the interests of the wounded and dispossessed, then people who are not poor have to be able to imagine other lives, to reach out with their consciousness and know what their own narrow experience has not taught them. For an individual to think generously about a cause, she must be able to think about the details of personal life, about the minute struggles with which people need help. When our students are among disenfranchised groups, they need urgently to be able to tell their story, because it is those stories, as much as it is high rhetoric or programmatic proposals, that will provoke change. So-called personal writing concerns itself with the human details that fuel the caring imagination and do so at a level diverse groups can more easily understand.

Yes, But . . .

Yes, it's important for classrooms to take democracy and associated principles, such as justice, freedom, fraternity, and participation, as primary concerns. But in our culture at present, it takes concentration, strategic planning, and deliberate language to keep such ideas foremost in our minds. Plenty of times we have failed:

- We have not helped students analyze the social and cultural assumptions in texts they read and write or in the world in which they live.
- We have neglected to look into students' thinking-on-paper and see the social and political themes in what seem to be personal thoughts.
- We have not been open enough with students about the political reasons for our teaching decisions or helped them think about classroom life in terms of democracy.
- Our classroom life is still insular, separated from the world. Even when we publish student work, that work tends to come from private life; it is rarely a response to social realities or a project to alter them.
- Even when we have tried deliberately to attend to issues of social justice, we have too often done so only under the teacher's guidance, too seldom handed the process of critique and action over to the students.
- Our talk with colleagues is too often apolitical. We act as if the grounds for persuading one another were only utilitarian ("this works better") or some hierarchy of quality ("this is a more effective way of improving kids' reading"). The democratic character of everyday life in our classrooms and the possible public futures we are creating should be at least as important as these considerations.
- We often have taken no part in political processes, paid no attention to legislation and policy that affects students' lives at least as much as our teaching can. We have let ourselves get mired in today's busyness at the expense of tomorrow's transformations.

We don't just feel guilty or downcast, though. Rather, we know that all our revisions to teaching have come from the sense that something was missing, from unease and some confusion. And so we have begun trying to address the problems we see so far, knowing that in a few years new dissatisfactions will emerge and we will revise our teaching once again.

What We Talk About When We Talk About Reading and Writing

Some classrooms include a lot of talk about skills, some talk about following instructions, some talk about standards imposed by outside agencies. Then again, some classrooms talk about beautiful language and aesthetic pleasure, some talk about personal memories, and some talk about self-expression and creativity. Though any of these things might come up in our classrooms, we have been working to place important concepts about social justice at the center of our discourse. Though we work on skills and discuss what others have said about standards, we talk *more* about difference and fairness. Though we talk about personal memories, we try to explore *more* how those memories illuminate aspects of culture and social relationships. In our examinations of language, we are concerned *more than before* with how power relationships bring out some features while silencing others. Holding democracy at the center of our conversation transforms the images and themes we see in books, the topics we write about, and the ways we look at the world. Chapter 2 looks more closely at classroom discourse and ways to heighten attention to critical concepts; Chapter 10 addresses the deep political content of even students' most personal writing.

Analysis and Critique

Every text, whether written by a twenty-first-century child or a thirteenth-century monk, is created from within a worldview. According to the author's particular perspective, some things are important enough to go into the text, and some things are unimportant enough to be left out. When a reader infers what parts of the social world are being omitted from the language of a text and what those omissions mean, that's critique.

Some texts are designed to make us look at the world and see things we have not noticed before. They point out blind spots in our big, national conversation. They push us to see things about the world that could be better. When we use these texts to think about aspects of the social world that are usually hidden from our view, that's also critique.

Some people raised in religious families learn to spot in texts, television, and movies the subtlest traces of values that contradict their beliefs. That is critique too. But in the United States, we do not and cannot have a national religion. What we have instead are shared political values that center on secular, public conceptions of the good life. Democratic literacy education succeeds inasmuch as it sensitizes students to these values and concepts, makes them aware when they are being compromised by the worldviews in texts, and helps them imagine ways in which to respond to those breaches. Our teaching is most democratic, as well as most relevant to our students' present lives *and* future citizenship, when students develop the habit of interrogating the word and the world in the interest of justice in public life.

A democratic imperative calls on us as teachers to imagine a new set of skills and concepts for young readers and writers (Christensen 2000). They need to learn to analyze not simply in some static, traditional way—identifying plot, character, theme, and symbolism—but rather for the more durable elements of public interest. They need to learn to evaluate their own writing not just in terms of whether they "have a good lead" or surprising language, but also in terms of the importance of their purposes and projects. Concentrating on significant social values angles students' literate activity toward creating more equality, fraternity, and liberty in our shared life. Chapter 2, in its discussion of concepts in critical reading, and Chapter 3, in its descriptions of growing classroom conversations about socially significant ideas, make these ideas clearer.

How We Talk About What We Do

We do not often enough induct students into a language of democracy by thinking through with them the policies, practices, and procedures of our teaching and learning environments. In classrooms, students get used to living publicly in a particular way, they become habituated to what Dewey called a "mode of associated living." An expanded conception of democracy and critical literacy is the subject of much of Chapter 1. When we create classrooms that honor students' decisions, support students' collaboration and concern for one another, and sustain their open-ended inquiry, we are applying democratic principles to our teaching. This is important because we want students to carry these habits of mind and activity with them into the larger world. To support this transfer, however, we need to share with our students the language that informed our decision making in crafting this kind of environment. Having the names of things, being able to use words as tools to think and communicate, is essential if students are to use that thinking to inform the communities in which they participate when they are away from us. We need to talk up democracy when we talk with the class about what we are doing, how we are living together.

Unfortunately, the term *classroom management* probably helps our minds remain stuck on "command and control." Leading in a democratic community is quite different. Issues of safety, order, work environment, and respect can be addressed in a democratic discourse just as well as they can in an authoritarian one of "because I said so." It takes more words, and it requires that we respect student reasoning about the shared community enough to take the time to bring them that discourse.

As teachers, so much of our talk is procedural: we are forever giving instructions. Fortunately, language about democracy is procedural too. When we make teaching decisions using concepts such as fairness, respect for difference, and freedom of expression, we are weighing the sometimes competing values of democracy. We have the opportunity, if we choose to take it, to discuss those ideas with students. If we don't discuss them and resort to "just do it," we give our students a little more practice at living in an autocracy, even when we mean it to be liberating. Even our instructions can be experiences for social thoughtfulness. Chapter 3, which discusses political conversations growing out of a classroom's shared life, and Chapter 4, which brings out the political reasoning behind a number of structures in the reading workshop, discuss these ideas more fully and specifically.

Relationship to the Outside World

Throughout our teaching, we have tried to make our classrooms "permeable" (Dyson 1993) by inviting students to bring their lives into their official schoolwork and by working to affect students' literate lives outside school. What we have not done often enough is position our classroom work head to head with the social world outside of school. We have not concentrated enough on learning about social problems, caring about them, and trying to do something to help. Even if a group of kids aren't going to change the world in one school year, they ought to be in the habit of thinking in dialogue with political and social realities. We want them to believe that the world will respond to their action, to learn the diligence of striving, to develop identities as democratic participants, to be willing to walk "the long haul" (Horton, Kohl, and Kohl 1998).

Most classes in schools define themselves partly through the conceit—"we here in this room are becoming enlightened in a special way." It's good that people who live in schools should think this way. But part of the learning process ought to include, as its necessary and logical extension, a passion for making the world better. That's not merely a pleasant dessert to be indulged in after the main course of "real learning"; rather, it is having a different idea of "what we are doing here" from the start. This agenda is clearest in Chapter 7, about teaching students to note social themes in a writers notebook, and Chapter 8, which describes a process of getting students writing for social action.

Teachers' Roles in the World and Their Professional Conversations

It has become almost commonplace to note that part of the National Writing Project's success is attributable to the fact that it gets teachers to pay attention to their own writing. Teachers teach best from within processes they understand from direct experience. The same principle applies to democratic efficacy and action. Once teachers have done some political work, have endeavored to affect public opinion and public policy, they have a much more detailed knowledge about what they are trying to teach their students when they educate for public participation. Teaching for social action grows right along with the realization that, as teachers, we have to be more a part of the larger political processes that shape schooling and other important aspects of children's lives.

In recent years, many teachers have begun to feel the need to be more politically involved, as professionals and as citizens who have a special role to play in our society. Recent efforts (some of them successful) to legislate reductive curricula and teaching (especially of phonics) and recent policies imposing high-stakes testing have conscripted teachers into the political ranks in ways most of us have not seen before. This is only the beginning. Ultimately, it will not be merely the wish to gain experience for our teaching that pulls us into politics. It will be the need to preserve public schooling, our best hope for anything approaching social justice. The standards movements, the high-stakes tests, the phonics laws—all are small potatoes compared with the move to privatize schools that's waiting in the wings.

It's lamentable that it took threats to our work methods to awaken teachers' public consciousness. Children were poor, hungry, and harmed long before there were phonics laws, and too many of us had never written to our congressional representatives, organized public gatherings, or contacted the media. Now that we have their addresses in our books, though, we need not limit our efforts to those directly related to schooling. We know that kids are more than a test score, and that their life chances are tied up in much more than their days at school. We know that getting them ready for the world involves just as much getting a world ready for them, one that will listen, negotiate, and welcome their participation as citizens. We need to recognize that being an educator consists not of installing skills, concepts, and information in kids' heads but of building lasting conversations, new relationships among people, and a responsive and ethical social world.

Educators also need to examine *what counts* in our conversations with one another. What convinces us to try something new? On what terms do we try to persuade one another or argue for the merit of our practices? So often, it seems, we are persuaded when we see examples of kids' facility with language or their astonishing insights, or when we are moved by a personal story. Certainly, these are better proofs of learning and quality classroom work than are test scores. Perhaps, though, we should pay more attention to the social and political importance of what kids contemplate and accomplish as writers and readers. Perhaps we should be more impressed by the degree of democracy a teacher is creating than the efficiency and organization of her classroom management. Perhaps we should look not for quick fixes to the social difficulties that vex us in our classrooms but for the slow fixes or nonfixes—the complex and indeterminate ways teachers and students manage to live together in the midst of difficulty and diversity.

CHAPTER 1

LITERACY EDUCATION FOR DEMOCRATIC PARTICIPATION

Katherine:

Any teacher would have loved having Ruth as a student. She was the image of what I wanted my students to become. Deeply thoughtful and considerate, she had a plan for her reading life at age ten that included broadening the kinds of things she read, imitating these styles in her writing, and improving how she talked about books with her reading partners.

Watching her read and discuss Letters from Rifka *with her reading club, I was impressed again with how seriously she participated as a reader and collaborator. She came to each club meeting with big issues to discuss, usually having stabilized her thinking on these issues by voluntarily writing about them in her reading notebook. In conjunction with the other group members, she negotiated understandings about this difficult novel. She shared her knowledge and experience of her Jewish faith with her non-Jewish partners. She would return to the words of the book when interpretations conflicted. She responded often to the poetic quality of the writing, once copying an apropos quote from a Pushkin poem into her notebook. She recognized that Rifka's dreams might be symbolic, insisting that the group interpret them ("Rifka's dreams usually have deeper meanings, remember?"). What more could a teacher wish?*

Ruth had mastered, to a degree worthy of a college English seminar, the art of textual analysis—reading efferently and aesthetically, connecting what she read with other texts and to her personal life. She even took the author of the book, Karen Hesse, as a mentor—a character in a story Ruth was writing began having symbolic dreams. Still, something was missing—and it was missing because I had never taught it.

The novel's clear political and social implications, what it says about power and injustice, passed Ruth by. Like so many readers, she seemed to keep oppression at arm's length, something experienced in the distant past in a distant land. Nothing she said or wrote about the book revealed her thinking about harm, fairness, and flight in relation to the world she lives in now. She took the novel as pure art, something to be enjoyed aesthetically and personally, and she was very good at evaluating it in terms of our classroom values and norms. But she could not let the book ignite in her a passion to make her world better. This was not something missing in her as an individual, something she should have brought to the text on her own. No, a social and political way of reading was not yet in place in the book club's conversation—or in my teaching.

Every teacher, in collaboration with her or his students, establishes ways of thinking that are valued in that classroom community. (In the same way, each family develops its own ways of doing holidays, and everybody else's family practices seem off base, or at least exotic.) The thinking in a particular classroom is influenced by many forces, but it is always specific and local. That is, *the things that matter here* never include all the possible things that could matter. In Katherine's classroom, of which Ruth was a prominent, accomplished member, highly literary, aesthetic thinking was valued, as were collaboration and personal knowledge. Those are great things, but a different kind of thinking had been left out.

Learning to think in terms of making a better world, to reflect habitually about social and political problems and possibilities—these goals should surely be among those we have for our teaching and learning. Like most of our colleagues, we have always been happy to see these kinds of thinking when kids exhibit them "on their own." But couldn't we, shouldn't we, support them more deliberately?

Kendra is a student in a writing workshop, and she keeps a writers notebook so that writing can become a tool for thinking. She has written about the day she saw a blue jay aggressively tossing twigs and leaves out of the gutter on her friend's apartment building and about how it feels to be on a soccer team that loses all its games. She has set down her memories of each room in her grandmother's apartment and reflected on her life history as a reader. She has entries about sunlight, icicles, and the sound of crows in the morning. Today, she writes about her ex-boyfriend, whom she makes a point of not naming, and how his jealousy whenever she talked to male friends made her break up with him.

On her eight-block walk home from school, Kendra may be thinking about any of these things. Or she may think about the things that surround her now. She may think about the housing project she walks past and the friends who live there. She may think about the air she breathes as she avoids the bus exhaust fumes that make her cough (she has asthma). She may notice the billboards advertising cigarettes. She passes a building in front of which she often sees the same couple fighting (once she heard the woman scream back at the man, calling him a faggot) and remembers hearing rumors that drugs are sold there. All of these sights, sounds, and interactions have something to say about social injustice, exploitation, and risk. But none of it finds its way into her writers notebook. "It just doesn't seem like it belongs there," she says.

Again, the conversations we sponsor in our classrooms frame our students' attention. Through our demonstrations, the literature we select, the questions we ask, the responses we make to student speech and writing, and our instructions for what students are to do—we say, "Here, look at this" and "This is good to think about." That's how some things come to "belong" in a writers notebook and other things are left out.

In some ways, teaching, like writing, is a composing process. Let's say you were going to write about the fireworks display you attended on the Fourth of July. To get anything down on paper, you would have to make a thousand decisions. You might tell it all from the perspective of personal experience: who you were with, what you all said, how you responded, how it brought you all closer together. You might decide to add some memories of other fireworks you'd seen and find some connections among those events that are more meaningful than the fireworks themselves. You might describe the program, what you could tell about the planning of the display. You could choose to write about the history of Fourth of July celebrations. You could write about whether or how people in other countries pay attention to the day. Another possible chunk of information to add would be the physics of the fireworks, why and how they make the designs they do. It would be possible to include some comparisons between fireworks and munitions in actual wars. You might consider what it means that Americans commemorate the signing of the Declaration of Independence with imitations of warfare. You could consider the demographics of the crowd and investigate what types of people turn out for these displays. And on and on and on. What you almost certainly could not do is write everything. Some process of selection is fundamental to the act of composing. And you could only know what to put in and what to leave out by returning to your purpose.

Of course, in teaching, you can't completely control the text. (It's pretty tricky in writing, too.) Still, each one of us does frame what counts in the human community we construct with students. And one important lens for helping us decide what's in and what's out of conversations is to return often to our sense of purpose. What are schools for, anyway? Maybe getting clearer about that will help us decide what is most important to include.

Schooling for a Possible Public

We are both public employees. Both our paychecks come from government entities, so most of our household income is provided by public funds. We get the people's money. What entitles us to this?

We work in public schools, and schooling is understood to be of enough significance to the public that it should be subsidized. Public elementary and secondary schools, unlike most organizations with which people interact, don't charge fees for their services. People in the United States have to pay for all sorts of important things. Most people do not eat for free; both grocery stores and restaurants charge for food. The public does not pay for clothing or most people's housing, even though these needs would seem to be more fundamental than the need for an education. In a democracy, though, education is so essential that the general public pays for it. Why? We used to assume, when we saw quotes from Tocqueville or Jefferson about the importance of an educated citizenry in a democracy, that it was all about voting. We figured people needed, at least theoretically, to be able to make sense of newspapers and platform statements and candidates' materials—not to mention the directions and names in voting booths. Elections could only be valid if voters had the technological competence to understand what they were giving their consent to. This typical conception of democracy, *liberal democracy,* emphasizes the election of political experts who do the real deliberating and make the decisions. (Liberal democracy is not the opposite of conservative democracy. This is a different use of the *L* word, and, in fact, reflects a conservative conception of democracy.) Here the role of the people is to select the experts. Having voted, the people rely on their rights to make elected authorities leave them alone. That's an oversimplification, of course, but it is the basic idea of liberal democracy, and it is the model most people have in mind when the word comes up.

But there are other perspectives. The most useful and persuasive for us has been the concept of *participatory democracy,* or deliberative democracy, or what Benjamin Barber (1984) calls "strong democracy." This perspective emphasizes ordinary people's participation in democratic processes. By investigating alternatives, understanding others' positions, trying to come up with solutions that appeal to the widest range of opinions and perspectives, we *create* our democracy as we go along. Democracy is not what we have when the process is over: it exists only when people deliberate together. By engaging one another in public, even though it's messy and frustrating and hard, we construct our social dialogue and continually coauthor the public will, of which elections are just one manifestation. Understood this way, democracy is the ultimate languaging process, a continual exchange and transformation of signs.

Participatory democracy can be hard to imagine as a practical method for governing a big country. It is most useful (and most evident) in the local groups we participate in every day. Nevertheless, work in these smaller democratic units affects our engagement in the larger political process as well. By giving one another the opportunity and respect the democratic ideal demands, by deliberating about important local topics and making decisions together, we build dispositions that make us differently attentive to politics in the larger sphere:

> The argument of the participatory theory of democracy is that participation in the alternative areas would enable the individual better to appreciate the connection between the public and the private spheres. Ordinary [men and women] might still be more interested in things nearer home, but the existence of a participatory society would mean that [they were] better able to assess the performance of representatives at the national level, better equipped to take decisions of national scope when the opportunity arose to do so, and better able to weigh up the impact of decisions taken by national representatives on [their] own life and immediate surroundings. (Pateman 1970, 110)

But our question is, what *justifies* public education? It's possible, in a darkly cynical mood, to say it's just one of the ways the government subsidizes corporations—it provides workers. Training the work force is a commonly invoked rationale for public education, and people typically think of functional literacy—with a focus on the skills necessary to get and keep a job—as being the most important graduation standard. However, this is not an adequate justification. Why should all the people foot the bill for training corporations' employees? If education is intended solely to prepare people to work in the private sector, then employers ought to pay for their own schools.

It is also true that the education system functions largely to sort people into successes and failures, closely following the social-class membership of their parents. But, of course, that does not justify the expense of the people's money. Far from it! The poor, after all, are being forced by the state to pay for their own oppression. In fact, if that is all the system can do, social justice would demand that we call for an end to the whole machine.

In *Democratic Education* ([1987] 1999), Amy Gutmann maintains that the only justification for publicly subsidized education lies in preparing children for and habituating them to democratic participation—building in them the dispositions, habits, abilities, feelings, and understandings they will continue to employ as adult citizens in participatory democracies. This includes not only basic literacy but also critical literacy: habits of listening and considering different sides; the ability to collaborate, deliberate, and differ; respect for others as civic equals; a commitment to avoid and resist repression and discrimination; the development of concerned social agendas; a deep understanding of the traditions and concepts that create and sustain democracy; and fluency in communicative and democratic processes. If a republic is to continue to exist, if a people is to reproduce its best principles deliberately, rather than unconsciously reproduce its most unjust practices, schools must focus on helping students develop civic virtues—the habits of mind the people collectively need for liberty, equity, peace, and stability. Public schools exist to create public selves, public purposes, and public habits. If we don't work hardest to attain those goals, we aren't earning our keep as public agents.

This commitment doesn't mean we teach only how to write petitions and editorials or how to read political tracts and newspapers; it doesn't mean political content determines our every word. It does mean recognizing that all we do has political meaning, from saying "settle down" to writing poems. It means highlighting, foregrounding, a lot of language and thinking about political meanings, much more than most of us are doing now. It means centering our work on democratic principles and critical concepts, using them as the main framework for deciding what goes in and what stays out of the environments we create in our classrooms.

Democracy and the Progressive Tradition:
A Glance Backward

These ideas are not new to American education. Perhaps every educator, in her or his journey of learning to teach, recapitulates educational history, as individuals in development recapitulate the history of the species and their culture. To help with our development as teachers, it is useful to be mindful of our ancestors in educating for social justice. We want to claim a tradition, learn from the past, and teach in conversation with others across generations. Too often, people associate ideals of participatory democracy and social justice with the 1960s, but this tradition is more deeply rooted than that. The ideal of educating for public participation is as old as public schools.

Horace Mann was the first Secretary of the Massachusetts Board of Education, a post he occupied from 1837 until 1848, when he became a member of the U.S. Congress. Mann did not invent the common school, but he was better than most of his contemporaries at articulating the rationale for public education for all children. In Mann's view, just as kings and queens, when they are young, are placed under the tutelage of a Regent in the statecraft of leading a country, so must all the people, in a democracy, be apprenticed into self-government. He wrote that children should:

> receive instruction in the great essentials of political knowledge,—in those elementary ideas without which they will never be able to investigate more recondite and debatable questions;—thus, will the only practicable method be adopted for discovering new truths, and for discarding,—instead of perpetuating,—old errors; and thus, too, will that pernicious race of intolerant zealots, whose whole faith may be summed up in two articles,—that they, themselves, are always infallibly right, and that all dissenters are certainly wrong,—be extinguished,—extinguished, not by violence, nor by proscription, but by the more copious inflowing of the light of truth. (Mann 1957, 97)

It is sometimes hard to read Mann and see a progressive vision. His morality was narrow by most modern standards, and his understanding of democracy was limited to Liberal Democracy. Also, the republic was still young and must have sometimes felt less-than-stable, so one feels in his writing a terror of anarchy and a need for stability. All around the preceding quote, he urges caution and voices apocalyptic fantasies about teachers taking doctrinaire stands on controversial issues (like slavery and universal suffrage) and the public consequently removing all the children and funding. Even in such precarious times, however, he exhorted teachers to induct students into the principles and practices of democracy:

> The will of God, as conspicuously manifested in the order of nature, places the *right* of every child that is born into the world to such a degree of education as will enable him, and, as far as possible, will predispose him, to perform all domestic, social, civil and moral duties, upon the same clear ground of natural law and equity, as it places a child's *right*, upon first coming into the world, to distend his lungs with a portion of the common air, or to open his eyes to the common light, or to receive that shelter, protection and nourishment which are necessary to the continuance of his bodily existence. (Mann 1957, 63–64)

Really meditating on that sentence, even today, outrages us with how far our schools have to go. When we remember that Mann wrote those words in 1846, it is hard to imagine his hand didn't tremble as he wrote. After two terms in Congress, Mann lost the race for Governor of Massachusetts, then became president of Antioch College in Ohio, a pioneer institution in the inclusion of women and African Americans. In his 1859 farewell address, he exhorted the graduating class to "be ashamed to die until you have won some victory for humanity." He died two months later.

In some of his earliest writing, an 1897 pamphlet called *My Pedagogic Creed,* John Dewey wrote:

> I believe that education is the fundamental method of social progress and reform. . . .
>
> I believe that education is a regulation of the process of coming to share in the social consciousness; and that the adjustment of individual activity on the basis of this social consciousness is the only sure method of social reconstruction. . . .
>
> I believe that it is the business of every one interested in education to insist upon the school as the primary and most effective interest of social progress and reform in order that society may be awakened to realize what the school stands for, and aroused to the necessity of endowing the educator with sufficient equipment properly to perform his task. (Dewey 1959, 30–31)

Like Gutmann almost a century later, Dewey explained that creating a better, more democratic world was what school was *for.* No other social institution stands as much of a chance of creating a better world. The moments and days children spend in school accustom them to a way of living together in public, and if they carry democratic dispositions into adulthood, a new world will result. As he wrote in *The School and Society,* "When the school introduces and trains each child of society into membership within . . . a little community, saturating him with the instruments of effective self-direction, we shall have the deepest and best guarantee of a larger society which is worthy, lovely, and harmonious" (Dewey 1959, 49). To get people ready to participate in a democratic community, they need a real democratic community in which to participate right now.

The democratic learning inside a classroom also must be connected and attentive to social life outside the classroom. Dewey cautioned that one could create a little democratic world sealed off from the larger society; a classroom or school could be as hermetic as a monastery. Without having thought about the world outside, students won't develop ways of thinking about problems that will need their attention there. Therefore, they cannot carry the social values they grow in school into the world (Dewey 1916, 359). Teachers, then, need continually to relate a class' democratic and humane ways of being together with those of society outside, applying shared values, concepts, and knowledge to the broader world with as much diligence as we apply them to our daily life together "in here." The notion that schools must be places where people can and should talk about thorny political problems is an idea that later educators, such as George S. Counts, developed more fully.

In 1932, Counts delivered an address to the Progressive Education Association titled "Dare the Progressives Be Progressive?" It was not enough, he said, for educators to provide environments, even democratic ones, and then silently hope that students would develop values and dispositions that might bring about a more just social order. He said educators need to define a political vision and become much less timid about teaching it. The speech caused quite a stir at the conference, and it appeared shortly afterward as a short book, *Dare the Schools Build a New Social Order?* In it, Counts took progressive educators to task for focusing so much on child-centeredness that they failed to map a social and political direction for progress. He critiqued their fear of "imposition" and "indoctrination," arguing that, in keeping silent about social problems, teachers actively lead children to believe that the world is just as it should be and that we should resist change rather than attempt it. We cannot help but impose the culture on kids, and that is what school is all about. Moreover, no matter how energetically we impose social values, the school is only one of many educative forces in society, and most of the others are not working for social justice. (He wrote this well before people had televisions at home.)

Furthermore, in valuing individual children's interests over social and political concerns, we impose the ideology of the upper middle class on all children:

> persons who are fairly well-off, who have abandoned the faiths of their fathers, who assume an agnostic attitude towards all important questions, who pride themselves on their open-mindedness and tolerance, who favor in a mild sort of way fairly liberal programs of social reconstruction, who are full of goodwill and humane sentiment, who have vague aspirations for world peace and human brotherhood, who can be counted upon to respond moderately to any appeal made in the name of charity, who are genuinely distressed at the sight of *unwonted* forms of cruelty, misery, and suffering, and who perhaps serve to soften somewhat the bitter clashes of those real forces that govern the world; but who, in spite of all their good qualities, have no deep and abiding loyalties, possess no convictions for which they would sacrifice over-much, would find it hard to live without their customary material comforts, are rather insensitive to the accepted forms of social injustice, are content to play the role of interested spectator in the drama of human history, refuse to see reality in its harsher and more disagreeable forms, rarely move outside the pleasant circles of the class to which they belong, and in the day of severe trial will follow the lead of the most powerful and respectable forces in society and at the same time find good reasons for so doing. . . . They wish to guard their offspring from too strenuous endeavor and from coming into too intimate contact with the grimmer aspects of industrial society. They wish their sons and daughters to succeed according to the standards of their class and to be a credit to their parents. At heart feeling themselves members of a superior human strain, they do not want their children to mix too freely with the children of the poor or of the less fortunate races. Nor do they want them to accept radical social doctrines, espouse unpopular causes, or lose themselves in quest of any Holy Grail. According to their views education should deal with life, but with life at a distance or in a highly diluted form. They would generally maintain that life should be kept at arm's length, if it should not be handled with a poker. (Counts 1932, 7–9)

Counts' words still describe the prevailing attitudes in most schools. Teachers must divorce their social vision and educational purposes from the interests of this class and embrace instead the best traditions that could make the idea of America worth striving for.

> A society fashioned in harmony with the American democratic tradition would combat all forces tending to produce social distinctions and classes; repress every form of privilege and economic parasitism; manifest a tender regard for the weak, the ignorant, and the unfortunate; place the heavier and more onerous social burdens on the backs of the strong; glory in every triumph of man in his timeless urge to express himself [*sic*] and to make the world more habitable; exalt human labor of hand and brain as the creator of all wealth and culture; provide adequate material and spiritual rewards for every kind of socially useful work; strive for genuine equality of opportunity among all races, sects, and occupations; regard as paramount the abiding interests of the great masses of the people; direct the powers of government to the elevation and the refinement of the life of the common man [*sic*]; transform or destroy all conventions, institutions, and special groups inimical to the underlying principles of democracy; and finally be prepared as a last resort, in either the defense or the realization of this purpose, to follow the method of revolution. Although these ideals have never been realized or perhaps even fully accepted anywhere in the United States and have always had to struggle for existence with contrary forces, they nevertheless have authentic roots in the past. They are the values for which America has stood before the world during most of her history and with which the American people have loved best to associate their country. Their power and authority are clearly revealed in the fact that

selfish interests, when grasping for some special privilege, commonly wheedle and sway the masses by repeating the words and kneeling before the emblems of the democratic heritage. (Counts 1932, 41–42)

Counts thought that teachers, if they would accept the power society had placed in their hands, could lead in moving America closer to this vision. He saw teachers as uniquely well-positioned to serve as midwives to a new, better social world. He also recognized that, to do so, educators would have to begin thinking of themselves and their relationship to society in a different way. "In order to be effective they must throw off completely the slave psychology that has dominated the mind of the pedagogue more or less since the days of ancient Greece" (Counts 1932, 30). We have to stop thinking of ourselves as working for bosses, and instead understand that we are leaders in the interests of the people.

What We Teach

Now we can return to what bugged us in those anecdotes about wonderful children reading and writing that opened this chapter. In much of what we considered our most successful teaching, our students became artists and scholars—but they did not become democrats. In our classes, communities of learners developed standards of quality, but not standards of justice. They crafted texts and readings with an image in mind of a "good one," but they did not also carry an image of a good society. We are not faulting our students; they enacted and internalized the conversations and practices we externalized. In truth, we are not even faulting ourselves as teachers; we just brokered into our classrooms the professional conversations in which we participated outside those rooms. But maybe we can do more justice to our public purpose as educators if we now bring a more informed vision of the socio-political fundamentals of teaching and learning into those professional conversations.

Teachers in a democracy have four complementary responsibilities:

1. *Teaching for social action.* Mann's notion of schools as apprenticeships in citizenry reminds us that we need to teach kids to use language as a tool for crafting a better world, to habituate them to activism. Primarily, this purpose relates to how we teach writing: the angles on the world we introduce writers to; the kinds of publishing and audiences we make available; the images of good writers we promote; and the level of significance we expect in students' thinking on paper.

2. *Teaching the language of democratic classrooms.* Dewey's emphasis on the environment in which students spend their days nudges us to be careful about the little communities we create in our classrooms. The language the class uses for talking about itself needs explicitly to develop political values. Whether students are reading or writing, they are participating in a social world right here in the classroom, and they need language as a tool for thinking about that world and negotiating their ways of being in it.

3. *Introducing the practice of cultural critique.* Counts' call for a foregrounding of socio-political problems and a clear vision of a better world makes us recognize the importance of critique. It is not enough to talk about the existence of things like corporations, factories, farms, and families. We need to help students examine the ways in which some people are more powerful than others, ask questions about what is fair, and name what is not fair. Nothing brings the world into a classroom like reading, so reading workshop presents the richest opportunities for teaching cultural critique. However,

once students have developed the conceptual lenses for effective social criticism, they can apply those same lenses to their own writing and that of others in the community.

4. *Conducting themselves as political agents.* Counts also challenges us to reframe our job descriptions. Only when teachers have a strong public voice can the interests of children and education be preserved. In identifying ourselves as educators, we need to realize we educate not just the kids in our classes, but also other educators, others in the community, politicians, and the public. We cannot simply install the idea of justice in kids' heads and believe it will stay there as they participate in an unjust world. Our work is also to make the world more continuous with the values we embrace in our teaching. Honestly, we cannot effectively teach students to be powerful democratic participants when we ourselves participate like sheep.

We have to pay attention to *all four* of these responsibilities in order to be true to any one of them. They are part of an interlocking system. Teaching cultural critique without teaching social action, for example, can lead students to a censorious dislike of literature and hopeless resignation that the world is a terrible place. Teaching social action or service without cultural critique can lead to lots of activity for its own sake, without a deep understanding of systemic issues, forcing students to sign on to agendas they have not really internalized as purposes. Teaching cultural critique or social action in a classroom that does not try to embody democratic principles is a kind of educational Stalinism: everybody has to be politically correct, but no one has any real agency. It also denies everyone the use of this immediate and formative community as a laboratory for democracy. And when teachers try to do any of these things without being actively involved in political life outside the classroom, teacher and students remain uninformed about the how, what, and why of social justice.

How We Teach

Say there's a loose screw in a chest of drawers in your daughter's bedroom and you want to show her how to tighten it. You show her the screw and help her look at it and assess the situation. You explain that there are two kinds of screws, some with straight slots and some with a kind of X, and that you have to get a screwdriver that matches the screw. You have her look at the screw to see which kind of screwdriver she'll need. Then you take her to the toolbox, and she picks out the screwdriver that best matches the screw. When you get back to the dresser, you take the screwdriver in your hand and show your daughter how to hold it, how to fit the head into the screw, and how to turn the screwdriver. Then you hand the tool over to her, so she can give it a shot. She does it like a kid, kind of fumbling around, but you let her do it. If there is some particularly disorganized thing she's doing, like not making sure the screwdriver is getting into the slot, you coach a little. You might even hold the tool steady for her if it starts wobbling. When she can't tighten it any more, if it's a screw that needs to be tight, you probably give it a turn or two more just to be sure. Then, if you're good, you go around the house and loosen a few screws so she can tighten them on her own. At that point, you pretty much hand over the whole process to her and go about your business, perhaps watching from a distance to see if she needs more assistance.

That's teaching, the fundamental process by which human cultures carry forward from generation to generation. It's such an ordinary part of life that it seems simple and unproblematic. Take a look at most schools, however, and you'll see that for some reason it's a hard process for people to conceptualize and carry out, especially with regard to the higher-thinking processes involved in literacy and citizenship. Nevertheless, the clear strategies in everyday apprenticeships also apply to teaching more complex activity: we demonstrate, we assist the learner's activity, we name and explain, we observe and assess together, and we hand over the process.

Demonstrating

When we demonstrate for students, we allow them to be spectators, to enjoy a holistic view of the activity they are supposed to internalize. In many cultures, this is the primary modality of teaching, although in modern schools, the separation between the roles of teacher and learner often represses the use of demonstration: the teacher questions and students answer, the teacher assigns and students carry out. In a demonstration, the teacher inhabits and externalizes the very kind of thinking and acting that students are to do themselves. Pure demonstration involves no questioning of students, no voiced participation on their part, but is simply an expert performance of the desired activity. The teacher just says, "watch me."

In teaching for social justice, demonstrations typically involve thinking through critical lenses, writing for social action, and community participation. To demonstrate thinking with a critical lens, a teacher might read part of a news article aloud, pausing frequently to think aloud about some particular critical concept or lens, such as representations of gender or individualism/collectivism. In demonstrations of writing for social action, a teacher might plan aloud and begin a draft of a letter to a newspaper editor, writing on a piece of chart paper or on an overhead. Demonstrations of community participation are, of course, continuous in classroom life, as the teacher shows kids by example ways of living among others. For a more formal demonstration, a teacher might ask another teacher to visit the classroom for a few minutes so that they can think together about a text or negotiate a course of action, providing a valuable image of collaborative thinking—of letting one's wishes be known but also letting go of hardened agendas in favor of creating shared decisions. Although demonstrations may strike some as being rather teacher-centered, they do not create passive learners any more than read-alouds create passive readers or reading itself creates passive thinkers. Rather, they help learners get a big picture of what they are trying to learn.

Assisting Learners' Activity

Educators working in the Vygotskian tradition know that the most essential form of teaching involves assisted performance in the zone of proximal development—helping learners do something they can't yet do by themselves but can do with help (Tharp and Gallimore 1988). Once learners have seen an activity demonstrated, even when they basically "get it," they still need help constructing the activity in their own bodies and minds. Sometimes teachers assist a whole class; sometimes they work with small groups who need particular kinds of help; sometimes they confer with and coach individuals. This is more than just helping students get the assignment done, clarifying directions, or reminding students about procedural rules. Rather, it involves observing and assessing the learners; identifying a teaching objective; and providing focused, ongoing assistance with regard to one or two particular aspects of the activity.

We assist learning for democracy when we ask students to keep a particular critical lens in mind as they read part of a short text, then talk about how the concept seems to apply so far, then read a little more and talk again, and so on. We assist writing for social action when we remind students of a sample petition in a shared file of class resources and ask them to plan aloud with us how the issue they are working on will fit into that format. Assisting democratic participation might involve helping a small group consider the subtle contributions of quieter voices in the group. In general, assistance like this involves interrupting the learner's forward motion by introducing a complication related to democratic values and processes that have not yet appeared on the horizon.

Naming and Explaining

We have all sat in classes where the only form of teaching was lecture, where the teacher went blah-blah-blah. And we are so sure we do not want to be that kind of teacher that we may sometimes be meek about naming and explaining concepts for students. But concepts that can inform how we live are organized by way of the words we share with one another, and the meanings of those words are linked to other words. There is no way to introduce the concept of justice through Unifix cubes, and it's irrational to expect that students will learn on their own, or even in their homes, how to participate in publics.

Learning to think critically about our culture involves gathering a network of words and meanings that we can use to deliberate regarding texts, world events, and relationships. We make these networks of words available to students by our oral explanations and by giving them texts to read that either explain the concepts explicitly or else open up conversations around a named concept. Stories can open conversations, but they usually do not name their ideas explicitly or explore their meanings in the same way that explanatory texts can. Acting for social justice involves first identifying those issues and problems that seem to call for action. It involves understanding the issues in language that can be used to persuade others. Crafting a democratic community, as opposed to one in which everyone is "nice" or "good," involves thinking about our associated living in words that correspond to democratic principles useful in the larger society. In educating for social justice, our hope is that our students will learn to think and act according to a diverse set of concepts that, when played out with others, will create harmony, fairness, and stability. These concepts, though they are revered in our culture, are not dominant, and they do not come naturally to people. Teachers must introduce these ideas in classrooms and use their authority to create a sanctioned language for conversations about meanings and applications. Without such dialogic, intersubjective explicitness, learners cannot become independent and intentional participants in the purveying of complex cultural ideas.

Dialogical Observing and Assessing

For a learner's activity or language use to grow, both the teacher and the learner must watch the language use or activity, checking regularly on whether it is improving, redesigning again and again ways to make it happen. For teachers this observing and assessing usually becomes almost habitual; because we understand what teaching is, we constantly monitor learners to see whether they are "getting it." Teachers need to make sure, however, that learners are on the same page we are, that we're all monitoring the presence or absence of the desired aims. Opportunities to reflect on when and how, over a particular chunk of time (minutes, days, weeks), we have deliberately performed the activity we're trying to learn are essential to active and purposeful learning. In other words, students must frequently, regularly, reflexively assess their own progress.

This reflection is particularly important in the normative, value-laden, against-the-grain learning of social action. Students need frequent opportunities to recall when during the last chunk of their reading they brought forward in their mind some critical concept to ask hard questions of the text. These invitations to reflect might be tendered at the beginning or end of a reading workshop. In their work for social action, students need to assess for themselves whether they have worked hard enough to bring others together around their cause, whether they in fact have taken substantial action to bring about change. To help bring this about, a teacher might ask students for homework to write-to-think about the extent to which they have so far employed a particular strategy in political action. Many teachers who try to build democratic communities in their classrooms use weekly class meetings as an opportunity for students to reflect on the quality of their shared life and to plan new actions. These assessments involve dialogue in that the teacher contributes what he has noticed about ongoing work while also expecting a learner to contribute her own assessment. Ultimately, it is the learner's habit of checking in with her own learning that matters most for lifelong learning: this is the kind of assessment we all must do all our lives in order to keep growing.

Handing Over

We can only know what learners know if they have a chance to perform without our sponsorship. This class is not always going to be together; individuals need to carry away habits they can use once the teacher is no longer in the room with them. For learning to transfer to new situations, the important tools, concepts, and habits for thinking have to be handed over to the learner (Wood, Bruner, and Ross 1976).

Edwards and Mercer (1987) found little handover in the progressive classrooms they observed: students demonstrated "ritual knowledge" about how to perform in accordance with the teacher's expectations for the day's lesson, but they never exhibited "principled knowledge," an awareness of the fundamental principles that would make a procedure or discourse applicable in other settings. These researchers argue that this stemmed from the teachers' commitment not to teach through "telling" but by allowing understanding to emerge within each child. Because the children never understood the principles of what they were doing and why, they could never take it over and do it on their own. Instead, the teacher maintained control over predetermined procedures for "discoveries" thoroughly planned in advance. Edwards and Mercer note: "A successful educational process is one which transfers competence to the learner. It is almost as if formal education, for most pupils, is designed to prevent that from happening" (1987, 159).

As we have thought about critical literacy, as we have watched ourselves and others attempt to construct teaching practices that might help children grow more critical, we have noticed that a lot of work directed toward social justice occurs in whole-class contexts. Much of the reasoning and planning stays in the teacher's hands. The teacher selects texts that he believes highlight themes of social justice, leads discussions of these texts, and helps his students develop critical thinking. Sometimes, in response to literary texts, or news articles, or community events, there is a class project of social action. Are individual kids the agents of these actions, or do they occur only when the teacher recognizes them, appropriates them, uses his authority to give them significance, and gets everyone to sign on? Are the students experiencing these emancipatory projects as simply more obedience to the teacher? If that's the case, then perhaps critical frameworks, critical concepts, and critical language are not being handed over to students as a matter of course.

Critical literacy has been handed over when a student, without teacher prompting, critiques the racial representations in a book he is reading independently; or when, in a notebook entry, she initiates her own thinking about the ways sports events create more losers than they do winners. Social action has been handed over when a young person notices a problem in the world that needs attention and, without prompting, by virtue of her own freedom and habits of acting, tries to do something about it. It has been handed over (at least for the moment) when, in a class meeting, students examine whether they have been treating one another justly. Each student needs the chance, on his own, to look at the world more critically, read with socially significant questions in mind, and sponsor social action.

Creating Possible Identities and Shared Worlds

When we and our students create the discourse of our communities, we deal with more than just vocabulary. We create the sentences it is possible to utter, the kinds of interactions it is possible to share, and our ways of thinking about the world and one another. Whether or not a particular topic seems worthy of conversation depends on whether those kinds of words can be spoken here. The discourse determines who gets to complain, correct, or "rise up." A classroom language is also the resource students draw on in order to think about themselves and their roles in the world. Discourse, James Gee (1990) tells us, is an "identity kit"—the words and interactions being the tools we use to construct who we can be in this community.

Randy:

> *I am working with an experienced fourth-grade teacher new to the teaching of writing, and we are conferring with students in her classroom. Joel is writing about his dog. As I kneel down to talk with him, I scan what he has on the page: a section about the day his dog ran away; a section about the day his dog came home; and a section about how he loves his dog. The story, as written, seems a little thin, like a synopsis rather than a real telling. I say, "So your dog ran away and then came back. That's such a great story to work with. Tell me about it." A set-up for a typical content conference.*
>
> *"Yeah," Joel says. "My dad doesn't like her. And he was always hitting her and stuff. And he didn't want her in the house or in any of the rooms." He pauses.*
>
> *"Really?"*
>
> *"Yeah, because she had these sores on her back. And he said if she kept coming in, he was going to kill her. He showed us his gun and said he was going to kill her. So my brother and me took the dog on the leash and we walked as far as we could over to [a different part of town] and then we let her go and scared her and ran after her so she would run away."*
>
> *"Oh, so it wasn't really like she ran away from home. I thought she just ran away. Really, you were trying to save her."*
>
> *"Yeah, but she came back." He looks stricken.*
>
> *"Oh, man. So it wasn't such a happy thing, since you were scared about your dad. I thought this was going to be a happy story. So—well—how's your dad doing with the dog now?" I am afraid to ask.*
>
> *"I don't know." Joel shrugs and looks off.*
>
> *There is no amazing turning point in this conference. I retell Joel the story he's told me and push him a bit to let that story come out more on the page. But he seems really uncomfortable. He is much more comfortable with the picket-fenced, boy-and-his-dog, Lassie-come-home version of his story than with the version that includes tyranny and violence, injury, sacrifice, and fear. This is the identity he prefers to perform to this community. And in this context, that's fine. It is late in the year, and his class has never even been allowed to choose topics before or to draft without worrying about correctness right away. Even writing about his dog in school, thinking about the reality of it as he casts it in the best possible light, is a new experience. This teacher and these students are already taking a risk by allowing me to open writing up this way. A much greater sense of safety and power will have to develop before he will tackle the hard material he really has on his mind.*

The point of this story is to show how dense with seriousness kids' lives are and how story-telling conventions can mask material that could come out a completely different way. The ways writers choose to frame their experience and knowledge arise from the discourse of the classroom, what it seems possible to say in this context. The roles they are expected to play inside and outside the classroom create the possible kinds of writers they can be. In a setting where power relationships and issues of fairness are frequently examined, where students take on roles of witness and activist, Joel's story and our conversation would have very different possibilities.

Jerome Harste continually reminds us that "curriculum [is] a metaphor for the lives we want to live and the people we want to be" (Harste and Carey 1999). In those words, "we want," he presupposes that we have a vision of a possible future. Curriculum, in that sense, is the desired future imported into the present (Cole 1996). The discourse we create in classrooms sets up possible future identities for our kids, and possible future worlds for them and us to inhabit together. That's what we're doing in all those minute-by-minute activities we plan and do every day in those schoolrooms: creating the future we want. As George Counts exhorted us to do seventy years ago, we had better get busy figuring out what worlds we desire. What, really, is the better world for which we work and hope?

We need to avoid the obvious fallacy of thinking we can predict the future: *if we teach in this way, the future will see more social justice and democracy.* We cannot possibly know that to be true. What we are willing to assert, however, is that it is desirable to live in a community where people are trying *right now* to make a better world. People presently engaged in making things better for others they do not know as well as for themselves are not preparing some better world down the road; they are that world today. Because the world we want to create is composed of richer compassion, more available democracy, greater equity, higher dignity for individuals and communities, and a more generally shared sense of plenty, we can take actions in this moment that start to make those things real. The only democracy we have is the one we make every day.

CHAPTER 2

JUSTICE IN SO MANY WORDS
Concepts for Critical Reading

When we notice something about particular values like fairness, social justice, and power relationships in something we read, we are applying knowledge gained from other reading we've done, from conversations we've had, and from the media to which we've been exposed. We also are testing the book's assumptions against the concepts, discourses, and communities of our experiences. For children to grow as critical readers, they must develop similar concepts and begin to employ them habitually while they read. Ultimately, we want kids to be able to initiate such inquiry in response to texts without a teacher's guidance. For that to happen, student readers have to participate in an ongoing conversation about social justice and critical action. They have to hold in mind a set of shared values against which they test all that they read. How do these values develop?

Discourses of Reading

Every classroom—elementary, secondary English, college history, whatever—creates a discourse initiated by the teacher and taken up to varying extents by the students. The teacher imports a primary reading ideology from groups to which she belongs outside the classroom (university classes, a community-based organization, a national professional organization, a teacher study group). Students then interpret and transform the discourse, partly in light of other reading ideologies they have encountered in other groups (their home, last year's classroom, a tutor). As the students change the discourse, it alters in turn in the teacher's mind. Ideally, through this process of negotiation, a definable discourse of reading emerges as the center of the class, work together, one that holds tight to some central themes.

The central themes of one classroom's discourse, for example, might include an intensity and seriousness about reading, the value of aesthetic beauty in text and response to text, the value of emotionally charged thoughtfulness, and a willing engagement in both social and solitary work. Most of the talk, writing, and nonverbal interactions about reading, across the whole school year, can be organized under these themes. These discourses "stick" partly because of the teacher's demonstrations, activities, and questions, but also because he explicitly names and advances these themes: he talks *about* these values all the time and asks the kids to do so as well.

In the immediate life of the classroom, the discourse defines "who we are and what we do." Members become insiders or outsiders by participating in or resisting the primary discourse of the group. But the discourse of reading is also a medium, a thinking device for individual members, the internalized language with which readers guide themselves through the reading process. For example, if there is a lot of talk in the classroom about texts creating pictures in your head (a common concept in many reading and writing workshops), then the students begin to create these envisionments as a matter of course when they read. Discourse creates thinking; indeed, it is the only source from which thinking derives.

Because reading discourses create reading processes and practices, the agenda of trying to create a more just social world can only be served by highlighting the importance of critical concepts and language in reading classrooms. We don't mean standing in front of a row of desks, lecturing about class consciousness, and testing the students on Marx, though such steps might indeed generate classroom talk with much more critical "content." In going this route, we would lose the ground already gained by the democratic dimensions of our teaching and submit students to the "little autocracy" we already know to be poor practice for participation in a democracy. To design a more effective social justice pedagogy, we need to look at how values like "gender equity" fit with a process that includes "drawing on the syntactic cueing system" and "envisioning."

When we look at reading as mental action, it may sometimes seem that we are describing reading as a purely psychological process, something that happens only inside our head. In order to think about what we are teaching when we are teaching reading, it is necessary to be able to talk about internal processes that are not, strictly speaking, visible in social interactions. This does not mean that reading is individual by nature. The ways readers think are conditioned and organized by their participation in communities that read in particular ways. In a group that values personal, autobiographical memory in response to text, an individual reader responds more personally when she reads. So our description of mental actions always depends on readers' participation in groups that value those particular actions and have their own definitions of what those actions mean and what they are for.

Critique and Other Mental Actions in the Reading Process

Good literacy teachers operate out of the theory that reading is always a process of thinking guided by print in which a reader reconstructs an author's ideas in negotiation with what she knows about the world and other texts. Reading involves mental actions that can be developed through active teaching. Readers *do* things when they read: they envision; they predict on several levels simultaneously (word, sentence, text structure, social interaction); and they form relationships of identity, opposition, or care with characters. In performing these actions, readers are not merely looking at the words of the text. They are also thinking about the world they know. If the text is describing a forest, then the reader, in order to understand, must draw on his experience of forests, whether actual or virtual. If the reader lives in a forest or has visited one, his experienced, lived world provides an intertext on which the reader draws. If the reader has only seen forests in movies or on television, then these texts become the intertexts. Either way, to picture things, the reader draws on visual memory; he does not require any new or specialized concepts, content, or attitudes to do reading's work. Envisioning is a relatively transparent mental action that teachers can coach students to do without a lot of explaining about how to do it.

Interpretation and critique, however, draw on more complex, less immediate intertexts than "how a forest looks." A student might interpret a story as helping us think about how alone people sometimes feel and how a new friendship can open worlds of possibility. This interpretation draws on a bundle of moral, social, and emotional concepts. The concepts of loneliness and friendship create a framework of quasiphilosophical abstractions that allow the language of the text to expand and connect with the world and with other texts. Abstractions like these are revealed through the explicit discourse of the dominant culture—conversations with significant adults, television, songs, church or friendship group discussions. An interpretation is not merely a reaction to the text; it is the intersection of aspects of the text with mediating ideas, or lenses, available in the "common sense" of the culture. The *interpreting* habit of mind continually taps this well of abstract, reflective lessons from life and literature.

Each habit of mind also has its own attitude or emotional stance, and acquiring these attitudes is part of getting the gist of the mental action and being able to put separate mental actions together into complete thoughts. Envisioning is often rooted in the expectation of aesthetic pleasure. Interpretation is reflective, philosophical, and often exacting about evidence (though different interpretive communities have different rules about what counts as evidence and how much evidence is necessary). A critical state of mind begins by feeling sympathy with the vulnerable, responds with indignation to oppression and unfairness, and is excitable into action for social change. A critical attitude clings determinedly to its own freedom and resists being captured by new discourses, especially if they sound as if they might violate core democratic values. At the same time, the critical attitude openly considers the ideas of others, listens, and inquires. Though values have to be settled enough for the person to act, there is, in the critical heart, a mistrust of too much certainty.

Like envisionment and interpretation, critique involves a habit of mind, as well as habits of the heart. The critical mind is one that questions, tests assumptions, considers claims in light of their implications, entertains multiple perspectives, and gravitates toward the interests of vulnerable people. A critical consciousness knows that the topics one has thought about the least, the ideas that everyone just assumes are true, are worth examining most carefully. It overturns assumptions in order to see what is under them, never completely satisfied that everything is understood. A critical mind is always learning, always inquiring, always in a state of disturbance. Paolo Freire calls it "unquiet" (1970).

To read critically one needs to pay attention to concepts that, although they are ever-present in daily life, usually go unexamined in most communities—things that seem to be the way they are necessarily, as if nature had made them that way. The details of our culture become what critical theorists call *naturalized* (even though the ideas are socially constructed, we take them as natural), so the most basic elements of our lives are as invisible as water is to a fish. The common sense of a culture involves things we think we don't have to ask one another, things we don't have to wonder about: We assume we all agree. For example, we all know that everyone is heterosexual, so we ask freely about marriage and boyfriends/girlfriends. We know what men are like and what women are like, and we assume respective interests in sports or clothes, money or food, tools or children. We know that successful people have gotten where they are through hard work and that poor people just aren't trying. We know that some children have to fail at school, while others have to succeed. We only pay attention to these assumptions when someone rips the fabric, disrupts the status quo. Only by deliberately applying critical concepts to naturalized assumptions can we increase the scope of mental freedom and allow people to choose who they want to become and how they want to live.

These critical concepts include power, force, gender, race, class, the flow of money, silence and voice, multiple interests and perspectives, fairness and justice, respect, otherness, hegemony, freedom, collectivity and interdependence, and the social sources of ideas, attitudes, and languages. This family of concepts provides a stable intertext that, when applied to texts, make critique possible. The richer that intertext is, the more thorough the critical reading can be. Critical concepts, then, need to be an emphatic theme in a group's reading discourse, named, explained, and hyped, if they are to become a durable thinking device for readers in the group.

Scholars and teachers who advocate a critical education frequently point out that such work is always *normative*—that is, concerned with a system of "shoulds." Education is not objective, disinterested, or value-neutral, but rather is always inherently ideological. That everyone gets to go to school for free is one ideological value. Furthermore, assumptions about what education is *for* always stem from particular philosophical and political perspectives. Values make school systems choose certain content over all the other possible content that exists. Education for social justice involves being willing to introduce ideology: to assert, for example, peace over violence, respect over an assumption of deficit, and justice over inequity. Education for liberty involves not only allowing more freedom but also talking about the meaning of freedom, making students conscious of their freedoms. Education for fraternity involves connecting students' interests with those of people they do not know and with whom they do not yet identify. As long as those words remain very general, few argue with them. Most teachers and administrators, however, are rather timid about saying out loud what we mean by these terms. We all know that the world, historically, has not been especially receptive to a detailed vision of liberty, equality, and fraternity. We risk being disagreed with, censured socially, or silenced when we say clearly what we mean.

But our silence about critical concepts exacts both political and cognitive costs. By leaving unquestioned the-world-as-it-is and the texts that operate within it, we silently assent to its unfairness and oppression. By sweetening, softening, smoothing over, and making excuses for social inequity, we naturalize injustice and defeat hope. Once we have convinced students that everything is finished and that hope is gone, how do we expect them to learn? Moreover, teachers' silence about the particular concepts that inform critical education deprives the teaching/learning transaction of a rational direction and scope. Thinking that all critical concepts will emerge "naturally" from students naïvely ignores the powerful working of naturalization. Likewise, imagining that literary texts like novels and poems will come right out and teach readers concepts of critique fails to recognize the nature, purpose, and structure of literary texts. Reading practices, and the concepts that inform them, do not arise from individual readers or from texts: they come from conversations in a stable social group, a discourse in which members affiliate with each other by affirming that some things matter more than others.

Concepts for Critical Reading

Over time, we have been inquiring into the understandings critical readers employ. The concepts listed here come from analyses of classroom conversations, interviews with readers, and reading group discussions, as well as understandings from literary theory, cultural studies, theories of democracy, and critical theory. We name the concept and list, as straightforwardly as we can, some of the norms that seem to inform people's thinking about that concept. By outlining concepts in this way, we risk oversimplifying them, but we assume people have participated in conversations about these ideas and that questions provoked by our outline might take readers to other discussions and texts for fuller, more open-ended explorations. We also simplify the language here, to get closer to the ways we talk about these ideas with kids. By doing this, we may risk simplifying the concepts, at times making them sound like moral platitudes. We do understand these risks, but we, like many other educators, have grown weary of reading about important ideas only in the most impenetrable prose. If we cannot say things clearly to children, we do not have the concept developed enough to work with it.

We would suggest that readers go through these lists with their own classroom discourses in mind, assessing what kinds of critical concepts are already part of the conversation, and what ideas might be as yet undeveloped. Our ultimate goal should be to increase the scope of students' language about the political dimensions of life. We can do this by bringing up these ideas in discussions with students, by explaining them directly, by holding back less of the possible material from which they can craft lenses for reading and visions of a better world.

Groups

- Individuals can be seen as the persons-they-are and also as members of groups. Part of the way people get to be the persons-they-are is by picking up the attitudes, beliefs, and feelings of the groups they belong to, by being like others around them.
- Some groups are pretty clearly defined in most people's thinking. These include males, females, Latinos, blacks, whites, Asians, poor, rich, gay, straight.
- Even though these categories seem rigid in our culture, they are often more fluid in particular people's experiences.
- People should be able to form purposeful, emotionally significant connections with others—in other groups and their own group.
- Individuals can choose many of the groups they identify with. We are members of a gender group, a racial group, and a class group; but many of us have complex, overlapping memberships even in those categories.
- We also choose to be members of other groups that overlap those categories. We may be members of the group "joggers" along with people from other gender, race, and class groups. We can act to make our lives better as joggers, without being divided by our differences.

Power

- When one group gets more money, more political offices, more control of media, more control of institutions like schools and churches, more chances to make decisions that affect other people's lives, they have more power.
- The group that has more power gets its perspective accepted as if it's the only way things could ever be.
- Because of money, control of the military, control of police, and control of information, groups in power can force others to accept their point of view, or at least force them to pretend to.
- Changes in power relationships can only occur through the work of groups.
- Because groups can change things, talking about people only as individuals helps to keep power relations just as they are.

Taking Things for Granted (Naturalization)

- There is not necessarily a group of people in power sitting in a room, planning how to keep themselves up and others down.

- Power works through a system of common sense, creating attitudes and beliefs that everyone accepts and no one questions, such as belief in individual heroes; theories about intelligence and entitlement; beliefs about the attitudes and actions of poor people; and stereotypes of women, racial groups, gay men, and lesbians. We also tend to take for granted our understandings of political concepts like democracy, freedom, and justice.
- All our thoughts, every day, are created inside these attitudes and beliefs, and unless we pay attention to them on purpose, we never see them. We think, "It's just natural. It's just the way things are."

Fairness/Justice

- People should have similar chances to have a happy life.
- People should not have to struggle too much just to keep their bodies healthy.
- No particular group should be more physically vulnerable to harm or deprivation than any other group.
- Being smaller, in size or number, should not reduce someone's chance at pursuing happiness.
- More powerful groups should not get in the way of less powerful groups' going after their purposes (assuming the less powerful groups' purposes do not include the oppression of some other groups).
- People should be heard, known, and understood by others in their group as well as members of other groups.
- People who hurt others or keep them from living fully should make it up to them. This applies to individuals as well as groups.
- Members of stronger groups should care about and work for the interests of more vulnerable groups.
- Other people's pain should always be significant, even if the other people are from a different race, gender, class, nationality, or set of beliefs.

Voice/Silence

- You can only get a fair and just society if all groups get to tell what their lives are like.
- Because of their limited access to publishing and media, it is important to clear special spaces for the voices of more vulnerable groups.

Multiple Perspectives (Different Sides of Stories)

- Because people live together, anything that happens can be viewed from the point of view of more than one person.
- In texts, there are always people, seen or unseen, who do not get to tell their side.
- Because texts move in a linear fashion, authors, in order to write, always have to select some perspectives and silence others. It's impossible to give every side of something, and even more impossible to give them all equal importance and have them all speak at the same time.

- In some texts, it feels very easy for the reader to "know" what's right. That's because some perspectives have been effectively shut up. In other texts, there are more conflicting sides, and the reader feels more unsettled about what to think.
- To bring out some of the voices silenced by the text, readers have to imagine what another side might be—not just an opposing side, but a side believing that completely different things are important.

Representation (Showing What People Are Like)

- Stories, paintings, advertisements, movies, news articles, and other texts represent people and relationships. There aren't real human beings there, just some words or images that are meant to show "what they are like."
- In making texts, people choose from words or images they have seen before that show what people like this are like. In this way, texts always reproduce pieces of other texts, blended or stitched together. "Authorship" always involves choosing this and that from what is in the culture and putting it together, occasionally in a way that looks new.
- Stereotypes develop of the groups who usually are not doing the writing that gets published and read by lots of people. In American culture, over history, the groups who ended up being represented by others have been most of the people in the world. These groups include women, races other than European, poor and working people who live in the city or the country, children and adolescents, and people whose intimate relationships take any form other than mother/father/children/grandparents all cheerful together.
- Critical reading involves, in part, recognizing those stereotypes. In doing so, we open up new spaces of possibility for how to be (for the represented groups) and new potential relationships among members of different groups (because they can try to understand each other as they live in the world, not as they are received in representations).

Gender

- Thinking about gender involves thinking about how both female and male characters are represented.
- *Strength.* Male and female characters are often portrayed as different in terms of their strength and vulnerability. It is not fair for females always to be vulnerable; it is not fair for males always to be strong.
- *Agency.* Male characters are typically the ones who do things, who have gumption, who make projects and have intentions. Female characters often wait for other people to get them going, or they respond to what males or adults are doing.
- *Centrality.* Male characters are often the ones whose actions are central to the story. Female characters may be doing things at the margins, but their story lines are less often central to the action of the story. Even when a girl is the central character, she may seem merely a substitute for a male stereotype—physically strong, action-oriented, "butch," and fantastically heroic. It is worth asking whether a mere flip of the usual roles really opens new possibilities for our thinking.

- *Repertoire.* Both male and female characters are limited in their repertoires of actions and responses. Girls may cry more. Boys may get mad more. Girls may care about others. Boys may make action plans.

- *Opportunity.* Plots of stories are made up so that chances to do different things are offered unequally to boys and girls. Boys often get to do a wider variety of activities, to go more places, to experience more new things.

- *Desire.* Female desire is avoided in many texts. Girl characters are not supposed to want something or someone too much. They hope, but they don't actively desire and pursue in the way boy characters do. When desire is central to a story line, it's usually a male's desire.

- *Relationships.* Different kinds of possible relationships are limited in texts. Boy/girl relationships either are or aren't romantic, but it is always significant if they are or are not. Same sex relationships are also limited. Two friends who are male are not permitted the same kind of relationship that two female friends might have.

- *Idyllic conventions.* Some texts rely on the reader's acceptance of all male and female characters acting in just the way they are "supposed" to. In some such stories, it seems like everyone is happy and that any suggestion that things might be otherwise would just be grouchy.

- *Looks.* Especially with pictures, television, and movies, it is important to notice who is looking and who is being looked at. Many feminists have pointed out that, very often, females are set up as objects to be looked at by males. Even in stories without images provided by someone other than the reader, there may be more discussion of how certain characters look—for instance, whether they are "pretty" or "ugly," "fat" or "thin," and so forth.

- Readers can critique the way gender is represented without also thinking that girls should be like boys or vice versa. They may think that people should be freer to create identities and personalities without merely conforming to typical cultural expectations. They may also think that different ways of being should be valued by more people, such as ways of knowing and being that are usually thought of as feminine.

- Many individual males or females do not feel that they "fit" with the usual ways of thinking about their gender. It might be that having two categories (male/female), especially if they are thought of as opposites, to describe gender is just not the most helpful way to think about it.

Race

- All of the preceding ideas about gender are also true of race.

- *Criminality and evil.* Especially in television and movies, a disproportionate number of African Americans and Chicanos/Latinos who are shown at all are shown as criminals or evil people. This is also sometimes true of other groups such as Chinese and Italians. This puts the viewer or reader in the position of thinking of members of these groups as scary enemies. This representation might make people think of members of these groups as valid enemies of the state.

- *Intelligence.* Ancient stereotypes about the intelligence of different groups still exist in stories and media. Plots of stories may operate on assumptions about African Americans, Native Americans, or Latinos being less smart or at least more naïve, less experienced than whites. Ideas like "street smarts" are substituted for thoughtful mental activity. Stereotypes of Asian Americans as brainy "model minorities" also keep people slotted in roles.

- *Bodies and minds.* Some groups, especially African Americans, are often portrayed as being bodies. Other groups, like Asians or Jews, are sometimes depicted as being minds. Either way, the members of the groups are limited and made less whole as human beings.

- *City and country.* Texts often show members of racial groups as being either from the city or from the country. Each category carries its own stereotypes. Think of the words "urban," "ghetto," and "inner city"—particular images of people and their lives come to mind. These are different from the images that come to mind about blacks in rural Mississippi, Latinos working on farms, poor whites in Kentucky, or Cambodians in Missouri.

- *Otherness/exoticism.* Sometimes, members of minority races are portrayed as being strange or exotic, as a sort of wondering entertainment for white audiences. One problem with this is that it doesn't allow the people being looked at that way to be human beings with their own points of view and purposes. It makes it seem like there's one group that is normal, in which everyone is pretty much the same, and then there are these strange others.

Class

- All of the preceding ideas about gender and race also apply to class.

- *Reasons for poverty.* Texts that have poor people in them will often hint at some reasons why they are poor. These reasons might include laziness, hard luck, the need to learn a lesson about what is important in life, or having had poor parents. Reasons such as these hide the fact that things are set up in society to make some people poor and to keep wealth in the hands of those who already have it.

- *Transience.* People who do not have much wealth or income frequently have to move. They may move in and out of shelters and subsidized housing. They may try to get out of "bad" neighborhoods for a time but be unable to keep paying the higher cost of the new place. They are more likely to be evicted from their homes when they cannot make rent payments. All this moving around makes it harder for people to form relationships with others in their community, which makes it harder to take social action or to develop a network of mutual support. When their children have to change schools frequently, it becomes harder to learn and to develop habits of forming friendships. Difficulties like this are common in the lives of many readers, but they are hard to fit into the structures of most written stories. Their absence is significant.

- *Substance abuse.* Vulnerable people who abuse drugs and alcohol are often represented as evil or weak. This representation ignores the fact that intense trouble, shame, and chaos makes people want some kind of relief from pain, hunger, and the consciousness of hopelessness. Schools are complicit in this simple-minded representation in their enlistment in wars on drugs, drinking, smoking, drunk driving, and the like. Restoring the logic of addicted people's lives is not only humane, it is also better education against addiction.

- *Idealization.* In some texts, poor people are shown as being very wise about money not being able to buy happiness. They know what is really important. In few texts, though, do you see rich people saying they wish they didn't have all this money so that they could get in touch with what really matters and then giving all their money away. Rich people in many stories manage to enjoy the sky, love their children, smell the flowers, and also have enough money not to have to be afraid of catching cold. The pattern of happy poor people in texts could be seen as a way of consoling everyone about things staying just the way they are. It is possible to critique this pattern without also saying that money buys happiness.

- *Significance.* In some texts, the ordinary lives and thoughts of the very rich are treated as very important and worth reading about simply because of their wealth. Even minor rich characters may be made important by their wealth.

Money

- Most money is in a few people's hands.
- It is useful to look at where the money is in a text. Sometimes, we may see money directly, people spending it, getting it, wanting it. Other times, we may have to understand its unspoken presence by noticing characters' ownership of land; buildings; technological devices such as machines, computers, video equipment; fancy clothes; or precious objects. We may recognize that money is involved in getting certain services like medical care, transportation, legal services, access to communication, or help with construction of houses or buildings.
- Looking at what the money buys and what it does not buy is interesting.
- In investigating political stories, reporters sometimes say, "follow the money." Critical readers can do the same thing, tracing where money starts out in a story and where it flows as the story moves along.

Labor

- Many people have to work very hard in jobs that do not mean anything to them personally. They have to stay in these jobs because they need to be paid, though the minutes they spend on the job do not help them get to their personal goals and desires. In other words, they work for other people.
- People should be able to do whatever they can to make the time they spend in their jobs meaningful and satisfying.
- People who work for other people should be paid enough so that they can improve the quality of their lives outside their work. The energy and time of workers should be valued by the people they work for.
- The lives of workers are often made worse by the desire of the people who own companies to make more and more money for themselves. They keep too much of the money for themselves and do not share it with the people who work to help them make it.

Language

- People have different languages in their lives. Some people, for example, speak Spanish in some places and English in others. Also, people speak one language at school, another at home with their family, and another to their dog. These language changes are sometimes hard and sometimes easy, but they are always important.

- The everyday languages of common people should be valued, because these languages are important tools for people's thinking and because people's sense of themselves—their identities—are tied up in the language they have used to form them.

- One thing to think about when we read a text is how the different languages work in this world. We can notice who speaks the different languages and who does not know how to. We can notice who talks and who keeps quiet in different language situations. Then, we can look at whether the different amounts of power that different groups have makes those voices and silences happen.

- Across a group of texts, we should expect to see problems and changes in languages. If we don't see them, we can wonder what is being left out of those texts and why.

Intimate Relationships and Families

- In American culture, the stereotype of a family has a mother, a father, a sister, and a brother—and maybe a dog—all of the same race, culture, and religion living happily together in a house. Some families are really like this, but most are not. This stereotype can make people feel that their lives aren't good enough. It can also make people think that *other* people's lives aren't right.

- Because of this environment, people who love differently are especially vulnerable, sometimes even to violence from others. For example, lesbians and gay men are often victims of hate crimes that do not happen to people who love in the ways most people think of as "normal."

- People put families together for themselves out of the possibilities available to them. The ways they do this show their genius and creativity for love and intimacy. Sometimes, the people who love each other are different genders, sometimes the same. People sometimes live in the same house; sometimes they live miles apart. Most people participate in a number of families and intimacies at the same time.

- Intimate relationships, whether between two lovers, between parents and children, or between small families and the bigger, extended families around them, always have problems. Stories that don't show these problems can contribute to readers' unrealistic expectations for their own lives.

- We can read critically about families and intimate relationships. Some texts might draw on a stereotype and make some readers feel like their lives are all wrong. We can question the assumptions in such texts. Others might tell stories that make everything seem possible and help readers to feel that a wide variety of intimate relationships could be satisfying.

Relationships to Nature

- Industrialization, which most clearly benefits the owners of companies, uses the earth's resources and, through its waste products, pollutes natural environments.

- Human beings share the earth with other species. It is not fair or moral for us to place our interests too far above those of animals and plants in the natural world. Figuring out where to draw the line is complicated by the fact that we do eat plants and animals, we do take space away from them, and we do attempt to protect ourselves and our property from them.

- The fact that human beings *can* wreck the earth does not mean that we *have* to. Rather, we need to see ourselves as responsible for the care of the earth and the protection of fragile ecosystems, balanced through complex negotiations with the needs of industrialized society. These negotiations with the interests of rich and powerful corporations often involve resistance, protest, and struggle.

- Ultimately, the government is the only entity powerful enough to interfere with powerful corporations. Individuals can attempt action through their elected representatives and whatever means possible of getting the government to act.

- Individuals do participate in the culture industrialization makes possible. People can make choices about their own ways of participating in the use of resources and the disposal of waste. Tiny actions like these will not ultimately solve the big problem. But these little things help to break up usual ways of thinking about waste, pollution, and the earth, and they give us a way to talk to others about the bigger issues.

Violence and Peace

- Violence occurs in cycles. One party is violent to another, and that brings a violent reaction, which results in another violent action, and so on. To break the cycle, someone has to choose not to react with violence.

- Violence on a large scale, such as war, rioting, and police invasion of a neighborhood, hurts the most vulnerable the worst: the poor, the small, and the powerless. Usually, it most benefits the powerful. Therefore, violence is rarely in the interest of justice.

- Living in peace requires the courage to stop responding violently and the ability to imagine other possible responses.

- Peace rarely means the total absence of conflict. We have to work actively, pay careful attention, and struggle for a peaceful world.

Acting Alone or Together (Individualism/Collectivism)

- Over time, ways of thinking that have grown up in Europe and America favor the strong individual who can do something in isolation or against the resistance of the social world.

- This belief in the individual sometimes might help us act courageously against powerful resistance; however, it might also make us all tend to stay separate from each other. As long as everybody is just working by themselves, no one has enough impact to change things in society.

- If ordinary people stay separate from each other, then the groups that already have power will keep it and those who are vulnerable will stay that way.
- Stories of collective action may be helpful in getting people to imagine what they might do together.
- Collective action is built on relationships, so it is useful to think about which relationships in a text might make the beginnings of collective action possible.

Teaching Social Justice Concepts

A teacher's decision to concentrate on a particular concept might stem from a particular conversation wherein students identify, even in a very basic way, a critical concept in something they have read or studied, or a social issue in classroom life. In other words, deliberate work on developing students' nascent conceptions might be a way of moving "everyday concepts" toward "scientific concepts" (Vygotsky 1962) or "interests" toward "aims" (Dewey 1916). On the other hand, a teacher can also introduce the abstract notion of the concept even before children have begun noticing it and then ask the students to use that idea as a lens for their reading over the next few days.

Getting students doing or thinking something they aren't already doing or thinking calls for active, assertive teaching. For most of us, the first image of powerful teaching that comes to mind is frontal teaching; that is, breaking down what is to be taught and explaining it piece by piece to students. Perhaps that is followed by images of tests with serious consequences. The trouble, of course, is that, while explanations may be part of teaching something new, teacher talk does not, by itself, ensure learning. We need teaching strategies that allow us to make sure we're constructing close to the same ideas, that we're all actively involved in the thinking, that we're all on the same page. Our goal is to make the concept clear and explicit in the learner's mind, not just in our words. That does not mean there is no role for explanation. Children listen. Every parent has heard their child say, *Ms. So-and-So says. . . .* To help young readers use critical concepts in relation to texts, we need to introduce critical discourse in our talk to them, to make it important in the language of the classroom community. (For a teacher to be comfortable talking about these ideas, it helps if he first has the opportunity to talk about them with other adults. Reading this book and others like it might help, but the language needs to be formed in the teacher's own mind and mouth for it to feel comfortable. Study groups, classes, meetings, and workshops can provide this kind of opportunity.) In addition, we can help kids develop the concept by demonstrating its use, helping them try it out, and asking them regularly to reflect on whether they have been using the concept in their reading.

Some teachers like to introduce a concept in connection with a text they are reading aloud to the entire class. It might go something like this. The teacher interrupts her reading to explain the critical concept—gender, say—and then goes on reading. Perhaps at the end of the next chapter, the teacher thinks aloud about how gender issues might pertain to this book—not lecturing but *reflecting*: using an uncertain tone, changing her mind, making on-the-other-hand statements, raising questions rather than advancing assertions. At this point, she might not even invite the kids to contribute: even if they are volunteering like crazy, it's sometimes useful to repress their externalized participation a little, suggesting they keep thinking about the ideas and questions they're forming about gender while the next section is being read. After reading a few more pages, the teacher asks the students to share with a neighbor what they're thinking about gender in the world of this book.

Any novel can support thinking about a number of critical concepts. As the class moves through the book together, it's possible to introduce two or three concepts and then develop them in some depth. (Trying to do more than that can make the application of critical lenses mechanical and perfunctory.) Of course, the point of working with a shared text is to teach students to think about these concepts in their independent reading as well.

Let's think through how we might introduce social justice concepts in a reading workshop in which kids are reading independently or talking with partners or in small groups. We might introduce the concept in a minilesson. That same day, the concept might come up in reading conferences, in which case we might also highlight it in the group session at the end of the workshop. For the next day's minilesson, we might bring in a carefully chosen short text (or section of a larger one), read it to the kids, and reflect on how the concept applies. Again, in subsequent conferences, we would look for opportunities to highlight the concept, individually and in share time.

A day or two later, we might bring yet another short text to the class, this time distributing a copy to everyone. First, we'd probably read the text aloud, in case some readers find it difficult. After a little bit of discussion, we'd ask the students to look back over the story and mark places where the concept we'd been talking about the past few days might pertain, spots where we could really think hard about *x*. Students could then share their thoughts with a partner, and the class as a whole could discuss a few people's ideas. (It's important to accept student approximations, to give any thought legitimacy, even if it means restating it in a way that makes more sense than the way the kids said it.) Now that we've talked about the concept, demonstrated it, and tried looking for it together, we might tell the students we'd like them to be on the lookout for chances to think about this concept as they read their own books. We might provide sticky notes or specially colored bookmarks so that individual readers can continue to mark spots to which the concept pertains and jot down their thoughts. Over the next week or so, we might reserve the class' shared discussion time for examples of students' thinking. The repeated appointment to share allows kids to think toward that time while they are reading or discussing; the conversation itself is valuable, but knowing the conversation is coming is even more so.

Another way of introducing concepts is to work with small groups using text sets (Short, Harste, and Burke 1996). The teacher chooses the texts with an eye to examining a critical concept from different angles. The texts may be in any genre—short story, picture book, poem, news article, folktale, a chapter from a history book, a summary of a legal decision, an advertisement—but each set should comprise only three or four texts. As part of each group of texts, the teacher includes a short, easy-to-read essay discussing the concept students are being invited to explore. Working in small groups over a number of days, students read the texts and the essay, then discuss the critical concept in relation to the examples they have in front of them. In addition, through their personal responses to the texts, they discuss the way this social justice issue manifests itself in the world. While the groups meet, the teacher circulates from group to group, assessing and conferring to improve the quality of the conversation, extend students' understanding of the concept, and prompt them to consider the concept from the multiple perspectives offered.

Teaching critical concepts, especially in classrooms where talk about texts has already been rich, collaborative, and intentional, does not necessarily involve creating new classroom structures. Rather, *becoming more critical* involves bringing newly intensified lenses to the practices already in place. It involves bringing new terms to the discourse of reading in the classroom. We are interested in students being able to ask themselves new sets of questions within the classroom, developing new frameworks for reading literature, nonfiction, and the world. The important question is, *what kinds of work will best help readers build these new concepts?*

Developing Concepts

Vygotsky (1962) distinguishes *everyday* concepts from *scientific* concepts. The child forms every-day concepts during daily activity outside of school; he or she forms scientific concepts in school with explicit, organized support from a teacher working within the framework of an academic discipline. (Thus, Vygotsky's term *scientific concepts* does not refer only to theories in the natural sciences such as biology and physics; it includes ideas that have been organized in relation to one another in any field of academic study. To make this clear, some writers have taken to calling them *scholarly* or *academic* concepts [Mahn and John-Steiner 1998].) Scientific concepts in the traditional study of literature might include character, setting, image, and symbol. Scientific concepts in the study of history might include revolution, technological change, and the relationship of culture to geography. Concepts related to critique and social justice fit with Vygotsky's notion of scientific concepts.

As with all scientific concepts, the central concepts of critique have their origins in children's everyday concepts. Our students already have ideas about gender, race, money, and fairness, and these ideas—and the experiences from which they are drawn—must provide, according to Vygotsky, the foundation on which scholarly concepts are built. Scientific concepts cannot simply be imposed from the outside. If we do not help students connect the language of the scientific concepts with their lived experience, their understanding of scientific concepts will be hollow and rote.

Also, as Howard Gardner (1991) has pointed out, everyday concepts are often naïve, simplified, and stereotypical, and these constructed misunderstandings have to be aired and addressed in order to be revised. (Even then, Gardner tells us, naïve concepts can be remarkably robust and resistant to change, in graduate students as well as young children. How much more so when they fit intimately with the broader culture and the home culture in which the child participates daily outside of school!) To work on revising everyday concepts, teachers need to invite students to talk not only about concepts and texts, but also about the ways they have thought about these things in their daily lives and how those ways of thinking might be changing now. No matter how strong the classroom discourse is, no two people will have identical concepts in mind as they discuss them, because their individual life stories, predispositions, and prior habits of thinking differ so much. The differences among people as they talk about these ideas is what makes the conversation endlessly interesting, inquiring, and unfinished.

Vygotsky also makes it clear that a scientific concept is usually introduced explicitly by the teacher, who names and explains it. Students then must have an opportunity to work on the concept, to apply it to specific problems. In the context of this work, the teacher goes on talking about the concept, relating it to other neighboring concepts in the domain, and helping students to understand the hierarchical organization of ideas—how one idea is part of a bigger one and so forth. For example, looking at gender in a story is part of the bigger concept of representation, which is related to taking multiple perspectives, which is all a part of the quest for fairness.

To be able to relate critical concepts to one another, the teacher needs to have an ever-growing, organized, deep understanding of critical concepts and to have examined her or his own assumptions and everyday concepts with a clear, honest, critical eye. Just as teachers need to have powerful experiences in reading and writing, they also need to have conversations about political perspectives on everyday life and literacy.

In developing critical literacy, we face a problem that does not exist to the same extent in, say, science or math. The concepts are language, and the material to which they are applied—books, news stories, and other texts—is also language. That makes the nature of "hands-on" experience, and the ways in which students can work with concepts, more problematic. In science, for instance, if a teacher were working with students on the concept of *mass,* he and the students might design an experiment in which they freeze a measured amount of water, thaw it, and measure it again, to see whether mass changed when matter changed state (Wells 1999). By contrast, when we introduce children to a concept and then ask them to think about it as they read a group of texts, the entire process is mediated by language several layers deep. It is hard to get concrete about these ideas; we may feel we never get to "the thing itself" since everything is language. Because language here is both the object of inquiry and the medium with which learners are thinking, it is especially important for every child to be generating language about the concept—in writing, with partners, and in groups. At least some of the time, partners prove most helpful, since that structure provides the most efficient means of getting a maximum number of people talking to other people at the same time. (Groups of four or five, by comparison, require a longer wait between turns and more competition for the floor.)

Furthermore, as seems always to be the case with reading, learning new practices is aided by complementary work in writing. If students are using the concept not only while reading books but also in their writers notebook as they look at their world, the conversation between word and world is heightened. They are better able to integrate the scientific concept with their everyday concepts and new experiences.

In every area of literacy learning, there are important connections between reading and writing. We get ideas about both form and content from what we read, and we apply that understanding to what we write. Reciprocally, our experiences with writing inform our reading as we recognize in texts things we have tried to do in our own writing. Reading critically is no exception. Once students have begun writing (and working in other, nonliterate ways) for social action, trying to make the world better in particular ways, they can read differently. Figures 2–1 and 2–2 diagram some of the ways reading is transformed when we reach out to touch the world, although the processes they diagram are not mutually exclusive.

In outlining the concepts discussed in this chapter, we have taken the approach that texts need to be checked out, that readers need to maintain an informed skepticism about the assumptions behind what they read. But often when we try to introduce concepts of social justice, we use texts that illustrate the concept deliberately. The author seems to share our vision of social justice, and the values we see in the text match our own. Certainly, this is a good use of literature, in that it makes the concept visible while also keeping it open for discussion. However, if students in school only read texts that fit with the political values of the classroom, how are they going to learn the critical habits of mind that help them deal with the much more common, politically incorrect sorts of texts they encounter outside school? If the discourse and the text always match harmoniously, might that not teach a sort of noncritical reading? We suspect that it is when texts and values do not match we can see ourselves being critical. For that reason, we may sometimes need to include books that we think are outrageously wrongheaded. It is perhaps simplest to find easily critiqued texts in the popular media. Television is full of repressed injustice, as are newspapers, magazines, advertising of all kinds, and many of the books in the children's sections of bookstores—you know, the ones you don't ever look at. Only when we stop censoring the texts we disapprove of can we help students take critical power over the texts they read, resisting authorial assumptions and recognizing and disrupting naturalization.

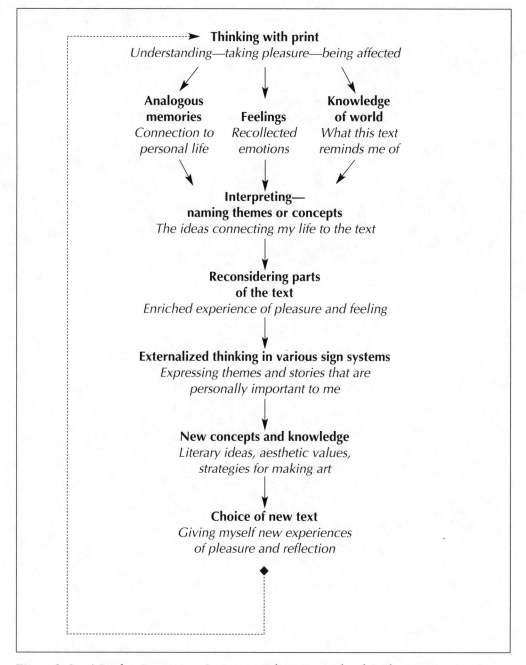

Thinking with print
Understanding—taking pleasure—being affected

Analogous memories
Connection to personal life

Feelings
Recollected emotions

Knowledge of world
What this text reminds me of

Interpreting— naming themes or concepts
The ideas connecting my life to the text

Reconsidering parts of the text
Enriched experience of pleasure and feeling

Externalized thinking in various sign systems
Expressing themes and stories that are personally important to me

New concepts and knowledge
Literary ideas, aesthetic values, strategies for making art

Choice of new text
Giving myself new experiences of pleasure and reflection

Figure 2–1   *A Reading Process in a Community Valuing Personal and Aesthetic Response*

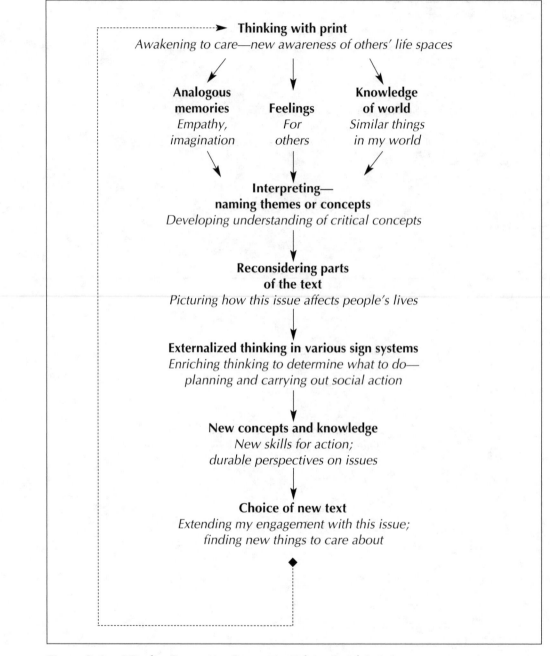

Figure 2–2   *A Reading Process in a Community Valuing Social Action*

CHAPTER 3

GREAT TALKS ABOUT IMPORTANT IDEAS
Strategies for Critical Conversations in Reading

Liz Howort goes to high school in New York City, where she is a member of a group called Students Organizing Students (SOS). Last year, the group took a two-week trip to Cuba to study the country's culture and politics. They have raised money for Doctors Without Borders. They have rallied to free Mumia in Philadelphia. Many nights Liz and her little brother Ben discuss the activities of SOS, and the intricacies of growing up in New York in the twenty-first century, with their parents, Anne Powers and Lou Howort. Liz says that her family has political discussions, but "it's not like I say, 'hey, Mom, let's talk politics.' Either Ben or I will talk about something that is happening at school, and it turns out to be political, whether I knew it or not. For instance, one night I said to my dad as he was washing the dishes, 'You know, it's weird. I have a lot of friends this year, but none are black males.' And my mom joined in and talked about how class plays into race. I thought of all my friends who are black, and I said, 'Wow, they're all middle class and female.' I hadn't thought of it until my parents and Ben and I had this discussion. My friends are all middle class, except one, and she is very articulate and smart, and everyone dresses alike, so that blurs class lines, and it's really hard to tell economic class in public school. Why don't I have friends in the lower class?"

Liz, clearly a deeply thoughtful, articulate, and socially aware young woman, attributes her ability to discuss issues like class, race, and gender to the ongoing talk she participates in at home. Many of our socially and politically active friends say they can trace the beginning of their interest and awareness to when they were small children, when they were asked to participate in dinner-table conversations about complicated and controversial social issues like welfare and war. When they volunteered an opinion, they were listened to. They talked with the adults in their homes during and after television shows, commercials, and movies, and they see this as a major factor in their ability to think critically, to see through sales pitches and the images that try to define the "cool" ways to look and act and be. They have a capacity to see multiple perspectives because they were encouraged to think about *What if?* and *How could it be better?*

One friend has said the most valued question in her family was *What will you do for the world?* Her parents lived their words by writing letters and making speeches, serving on committees and canvassing, sometimes taking part in protest marches and sit-ins. Anne Powers remembers:

> At every big holiday dinner we debated political issues over "pass the turkey." There was a lot of commotion—a high energy level. Being surrounded by people who think and talk about ideas is really important. The notion that we shouldn't just take things in passively or float through life, but that we have an opinion was always part of our family. It never occurred to me that there were families that just sat quietly and ate their dinner!

But Anne also points out that the political climate in her family did not end at the dinner table, but found action in their community. "So it wasn't just the talk, but the activity, too." Her parents expected that their children would also search for ways to help others, and they provided the ways and means to do so. Now Anne and Lou provide this same kind of open, honest environment in which their own children can learn and explore, and they show Liz and Ben how to move from talk to action through their own political work.

Imagine another kind of dinner-table conversation in which the children are given the message, literally or more subtly, that they should be "seen and not heard." At this table, the child hears the adults most influential to her or him state that welfare is simply "paying people to sit on their lazy butts all day. Those people should get up and get a job like the rest of us." What a different conversation it would be if an important and influential adult asked the child, "What are some reasons people might not be able to work? What should we do about people in this country who are not able to earn enough money to feed their children? What if they are sick or disabled?" And if the child then says something egregiously wrong or naïve, imagine that the adult says, "It's interesting that you think that. I think differently, because. . . . " Or, "I'm not sure of the facts myself. Where do you think we could go to learn more about that?" Liz's earliest memories include her parents asking open-ended questions and then really listening to her answers.

> At first, it was questions like, "What was good about your day today?" and "How did you feel about that?" Now it's just natural. I say, "Guess what happened today?" and we're off. It's not just the kids either, anyone at the table might have had something outrageous happen that day, and we all listen and ask questions and talk about it all dinner long. In school, you know how teachers ask a question and then interrupt if you don't answer soon enough? You want to say, "Hey, I don't know exactly what I'm saying yet, but I'm trying to work it out in my mind." At home, we all have the liberty to talk as long as we need to.

Perhaps dinner tables like this exist mostly in our idealistic fantasies. In the world of fast capitalism, so many parents and children reel through their days at such a rate that the idea of leisurely, open-ended dinner-table conversations seems merely quaint. If that is so, then it is all the more important that children be asked to think and inquire and discuss in school, that they be asked the simple, open-ended question, "What do you think?" And it has to be asked without that invisible blank at the end for the child to fill in with the answer the teacher wants.

After a lot of practice as a whole class, these types of discussions begin to appear in other social configurations—during Reading Workshop, in book clubs, partnerships, and individual responses to texts. Critical conversations do not take shape naturally, however. Keeping them productive, inclusive of all voices, and somewhat sane involves a lot of hard work. Therefore, students need to learn and practice strategies that help create significant conversations in response to reading.

How to Build Critical Conversations

To involve children in critical conversations about the books they read or about the world they live in, the teacher has to be a critical observer of the word and the world as well. She has to have an ear tuned to issues of race, gender, class, difference (Shannon 1995, 275). She has to want to weave political ideas into an already overflowing literacy agenda and believe these are important issues to discuss. She also has to help children move their critical stances from texts to the living, breathing world. Opportunities for conversations about socially important ideas arise any time a group of people is living together and studying together. Here Katherine describes an incident in her multiage classroom (kindergartners, first graders, and second graders).

One day I overheard six-year-old Daniel say, "Sherrisa can't be President of the United States." It was a split second in the life in our classroom. We had an agenda that morning. We had "work" to do, a book to read aloud, math, writing, the usual. I could have ignored the comment or said "Of course she can!" and moved on. But because Sherrisa is both female and African American, I wanted to know what Daniel meant. So I said, "Let's go to the rug [our meeting area] and think about that statement."

Once we were in our circle, I asked Daniel to repeat what I'd heard him say. "I said Sherrisa can't be President, 'cause girls can't be President," he said. I must have stared at him open-mouthed, or raised my eyebrows, or in some way signaled that this statement was preposterous, because he "read" me and said, "Maybe . . . well, they can, but I've never seen one on TV or heard of one."

This was a true statement from his point of view. He had never seen or heard of things being otherwise. (If anyone doubts the power of the media to construct social identity, listen to children talk sometime: what appears on television must be real, they think, so if something does not appear on television, then it just doesn't exist.) Apparently, Daniel was only objecting to Sherrisa's gender unsuitability, not to her race. In some ways, gender is such a constant line of discrimination for young children, so in their faces, that it arises as an issue to be discussed and negotiated throughout the school day. Race seems to remain a shadowy, almost taboo subject with young children, as does physical appearance and social power. Discrimination along those lines is ever-present but is more difficult to define than gender and much more threatening to discuss.

The issue of Sherrisa's suitability for the office of President stacked up along gender lines primarily, with only one or two boys suggesting, bravely, that "girls can do whatever boys can do, there's nothing wrong with it." Jake compared it to his life experience: his baseball team "has a girl and a boy coach, both, so they were working together." I asked if it were in "the rules" that a President had to be male. They responded no, the rules were only that the President had to be "honest" and "loyal." I asked why we haven't had a woman President then. They responded that maybe women don't believe in what people want, so they don't get enough votes. Or maybe girls just don't even want to be President.

At this point Elijah wondered aloud, "What do girls want to be, mommies?" His question triggered a mini-inquiry into what women want in the real world, and what the girls in our books seemed to want. After that day, whenever a child found something on a commercial, in a book, or in a friend's remark that struck him or her as sexist, the child reported it to the class and we discussed it.

In the end, the whole class agreed that Sherrisa would make a great President and promised to vote for her when they grew up. Near the end of the school year, the kids *decided they wanted to have a class president, and voted by secret ballot, just like in the "real" elections. Sherrisa won by an overwhelming majority. She was extremely well loved and respected in our community, and her social power was palpable. What would happen to the question of her efficacy as a presidential candidate when she left our classroom? What would happen to Daniel's opinion of whether or not a "girl" can be President? Had we really succeeded in changing his worldview, or did we just "catch him up" in the discourse of our particular community? I can't know the answer to that, but I'm lucky I overheard Daniel's comment and lucky I decided to push through it to find out what his and other children's assumptions were. I hope our inquiry opened up possibilities for their future.*

In addition to asking critical questions and taking a critical stance, children need to know how to have good conversations that build on and follow a line of thinking. Children need to be taught and need to practice how to look at one another, how to talk to one another, not just perform for the teacher. They need to learn how to listen and respond to one another in a way that creates connections and builds a conversation history over time. They need to become interested in and accepting of difference and diversity in order to create a more democratic classroom environment (Chapter 6), in order to find issues and concepts worth investigating and acting on (Chapters 2 and 7), and also in order to engage vigorously and successfully in critical conversations. Talking about difference makes most teachers (most *adults,* in fact) nervous. We have been taught to fear, hide from, turn away from ("Don't stare!"), and be ashamed of people who are different from us. Yet even the youngest children can learn a language for difference, and can begin to respect rather than retreat from the "other."

Learning how to do all that takes time and requires explicit help with and instruction in everything from physical structures and arrangements to conversational moves that help children engage in lively, reflective, critical classroom talk. The following sections describe some strategies for developing such conversations.

Texts and Text Sets

As we discussed in Chapter 2, there are a number of texts—*Bud, Not Buddy* (Curtis 1999), *Just One Flick of the Finger* (Lorbiecki 1996) are two—that inevitably will trigger dynamic discussions.

But critical concepts and questions can reveal social issues in texts that many of us thought were just nice stories. For instance, *Charlotte's Web* (White 1952) can be read as a novel about loving across difference. *Matilda* (Dahl 1988) can inspire fascinating conversations about the power adults have over children and how they can abuse it. *Stone Fox* (Gardiner 1980) raises issues about economics, government, racism, and colonialism. Almost any text can reveal concepts and issues about racism because the story of people of color is either conspicuously absent from the text or is the assumed center of the text. In the same way, almost every text can raise gender issues: "Could this have happened if the character were a girl [boy]?"

When a class is reading complex stories related to historical events and eras, it is often helpful to layer the experience by introducing other texts—nonfiction articles, poems, and pictures books—around a similar topic. For example, when Katherine's fourth grade class read a biography of Harriet Beecher Stowe, the students wanted to find out more things about slavery and about abolitionists. The picture book *Nettie's Trip South* (Turner 1987), a biography of Harriet Tubman, and a bit of Stowe's famous novel *Uncle Tom's Cabin* helped deepen students' conversations. As they worked their way through the story of Stowe's life, the children were able to understand that her actions and her writing were out of the ordinary for her time, social milieu, and gender.

The good news is that once children get accustomed to looking at issues with a critical lens, they can do so with almost any text, from ads to comic books to Pokemon® cards!

Intertextuality: Creating Conversation Across Texts

A history or timeline of the texts a class has read together, posted in the classroom, is a concrete conversation piece and one that allows children's ideas to accumulate and deepen. In Katherine's multiage classroom, children created postcards for every book they had read together as a class, and the cards wrapped around the classroom near the top of the walls. The students referred to these cards often, and those who had been in the class for two or three years were able to connect ideas to novels they had read in the past.

Connecting ideas to other books is an important and powerful reading tool. Ideas build on one another to create worlds of meaning in readers' minds. In critical discussions, the layers of text take on even more importance because they help show patterns of human behavior and oppression throughout history. They show the influence of one social justice movement on another—the influence of Ghandi on Martin Luther King, Jr., for example. Multiple texts shed light on one another, and they help deepen the discussion by filling in facts and details; by presenting another perspective; and by treating similar issues through different styles, genres, and points of view.

Reminders for How to Talk

Collaboratively, the classroom community devises practices that lead to better conversations, and these practices become the expectations for how talk will go. Katherine listed these practices on charts and hung them in the meeting area, and the class would often measure the day's conversation against these guidelines. They also revised these expectations as they became better conversationalists. For example, one year's group put "Look at each other when talking" on their reminders chart in November. By January, they had gotten used to doing that. An especially aggressive pack of talkers decided to replace it with a different norm: "Wait for the count of ten before jumping in." Other reminders have included:

- Watch for people wiggling or opening their mouths to try to speak.
- Pick up on what others say.
- Jot down points you want to get in later.
- Tell people when you are changing your mind.

Teacher's Role in the Discussion

The teacher's role should change from discussion leader to facilitator to observer/participant as the year progresses. Many times Katherine steps out of the discussion completely and gives feedback at the end: the major topics of conversation, how people managed the conversation, who dominated, how many times someone talked or interrupted. Eventually, she hands over the entire conversation, including reflection/feedback portion, to the children, who will use their notes and observations of how things went to inform future discussions. Sometimes she introduces critical questions at key points in the discussion or writes critical questions on the board for children to think about as they prepare for a discussion. She teaches children how to ask a "turning point" question that will force the conversation to go deeper or to take an energizing twist (See Figure 3–1 later in the chapter).

Connective Language

Children can signal that they are really listening by using phrases as bridges to others' comments:

- I agree with [I disagree with]. . . .
- I want to go back to what so-and-so said.
- Could you say more about that?
- I'm not sure I understood you when you said. . . .

One approach is to write these and similar phrases on chart paper and tape it to the wall. At first, the phrases may seem stilted and artificial, as children look up at the list and fumble for which one to put at the beginning of their sentences, but all learning fumbles and feels awkward in the beginning stages. The expectation is that everyone will be listening to one another so well that they can link their comments to what someone else has said. The phrases merely grease the wheel. Once the idea of listening and building a line of thought takes hold, children begin to make connective language their own and use it more naturally.

When Katherine asked the members of one book club that was going particularly well, and seemed to be having thoughtful, transformative conversations, to share with the rest of the class what their "secret" was, Ewa said, "We get along because we are really interested in what people are thinking about the book. We discuss ideas in the books until we come to an agreement, or else we debate until we all understand each other's point of view."

Fred added, "We actually listen to what each other says, and if we disagree, we say 'That's so interesting that you think that! I think this other thing. . . .'"

Conversation Partners

Talking in pairs allows everyone to share their ideas. Children can be asked to choose with whom they wish to talk during the book discussion (and be asked to sit next to this person on the rug if the book is being read aloud). These partnerships help get kids warmed up, help jump-start a larger conversation. They allow children who have a lot to say more time to talk, while also granting children who have trouble speaking in a larger group a safe, familiar audience of one.

If the teacher is reading the text aloud, she can stop from time to time and say, "Turn to your partner and talk about what you're thinking right now." Or she can raise a particular focus question ("Who has the power in this story?") and have the children discuss it with their partner. Occasionally, partners should be asked to report to the whole group, but only to introduce a lot of different voices, help layer the discussion, and build on everyone's ideas.

Fishbowl Conversations

A fishbowl conversation, in which a small group holds a conversation in front of the rest of the class, is a physical example of conversation and provides a different kind of shared "text" for the community to reflect on. (It also allows those students who can only speak in small groups a chance to be heard by all.) The conversation the class observes is a "science experiment" everyone can work with. The fishbowl group can be asked to use a particular strategy so that the class can see how it goes and learn from it.

Here's how it works. A group of four or five students sits in the middle of the circle. They have a conversation, usually about a book the whole class has read. Everyone else observes, takes notes, keeps tallies, or makes some other record of what they see. After the fishbowl discussion, the floor is open to the whole class to say what they noticed.

This is what students said after one particular fishbowl discussion in Katherine's class:

GERALD: I did a tally. I marked who talked and for how long.

TOMMY: I noticed the first person to talk also talked more than once.

MIN: There were outbursts, but then everyone would stop and let each other talk.

AARON: I noticed Walter and I finally backed off, and I also congratulate Judith for inviting other people in.

ANGELINA: Aaron only interrupted three times today!

ANIA: They stuck to one topic!

LEAH: This was the best conversation of the year! Everyone who usually doesn't talk, did talk. And everyone was connected to everyone else.

Thinking Devices

Common ways of thinking or responding in a particular classroom get readers' minds going and enrich their conversation. In many classrooms, children keep reading notebooks in which they record thoughts, questions, responses, and connections as they read independently or listen to books read aloud. They can also make webs, graphs, or Venn diagrams to keep track of characters or events. Students can rehearse different note-taking styles as a class and use what helps and makes sense to them. A teacher's request to "stop reading and write what you're thinking" allows less dominant children to voice their ideas and is a way to manage a "hot" discussion when many children are eager to talk at once. Children can use these notes as a basis for a conversation with their partner and then report to the class similarities, disagreements, and interesting issues.

Occasionally, a teacher can ask students to respond to a "focus" question in their notebooks. The few minutes it takes students to slow down their thinking and redirect it to a particular question helps unfreeze a discussion, open it up, add a new layer, complicate things. For instance, one of Katherine's classes read the part in *The Watsons Go to Birmingham, 1963* (Curtis 1995) where the family fears their little girl was in the church in which a bomb exploded. After discussing the event as it happened in the novel, the students read an account of the real bombing. Katherine then asked the children to write for a few minutes about whether they thought something like that could happen today. At first, most of the children said absolutely not, such a violent thing couldn't happen in the United States, and besides, "we don't have slavery anymore, and we don't have separate bathrooms." But then Ewa reminded everyone that James Byrd was dragged to death by white men in Jasper, Texas, and José brought up the four white New York City police officers who shot Amadou Diallo forty-one times because they mistook his wallet for a gun.

One of the most useful and rewarding aspects of talking with others about a book is that it adds perspectives and interpretations you haven't seen on your own. William Ayers (2000) believes that it is a democratic virtue when we listen with the possibility of being changed. Knowing that reading is made richer by the thoughts and responses of others, teachers can ask children to highlight publicly how other children's thinking has affected their own. One way is to ask them to write down their thoughts about a book before a group conversation, then list who changed or added onto their thinking during the conversation.

Building Up a Topic

Once conversational routines and mechanisms for written reflection are in place, the classroom should be buzzing with exciting conversation. At this point, one of the teacher's roles is to help children hone one topic, delve into it more deeply, perhaps sustaining discussion over several days and feeding it with written responses and rereading. The teacher identifies a topic that many of the children have touched upon, a topic that keeps rearing its head. (This isn't so much a matter of reducing the book to a "theme" or "main idea" as it is picking up on this particular group's thinking about an issue that keeps "biting you in the brain," as one student put it.)

This topic, perhaps expressed as a burning question, an overarching idea, or a critical concept, is posted on a piece of chart paper, and the class focuses only on that topic for a time, having discussions, looking for evidence in the book to support and add to the topic, stopping from time to time to write about the topic for a few minutes. These "big ideas" often remain focal points during the year; children will say, "That relates to such-and-such, which we were talking about the other day."

Making Conversation Visible

An effective technique is to transcribe children's conversations, make copies for each student, and ask them to underline and write in the margins things they notice about the talk. For quite a while, children may get into quantitative rather than qualitative research, such as counting how many times boys talked versus how many times girls talked. (Usually, boys win.) They may want to quantify who was interrupting and how many times. As they become more sophisticated at conversation and also at processing the conversation, they make more qualitative, descriptive comments:

> "I noticed that when Peter began the conversation, he talked a lot more than usual. Maybe he set the topic for the conversation."
>
> "I noticed that Leah kept inviting quiet kids to talk."
>
> "Those who are good at getting the floor should learn to pass it along."

Students also profit from listening to their discussions on audiotape and watching themselves on videotape.

The "fixed" quality of audio- and videotape allows students to rewind to specific places, stop, and talk about what they are hearing. Sound quality can be an issue, but children are often good decoders of talk, especially if they participated in the conversation. Videos prove fruitful for noticing things like someone repeatedly getting up during conversations, or someone reading her own book while her friends are talking, or someone with his back turned. Face-to-face communication often improves after a video replay of a discussion.

Helping More Children Talk

In every group, there are people who are willing to take risks and put themselves "out there," and people who hold back. It is always quite evident to everyone who are the "quiet voices," and who are the "often heard." Teachers should never push the quiet voices before getting to know the children well. Some children are terrified of being "wrong," and would rather not say anything. Others have trouble getting the floor from more aggressive voices. Others come from homes where they are not used to or even not allowed to speak up. Then, there are some who may not be "on the same train": they need time to write or talk to a partner before they can bring their focus back to this particular conversation. Quiet students may need a great deal of time before they feel safe in a large group, and when a quieter child does finally offer a thought, it may be a nice opportunity for the whole class to celebrate it.

Sometimes the problem resides in the physical arrangement of the meeting space, the circle, who sits next to whom. Quiet children tend to find a friend in someone more dominant and then lean on that person to do all the talking. It's probably a good idea to adjust seating arrangements every few weeks to see whether that will encourage some children to function on their own in the conversation.

One year Katherine had a particularly gregarious group of six very loud and aggressive boys and girls who owned and operated the daily discussions. The problem continued for a long time until Anne Powers, visiting the classroom, gently suggested, "Have you noticed the dominant talkers sit in a clump in the middle of the rug? Perhaps if you made a large circle or two concentric circles [there wasn't much floor space], it would break that group up." Katherine had been reluctant to force these fourth and fifth graders to sit in a certain arrangement, believing that their "choice" of where to sit was crucial to their participation. Yet she could see that clumped seating made it easy for those on the fringe to remain outside the conversation. Katherine broke up the "core" group and that went a long way toward solving the problem of sharing the floor.

With this same class she also used a physical object to signal who had the floor. (In a previous class, her students had used a "talking stick" while studying Native Americans. Whoever had the stick had a turn to talk and then would pass it on to another person.) With this class, children received a card in one of three colors: everyone with a green card could talk on one day; everyone with a pink card, the day after; and everyone with a yellow card, the day after that. The children loved this strategy, and they invented many variations, including allowing students with a particular colored card to talk for fifteen minutes, with the whole class joining in after that.

Katherine's goal was for students to recognize one another in their conversations. She congratulated kids whenever they would "pass the floor" to someone else or "invite" others to talk ("Joan, what do you think?"). This progression, in which students appropriate what might be a "teacher" role in less democratic contexts, is crucial. It shows that they are no longer thinking of a class discussion as a time to wait for their chance to say their thing but are beginning to see discussion as *thinking together*. They cannot go on with an idea without hearing from someone else, without knowing what *everyone* thinks, collaboratively. Eventually, they may even congratulate each another on making good conversation moves.

Critical Questions

A priority for many educators is that children learn to read with a critical eye. We want them to understand that texts are always social and political, that even stories are told from a particular perspective and that other perspectives are possible. We want them to learn that texts always encode cultural values and that it's possible for readers to step back, weigh these values on the balance of their own experience and knowledge, and sometimes reject the version of the world encoded in what they have read. We teach students to read questioningly, using lines of inquiry like those listed in Figure 3–1. These questions are not a checklist to "get through" in connection with each and every book the class reads; rather, they are part of the group's ongoing way of looking at and talking about everything. Children are especially keen at spotting issues of fairness. They face critical gender issues daily; girls often want to hear about and read about other girls having the same benefits and possibilities and doing the same activities as boys. Children are sympathetic to characters being treated unfairly, and they tend to take a moralistic view on how the world should be.

Like adults, children understand the world from within the limited social perspectives of their race, class, and gender. Only by beginning to apply certain critical stances can they begin to cross some of those boundaries and recognize that there are entire other worlds of meaning, depending on how they look at things. A habit of applying critical questions to texts helps readers loosen their assumptions. The more we emphasize such critique in our conversations about our own reading and the texts shared by the whole class, the more students come to think of this way as part of their work with texts. Critical educators hope that students will come to critique not only

"critical cyeglasses"

- Is this story fair?
- How does this text address the points of view (perspectives) of other groups, especially those who usually don't get to tell their side?
- How does this text make you think about justice in the world?
- Whose perspective is missing in this text? What would it be like if we put it back?
- How does this text deal with individuals and groups? Are the people acting alone and in competition with one another, or does the text help us imagine people working together?
- How does money figure in this text?
- Are there groups you belong to in this text? What do they look like here? If your own groups are missing, what would they say if they were in the book?
- What really hard things are happening in this text? Are these things happening in the world now? Where?
- How different are people allowed to be in this text? Does it assume everyone is happy and good in the same ways?
- If the character in your book has problems, can you see how those problems are about having or not having money, struggling with others for power, or being cheated or helped by society's rules?
- Who has "power" in your text? How does that power get shown?
- At what points do you notice yourself resisting the book, the characters, or the author? What does your resistance say about the book, and what does it say about you?
- How does this book help you think about social issues you care about or causes you are committed to?

Figure 3–1 *Some Questions for Critical Reading*

the texts they read but also the subjects they study, the media messages they watch and hear, the things that happen in the classroom and the world. To that end, the teachers ask whose perspective is present in any given event and whose is missing. They invite children to take different perspectives on a situation in order to understand how things got to be the way they are and possibly how they can be changed.

Role-Playing

Linda Christensen and Bill Bigelow have used role-playing as a strategy to help high school students understand issues of injustice and inequity (Bigelow 1994). One curriculum they teach centers on the nature of public schooling, including what lies beneath the surface of school life—how the social realities of a school day were constructed historically, and why. Students role-play Hungarian immigrants, corporate executives, members of the middle class, black activists, and school administrators in the early twentieth century—the people who created or succumbed to what has become the way school goes. As part of the project, students evaluate an actual test from 1920, asking what kind of intelligence was being measured and valued by its multiple-choice questions.

Critical conversations are enriched by any kind of role-playing or perspective taking. Literature, history, and concepts come alive when they are embodied by actual minds and hearts living out all sides of the issues. In one of Katherine's fourth- and fifth-grade classes, a group of girls chose to spend several months reading Holocaust books. They also wrote poems in the voices of persons in train cars being taken to prison camps. The poems were quick, dramatic sketches in which the girls tried to imagine in dialogue and action what it was like to have been taken captive by the Nazis. Two of the girls, incredulous that the Holocaust had been allowed to happen, attempted to see the situation from the Nazis' side. They wrote poems reflecting some of the things they were reading about young German soldiers and others who felt they were simply following orders. One girl even attempted to write a "hate piece" against Jews. She was Jewish, and her parents were very concerned about her spending even a second on the side of evil. She argued that she had read everything from the victims' point of view (she had read at least twelve Holocaust novels, for children and adults; she had seen movies and visited the Holocaust Museum in Washington, D.C.) and still could not grasp why it happened. She wanted to try to get inside the persecutor's skin, to look at the world with hate in order to understand hate. Katherine's class "held her hand" and talked with her throughout the exercise. In the end, she learned that she wants to spend her life teaching children not to hate people who are different from themselves. This child's empathy and ability to get inside another person's skin is an extraordinary tool that will enable her to live a life of social consciousness and activism.

Critical Conversations in Multiple Configurations

In whole-class discussions, we teach how to read, how to make meaning, and how to employ critical concepts. We expect this learning to transfer to independent reading. For many it will. Many of the strategies we've talked about in this chapter can be used with independent, partner, and small-group reading. A teacher can help by posting critical questions on a chart as a reminder that these are things students can respond to when they talk, think, or write about their reading. She can also provide individuals and groups with photocopies of the list to help scaffold their written or verbal responses.

Let's look at a specific example. A reading club was reading the short story "Eleven," by Sandra Cisneros (1992), and had decided to focus on who has the power in this story.

HEATHER: I think this story is about injustice 'cause the teacher refuses to let Rachel speak and says, "I'm right, you're wrong."

ISAIAH: But you have to respect your elders!

HEATHER: But no one should treat you badly just 'cause you're younger.

LAWANDA: Why is the teacher so mean?

GRETA: In Laura Ingalls Wilder, they went to school in a one-room schoolhouse, and the teacher used whips on children who were acting bad. I think they were more strict then. So maybe this story is old—well, it's not a hundred years old, but maybe twenty years old.

CANDACE: When I put on my "critical eyeglasses," I tried to relate to how Rachel felt. Every single time you get older, you expect to be smarter, taller, but it doesn't come. She felt like all the years came back and she was little again.

LAWANDA: I want to go back to what Heather said. You know how sometimes little kids pester you? Maybe the teacher felt pestered by Rachel. Maybe the teacher thought she *was* right.

GRETA: Rachel gives up on her teacher. The teacher is trying to make her feel small, and it works. She feels all those little ages inside her. She said in the text, "If I was older, I would know what to do."

CANDACE: I agree with Heather. Some grown-ups do that, just because you're a kid. It happened
          to me before. I was in a long, long line, and this woman skipped me like I was thin air. Maybe
          she wasn't a parent, maybe she didn't have children.
GRETA: I think the teacher was abusing Rachel. She wouldn't let her speak. Like, "I'm older, so
        I'm right." Why people abuse kids is they forget what it feels like to be a kid. Like children
        are aliens and grown-ups can do whatever they want to them.

A teacher can also bring critical questions to her reading conferences with individual children, prompting and reminding them to consider these questions in their independent reading.
As with all instruction in reading, the object is to invite children to respond to their reading in rich,
multilayered ways. Critique is one layer, along with envisionment, personal response, textual analysis, and interpretation. Children find it particularly difficult to assume a critical stance, and teachers can give them a framework by way of critical questions. Katherine brought several critical
questions to a conference with Greta, age nine, who was reading *We Shall Not Be Moved: The
Women's Factory Strike of 1909* (Dash 1998). Greta copied the questions in her reading notebook
and wrote quick responses to them:

> These women are thinking about striking. It doesn't seem to me like it's actually gonna help them.
> They're just teenage girls. They don't get enough money. They want higher wages; they only get two
> cents a day, and they have to buy their own supplies—needles, oil for the sewing machines, thread.
> They're not allowed to talk, and I think they only get fifteen minutes for a lunch break.
>   Who benefits from this? Their families do because the girls send money back to their families. But
> I think the boss benefits the most. He makes them do all the work, and he gets all the credit and
> money. Rich ladies beat the girls. They're trying to get help from the rich ladies, but I think if they
> just stayed with each other, they could get power. The boss has the power, but that's why they're
> going to strike—to get power back.

During the conference, Katherine asked Greta if she could imagine a situation like this happening today. Greta said she knows it does happen in countries like India, where children are made
to work for no wages. In America, she said, it probably couldn't happen anymore, or if it did, the
workers would strike right away.
      When Angelina read *Will You Sign Here, John Hancock?* (Fritz 1976), she told Katherine she
noticed two big things: first, that Hancock risked his life for the rights of our country. "That's what
I call social action!" Angelina said. The other thing that stood out in this biography was that "the
only sign" of women was as "maids, lovers, cooks. This whole story is just about what men did,
and the women seldom stand out." Angelina also noticed that the illustrations portrayed only black
men serving white men, and that a little black boy looked more "poor and ragged" than the white
boys he seemed to be playing with. Her feeling was that neither blacks nor women were given
enough space in the story to make it a fair representation. Katherine asked Angelina what kind of
role she could imagine herself playing if our country were trying to win its independence today.
"I would fight if I had to," she said, "but in modern times, maybe we could find another way
besides war. Maybe we could have a conversation or maybe write some letters to the King that
would convince the English to let us go."
      Greta and Angelina couldn't possibly understand everything about the complicated social
contexts of the historical periods portrayed in the books they were reading. But they did understand how to read critically, how to look for whose perspective takes center stage, and what kind
of roles are being played by the more vulnerable members of our society.

Possible Justice: Responding to Narratives by Imagining a Better World

Our conversations about literature are only important if they help us read our classroom better, if they connect to the ways we live together. How can we extend the imagination it takes to live inside a book—the ability to make meaning and build the world of the story—to a social imagination, a belief that we can make lives better and more just for people? How can we do what it takes, as Maxine Greene says, "to invent visions of what should be and what might be in our deficient society, on the streets where we live, in our schools" (1995, 5)?

A leap of social imagination can happen in response to story. Stories of collective action can help people imagine what they might do together to make things better. Just as Sartre would have readers become the fiction they are reading, to give it life, we can give birth to freedom and possibility through stories of social action and caring. We can rewrite our own lives in the wake of the texts we read, and we can write ourselves into action toward a world better than the one we read about.

One year Katherine read *Charlotte's Web* to her multiage primary class. She read it twice, the second time skating across the story and looking at the relationship between Wilbur and Charlotte, reading it as a story of loving across differences. The children listed the things that are the same and the things that are different about Wilbur and Charlotte. They began with Wilbur's initial doubts and fears about Charlotte:

> "Well," [Wilbur] thought, "I've got a new friend, all right. But what a gamble friendship is! Charlotte is fierce, brutal, scheming, bloodthirsty—everything I don't like. How can I learn to like her . . . ?" (White 1952, 41)

How, given so many seemingly impossible obstacles to friendship, did Wilbur and Charlotte manage to become best friends? Jennifer and Elijah saw themselves in the characters: Jennifer threw her arms around Elijah's neck and said, "I'm white, and I'm a girl, and Elijah's a boy and he's black, and *we love each other a lot!*" This pronouncement was followed by much hysterical squealing from the other kids. Another child volunteered that he was in second grade and his favorite friend in the class was in kindergarten, so age doesn't matter.

It's easy to allow animals to be best friends in books, no matter their physical, social, or economic differences. But stories about animals are not necessarily naïve. When *Charlotte's Web* is read through a critical lens as a story about differences, the difficulties in relationships become apparent. Katherine asked her students to make a giant leap of response, to generalize this concept from the text and then ask, "Where is this happening in the world now?"

Katherine read the first pages of the book, where Fern is trying to save Wilbur from her father's ax. Her father explains that Wilbur is a runt—small, weak—and any farmer knows a runt will not amount to much; keeping him will only be a burden of labor and expense. Fern believes this is a "most terrible case of injustice." She cries out, "But it's unfair. . . . The pig couldn't help being born small, could it? If *I* had been very small at birth, would you have killed *me*?" (White 1952, 3). Katherine extended Fern's premise and asked, "What if Wilbur were human? Wilbur was a vulnerable member of his community, saved ultimately by Charlotte just because she loved and cared for him. What if he were a human that would not amount to much and someone wanted to kill him to save his family from the burden?" Adam suggested that every time Katherine saw the word *pig* on the page, she could read *human*, so she did.

SHERRISA: Yeah, what if Fern didn't care, and she said, "Go ahead, kill him." Or "Send him to a foster home"?

DANIEL: My little brother Jacob has cerebral palsy and he knows how to do something better than me—cry.

ADAM: If you don't let those people like that die, they could grow up and get a job!

KATHERINE: Do you think getting a job is what makes a person valuable?

PETER: No, it's that the person is good. The person is alive.

DANIEL: And one more thing Jacob's smarter than me at is flying dinosaurs. Every time I pretend this toy is flying, and I put the dino's mouth to his hand, he laughs.

KATHERINE: So Jacob is smarter at laughing and smarter at crying than you?

ADAM: Daniel loves when his brother can laugh or cry because he can't *talk*. If you know a person, you love them and want to take care of them.

KATHERINE (*responding to Derrick and Peter, who have begun to hit each other*): Well . . . several of you know each other very well, but you fight so much.

ADAM: That's the hardest part. To know why. They're sitting on the rug, and one of them starts teasing, and that starts a fight.

ELIJAH: Maybe they just don't care about each other. Derrick said he doesn't like himself when he was telling us his life story at the beginning of school.

ADAM: I think Elijah's answer is the truer answer. They always want to move away from each other; they don't care.

KATHERINE: So remember again how Charlotte is so different from Wilbur, and she has a busy job laying her egg sac. Why does she take time from her life to become Wilbur's best friend and to help him? He doesn't do anything for her. He just eats and sleeps!

SHERRISA: She feels sorry for him. He is going to get killed.

DERRICK: Wilbur doesn't have anything. He has no friends.

PETER: Charlotte is a loving spider, she cares about Wilbur.

DERRICK: Charlotte should be our mother.

Katherine hoped that reading the story of Charlotte and Wilbur as a story of accepting the most vulnerable in our society will help the children become "loving spiders." There is only one "rule" or expectation in her classroom community, and it blazes across one whole wall: "Our Community Pledge: To be a good friend." Katherine knew that her years with the children in this classroom would be a journey, an inquiry into what it means to be a good friend. She used story after story to guide and shape the community in its journey.

To sustain itself, a democracy must convince its young people that our story is not yet at an end, that there are chapters still to be written, drafts still unrevised. They must know that there is much work for them to do. Classroom communities are always in the process of becoming. The ways we are together, the stories we read and tell, and the ways we push for deeper and deeper response create a place where children are not speaking to each other as what but as who, creating an opening among people in a community—what Hannah Arendt called an "in-between" (1958, 182). Can they reach across this in-between space to shape their world? Can they work together to imagine a better community formed not by a teacher's rules and standards but by their common needs, their caring for each other?

Katherine read *Peaceful Warrior* (Clayton 1964), a biography of Martin Luther King, Jr., aloud to her fourth and fifth graders. She wanted to give them a vision of what Maxine Greene calls "the transcendence that came from King and his followers being together in a particular way." Greene calls King's community "a community of *beginners*, moved to imagine what *might* be if they took action together" (1995, 40). Katherine wanted her students to use King's story as a model for collective action toward some greater good in the school, the community, the city, the world.

What she did not anticipate was that her students would be able to see their individual circumstances mirrored in the life of Martin Luther King, Jr. At least she didn't anticipate that a white child would. Yet Ben saw himself in King's story. Ben was very much an "other" in her class and in the school. He had been diagnosed with ADHD, depression, and mild autism. He was heavily medicated. He did not write or do any class work, almost never talked, and when he did it was only to whine loudly, or to shout out angry accusations and curse words. Some children tried very hard to include him in their collaborations, even though he often sat with his head on the table or directed tirades at them. Many others begged not to be Ben's partner, and Katherine had to mediate whenever she placed him in a group.

When she read the story of King's childhood, the times he was persecuted for his skin color, how he was kicked down, received death threats, had a bomb thrown on his porch, and never fought back, Ben was listening closely. He followed Katherine out the door as she was leading the class to lunch and said, "I'm just like Martin Luther King, Jr.," his one and only contribution to a book discussion.

"What do you mean?" Katherine asked.

"Well, the way people picked on him, they pick on me 'cause I'm different, 'cause I'm something they don't like. They're prejudiced just the same way as white people against black people. I'm just not black. But I feel the same way."

Ben's words were a slap in everyone's face. Katherine remembered what Greene said about children with labels like Ben's, the disabled, the "at-risk" kids who receive "treatment" and "training" from the outside but are never allowed to be agents, never given freedom to choose and to act from their point of view of difference (1995, 41). Ben's personal response to King's story became a political response. His voice in the community finally created the possibility for dialogue, and it gave Ben a way of seeing not just for himself but for others.

King's story created a script for Katherine's children to inhabit, a good, loose script they could use to reshape their community and their way of living together. They began to look for ways to take action in the world. They invited friends and family members to talk to the class about their lives as political and social activists. These were not typical guest speakers but possible role models, possible scriptwriters for the children's own life stories. Their stories were a frame on which the children could hang their own details. Richard Rorty writes, "Each new generation of students ought to think of American leftism as having a long and glorious history. They should be able to see . . . the struggle for social justice as central to their country's moral identity" (1998, 51).

Katherine's students were fired up by the story of Martin Luther King, Jr. They were aghast at the injustice of segregation laws, and they never quite understood or believed that this story took place during Katherine's lifetime! They conflated the period with slavery, back a long time ago when white people were just so bad. No one could be that bad anymore! They talked a lot about how Martin Luther King, Jr., and their friends and family members actually lived the words they spoke and wrote about. Theirs were not empty words, but words backed by action, words full of personal risk and sometimes tragedy. Harste and Carey (1999, 2) propose that we help children realize that reading isn't really finished until we take social action in response to it: "It is not enough to read about women's rights. You have to act and talk differently too."

Katherine's class decided to make a wall outside their classroom with quotes from King's speeches and a list of actions and events that demonstrated how he "lived" his words. They wrote their own pledges to "live" their words, words they could back up with actions, not vague, sentimental proclamations. Maria wrote: "I pledge to try to look at Ben and notice him." And she did.

She noticed that he was an amazing artist, and she asked him to draw posters for their "Students Against Student Violence" social action group. She noticed that he always sat alone in the cafeteria, and she moved her group of girlfriends over to his table. He still would not talk to them or look at them, but he did not sit alone.

Stories of caring, stories of collective action, stories of love across differences, these are what we wish teachers would fill their classrooms with. We want the stories to open children to the possibilities of freedom. We want the stories to inform who they become. We want children to carry with them into the world the image of how to make peace, how to reject racism, how to help someone who is in trouble, and how to guard the earth. We want them to become parents who sit at dinner tables with the children of the future and ask, "What will you do for the world?" And then, to listen to the possibilities.

CHAPTER 4

DEMOCRACY
BEYOND WORDS
Social Structures in the Reading Workshop

Unless we make critical conversations available to students, unless we set the discourse in motion in the classroom, we cannot expect children to develop questions and stances related to social justice either now or in the future. The content—what we talk about when we talk about reading—is crucial. But we can't just talk about democracy and justice; we have to enact them within the structures of the classroom. And then we have to talk about them again, in political language that describes what we are doing here, in this room.

There is no reason to think that crafting democracy in classrooms will be easy. People have been working for at least twenty-five hundred years on how to live together in ways that create strong, stable, self-governing communities while still protecting the interests and desires of individuals, and no one has ever gotten it right. But, like many others, at least since John Dewey, we believe that the principles of democracy, and the struggling interactions they invite, are the best process for creating classrooms in which people learn how to learn, in which inquiry flourishes, and in which citizens are socialized into productive engagement with possible publics.

A big part of teaching is deciding what relationships people in the classroom will have to one another. As reading teachers, we might decide that everyone will read the same text, or that everyone will choose her own, or that students will read together in pairs or groups, or that we will use some combination of these approaches. We decide whether questions about texts will come from the teacher to the students, from the students to other students, from one reader to himself. We decide whether responses to texts will take the form of writing, art, drama, or a combination of media, and whether the mode of response will be prescribed by the teacher or chosen by readers. Teachers tend to think of these decisions as methodological, as structural, and have a cultural predisposition to evaluate them on the basis of whether they are likely to "work" or "not work." Some teachers, in addition, have become used to the notion that these practices embody theories of reading.

But these decisions are also political. Because teaching involves the creation of social arrangements, teachers are always, inescapably, involved in political work. Every day's lesson plan encodes a set of unequal relationships and a political theory. We cannot choose to leave social relationships out of a particular day's plan. Our structures or methods are the students' relationships—to each other, to texts, to knowledge, to their teacher, to the world outside the classroom. We demand of them that they practice ways of associated living every day; we can only assume that they internalize those habits. The nature of this togetherness matters.

Not only that; it also matters how we talk to students about the ways the class is expected to work together. Our instructions to reading groups are as much a part of the discourse of reading as our talk about texts is. Our response to an individual student's trouble choosing books embodies themes about the possibilities of independent action within a democratic community, about the nature of freedom. Coaching reading partners in how to talk and listen to each other while moving together through a book involves not only introducing procedures (though that's part of it) but also helping students internalize theories of dialogue and difference. Most instructions, redirections, corrections, and solutions to problems are opportunities for us to highlight political values, think with students about the world we are building together, and become a little more wide-awake to the critical dimensions of our everyday lives. We encourage this thinking by talking plainly about the principles we are trying to live by in our classrooms and also about how they either do or do not apply in the social world outside school. Thus, our teaching can become less politically innocent or transparent, and we can foreground important themes of social justice. This interdiscplinary work differs from the usual read-a-book-about-the-historical-period-we-are-studying approach. It involves bringing government/civics/political science ideas and concepts into classroom management and reading workshops and bringing the problems and experiences of our work in reading and writing into government/civics/political science inquiries.

In this chapter, we describe some of the classroom structures, or planning elements, we have found useful in building reading workshops. We also relate some of the social reasoning that we and students have discussed while working out how to live and work within these structures. For each particular planning element, we provide the following: a description of the structure; examples of the sorts of trouble that typically arise; reflections on the political meaning of the structure and themes teachers might discuss with students; and some thinking about how those same themes work in the larger world of the United States. We describe each structure so that teachers can, if they so choose, establish them in their classrooms. We provide examples of predictable problems because it is sometimes in the difficulties students encounter that the social meaning of the structure becomes apparent. Often, it is in the responses to what real students do that the details of teacher decision making are tested. We reflect on the political meanings relevant to the structure partly because they provide the most important rationale for implementing the structures and partly because we want to make the case that teachers must talk to and with students about such matters in order to develop the classroom's critical discourse. (Originally, our reasons for using the structures we're describing was that they seemed the most effective in helping kids become strong readers. We are not, for the most part, presenting that rationale here. Rather, we are highlighting the democratic themes that inhere in these structures.)

The political work we do in classrooms has meaning only in the ways these patterns and practices work out in the larger social world. Progressive teachers sometimes create little democratic utopias without ever examining with their students how *what we're trying to do in here* contrasts or corresponds with *how things go out there*. For one thing, this keeps us from helping kids transfer the structural thinking at which we work so hard together to their wider experience. For another, our silence about larger systems allows students to gesture superficially toward the "democratic" structures, never buying into a vision of social justice (or even confronting and resisting it). Finally, by considering the broader social enactments of ideas like choice/intention or dialogue, we may, as practitioners, complicate and revise our understanding of how such principles work, revise our expectations, and solve problems in our own teaching and learning.

Exploring Reading Lives

Description

Every person's reading life is unique to her or his own circumstances, life history, relationships, interests, needs, and habits. Readers are as different from one another as human beings are. Too often, reading in school is taken as a single thing, a goal everyone shares in the same ways. A community of readers can only develop a shared, intersubjective understanding of reading when each individual brings her or his particularity to the conversation. Therefore, we need to begin the school year by investigating *who we are as readers*.

There are lots of ways in which readers differ. What comes to mind immediately is that different kids like different books. That's part of it, of course, but it's only one of the ways in which we construct our reading identities. Location, body position, light source, stillness or background noise, the presence of food and drink, ways of keeping some part of the body moving, all contribute to what Marie Carbo (Carbo, Dunn, and Dunn 1991) refers to as reading style. In addition, each person has a reading history, a story series of memories that contribute to one's current relationship to reading. Reading is thinking, and everyone's mental style is different: some of us visualize still pictures, some see action and movement, some of us zero in on voice, some of us relate to characters as if they were real people, some of us notice pattern and design. Our goal is flexibility across many modes of thinking in reading, but every person brings particular dispositions and strengths to the project of growth in reading.

We can ask students to think about themselves as readers by asking:

- What do you remember about your earliest experiences of reading? Did someone read to you? What was that like? Did you have books? When do you remember first noticing reading?

- Tonight, look around your home for possible reading spots. What kinds of places can you find? Think about whether certain places might be better for different kinds of reading. For example, the kitchen table might be good for some things; your bed might be good for other things; the steps outside might be good for still other kinds of reading.

- Who knows what you are reading now? Who recommends reading material to you? To whom do you recommend things? Whom do you sometimes tell about what you are reading?

- When you are reading, what do you see in your mind's eye? How does your envisionment usually go? What kinds of things are easier to see and that make richer pictures in your mind? Is it like a movie or like a painting?

The following are some areas to explore on the map of a reading life:

- *History:* early memories; school experiences.
- *Social network:* reading friends; family relationships surrounding various kinds of texts; recommendation networks; the role of reading in clubs and church/temple groups.

- *Habits:* light, sound, body position; food and drink; need to wiggle; proximity to other people; duration of reading sessions; special places.
- *Reading as thinking:* how you see the text; how you hear the text; how you picture characters; the kinds of things you think about characters; what you notice about how the text is written; how you respond to confusion or difficulty; the kinds of feelings generated; whether other texts come to mind.
- *Pleasure:* the sorts of things that give you pleasure in reading; the relationship between the text and the real world; the language that pleases you; the kinds of textual organization that click with you; times when you have the impulse to try writing in a similar way.
- *Social groupings:* aspects of your reading that might have to do with being a female or male: aspects of your reading that might have to do with the racial and ethnic groups you belong to; the ways in which the amount of money your family has, and the kinds of jobs people in your family hold, may contribute to your being the reader you are; other social groups you belong to that may orient you to reading and thinking in particular ways; the ways your sexuality and affectional preferences affect the ways you think about texts.

This is a lot to examine, and it's not something you have to "get done" before students start reading, nor is it just a unit to cover. Rather, it is a line of inquiry to focus on early in the year (usually during independent reading) and is then ongoing. The idea is not that each reader is a type, like a zodiac sign, fixed for life; rather, we expect transformations in our reading identities as we grow together through the year. Our identities are fluid and continually in evolution. For example, students often begin with statements like, "I'm the kind of reader who hates to read." To claim that as a fixed identity would be more hurtful than helpful, and it would be better never to have brought it up. But if the inquiry continues with questions other than simply liking/not liking, the possibility for transformation is present.

We use a variety of activities to help students think about their reading lives. Using multiple sign systems, or intelligences, or thinking devices, provides points of entry for different kinds of thinkers and also extends the reflection of everyone. Some typical activities include:

- Student/student interviews.
- Public interviews in which everyone questions a particular reader.
- Writing about the differences among readers.
- Writing answers to questions about ourselves as readers.
- Keeping a journal in which we "spy on ourselves" as readers.
- Focused ethnographic investigations of one another's homes, rooms, habits, and reading conditions.
- Drawings of ourselves at a representative moment in our reading lives.
- Metaphorical drawings of what reading is like for us.
- Drawings representing ourselves as readers now and at some time in our lives when we were different.
- Acting out critical incidents in our reading lives.
- Acting out private moments in our reading lives, with props, to show the conditions we set up for reading or times when reading is hard to accomplish.

- A letter-writing cycle about life as a reader initiated by the teacher writing about her or his own life as a reader, with students writing back in dialogue.

- An invitation to bring in landmark books in your life history as a reader and share them with a small group.

- An invitation to bring in books that are easy and books that are hard and share them with a small group.

- Sociograms—or any kind of diagram or chart—representing the social networks of our reading lives, or the social groups that make a difference in the ways we think.

- Using sticky notes on every other page to keep track of what we see ourselves doing, mentally, as we read.

These activities make use of common inquiry strategies—direct observation, note taking, reflective writing, examining artifacts, graphic representations, dramatic reconstructions, interviewing. What makes them especially valuable is their application to reading as an area of ordinary but unexamined experience: students are asked to become conscious that they have particular identities, preferences, experiences, and styles as readers and that they are constantly making choices and *doing something* other than "just reading."

Predictable Problems

Getting this investigation going is relatively easy: students are thinking, talking, and writing about themselves, taking their own personalities as objects of study. The information they need is already known or right at hand. The work is to notice what usually goes unnoticed; as such, it fits with habits of mind many of us try to build through firsthand science investigations, writers notebooks, and other curricular areas. There is teaching to do, but the topic itself is inherently motivating.

Problems arise because of a couple of persistent "commonsense" attitudes toward reading (Gramsci 1991; Mayher 1990; Varenne and McDermott 1999). The first is an almost quantitative description of oneself as a reader using the binary terms of success/failure: "I'm a bad reader"; "I'm a pretty good reader"; "I was in the eighty-ninth percentile on the reading test"; "As a reader, I'm about a B+"; "I couldn't read until I was in second grade, but then I started to get better." Varenne and McDermott (1999) find this the most persistent theme in our cultural conversation about education. We all buy into it and enact it constantly. They also suggest that we educators need to try as much as possible to set aside those terms—and the system they represent. This isn't easy, but the specifics in the investigations described previously do help us move beyond the initial impulse to reproduce this vertical measurement of a singular, unproblematic entity assumed to be "reading." The question is not *do you like to read?* or *are you a good reader?* We are after a more qualitative, descriptive investigation of the people in the classroom as individuals and members of overlapping communities.

The second problem in student responses to these investigations is the tendency to "shop." Committed readers, particularly, often think of reading only as consuming products, picking flavors. It's often hard to get them to talk about anything except *why I like science fiction* or *why I don't like Katherine Paterson*. Difference is about more than preferences, and the possibilities of transformation are limited when these are the only terms in which we describe ourselves. Again, focusing on many areas for investigation helps students move beyond this consumption mentality.

That's why the invitations for investigating oneself as a reader aren't wide open; they are directed toward aspects of reading lives other than the ones that are most insistent in our culture.

One other common theme is problematic, and we have already touched on it. The first thing many people say about themselves as readers is whether or not they like to do it. Again, this is a description of an attitude, not of how one goes about it. People who say they don't like to read aren't resisting reading "walk/don't walk" when crossing the street or the URL address of a website on a television screen. Quite often, they aren't talking about newspapers, magazines, baseball cards, comics, song titles on CDs, notes from friends, or their own writing, either. Most of the time, they are talking about reading in and for school, which is perfectly reasonable, since that is the context of the conversation. They may also be equating reading with reading books or novels, another reasonable miscue, since those sorts of reading are going to be the focus in most reading classrooms. One way past these binary alternatives is to break "reading" open and think about it as a more diverse activity than the students originally expected.

Related Social and Political Themes

Difference and diversity are obviously important notions here. The basic assumption is that people are different, seem strange to one another, and that celebrating those differences is part of why we're in the classroom together. This is a fundamental change from assuming that reading consists of predefined skills that everyone must perform to a standard. While we are not suggesting that people's reading processes have nothing in common—of course they do—highlighting the differences in the ways reading occurs in multiple worlds and minds makes new connections (across gender or race, for example) possible. An African American boy and a white girl might both be very visual readers. Introducing different kinds of difference helps break down social categories that the culture and its history have fixed for us in advance.

Investigating reading differences also helps create community. It may be a paradox that by attending more closely to individuals, we create a group, but it can be so. It is usually easier to become a member of a community when you are known for who you are. We feel a sense of belonging by being understood and recognized, and this sense of belonging releases our energy for action in the community: *since people know me here, I may be able to act to change things, especially if my identity is assumed to be one of potential and evolution.*

By bringing many of students' life experiences outside school into the reading curriculum, we are honoring their ordinary lives outside of state institutions. Valuing the lives and work of ordinary people is a democratic theme, since it empowers the knowledge and folkways of the people against the agendas of authority (Christensen 1995; McDermott 1997; Moll 1997).

A qualitative descriptive conversation about reading lives helps move our shared values beyond identifying winners and losers. Recognizing the diverse way reading happens in different people's experience lets us create more interesting, not simply "better," ways to grow as readers. Even if the cultural assumptions are too intense in the subtext of the classroom, we can resist the explicit vertical listing of members from best to worst. There are other things to think about than how good you are. This seems pro-justice.

In order to become a reading community, members of the community have to assume they know what others are talking about when they use the word *reading*. Unless we reveal the unspoken, unexamined reality of reading in each person's life and mind, we all just pretend to be on the same page. Only when we get our assumptions out in the open can things be negotiated and shared. This applies to any area of the curriculum, but reading's invisibility (as an individual act) requires more than the usual explicitness. By bringing out and thinking together about our reading lives, we are moving from the personal, subjective, solitary world of reading toward a social, intersubjective, shared life.

Relationship to the Wider World

Perhaps the most overwhelming source of injustice in our world is our obsession with success and failure, winning and losing. Our society's mild acceptance that so many of its children live in poverty does not stem from a committed belief in the divine right of the rich. Rather, we allow ourselves to think that the rich are somehow better than the poor, that they are smarter, harder working, luckier, more talented. If there are successful people, there must be people who are failures. If there are winners, there have to be losers. If there is a ninetieth percentile, there has to be a tenth. We apply this sense of competition to every facet of life—sports, of course, but every other area of experience as well, even the arts. We compete in our love relationships. We give our mothers cards that say, *The world's greatest mother*. We rank graduates; we count honors; we spin and spin and pad our resumes. All to be better than someone else. Learning to think qualitatively goes against this grain.

Anyone reading this book will probably agree that "respecting diversity" is important in a democracy. But maybe the phrase has been overused to the point of becoming hollow. Explicitly investigating differences refreshes the wonder at another's peculiarity that is the emotional heart of honoring difference. Our culture becomes more homogenized by the day, as more and more of us work for the same companies, wear the same clothes, expect the same satisfactions in our lives. If we are to continue to experience the meaning and satisfaction that knowing who one is can bring, it is ever more essential for us to look in detail at the peculiar ways each of us interacts with her or his environment.

Maybe teachers, even our whole culture, have talked about reading so much, weighed it down with so much baggage, that we cannot see it anymore. When very large groups of people have talked a lot about one thing, the shared definition can prevent intelligent conversation, because every concept ends up stereotyped and shorthanded. A single word like *love* calls up for millions of people a set of definitions and assumptions—gender roles, images of good relationships, rules about how to feel—that condition our ways of thinking about even our most intimate, intricate moments. In order to be in a community where the possibilities for love are transformed, extended, and really known, we would have to feel safe to disclose, to talk about, how love goes for us. Categories of culture like reading (but also like gender, race, class, power, money, relationships to nature) need to be examined intricately by people in the process of talking about their lives. Without conversations like that, we are caught within unchosen boundaries.

Independent Reading

For us, independent reading is both point of departure and destination. It is more than "outside reading," more than choice, more than solitude. This is the classroom structure in which members of the community work on their reading lives. All investigations into reading differences begin in independent reading. We set up whole-class, partner, and small-group reading experiences with an eye toward affecting the reading lives kids construct independent of authority. After all, if students can't create rich reading lives without our influence, what's it all for anyway? We do not think of independent reading as individualistic or solitary; rather, it is a continual negotiation with others, a way of being with both local and virtual communities. It is a way of participating in important conversations and setting agendas for social action. *Independent* is really a misnomer. Reading lives are inherently dependent—if nothing else, on a writer and the people who produce the physical texts. Readers always read within communities, always choose particular texts by way of some social route, and always think with others (even if only internally) while they read. But we want individual students to be able to plan and build reading agendas without help from an authority. Consequently, as a school structure, independent reading has special meaning.

Practically speaking, setting up independent reading is pretty familiar and also pretty straightforward. The first consideration is where students will get the books they are going to read. At any particular moment in an independent reading workshop, there are as many books in circulation as a teacher has students. (For teachers in self-contained classrooms, that's around thirty; for teachers in departmentalized setups, the number may approach one hundred and fifty.) If students are going to be able to choose books all through the school year, there have to be a lot of books available. Of course, some students may have books at home or be able to buy them themselves. Forming partnerships with school and community librarians, letting them know that the students need books they're interested in and able to read without much assistance, provides an extra source of support. Having a well-stocked classroom library is also important. Teachers can build these libraries using a combination of their own money, school budgets, donations, and points awarded by book clubs.

The classroom library should be set up physically in the room so that a number of students can browse there at the same time. It's often helpful in the long run to have students help set up the library rather than having everything organized the first day of class. Like many instances of shared decision making, this is a messy business, but the students are better able to find what they need, even when the organization they've come up with isn't the most logical. At the beginning of the year, teachers often include a special section for easier books, labeling it "light reading," "quick reads," "easy and breezy," or a similar name that carries little stigma. Though the purpose is to make sure struggling readers can quickly identify texts with which they can feel strong as readers, other students, too, sometimes select a book from this section for a quick read. Teachers who want to raise the literary quality of students' choices by highlighting some books keep in mind how bookstores get our attention—by setting certain books face out in an easy-to-reach place. Frequently, that's all it takes to get a book circulating through a class.

The independent reading workshop schedule follows that of the writing workshop. Usually, there is a whole-class meeting at the beginning in which the teacher presents a minilesson. This short meeting is followed by the heart of the workshop, which lasts from twenty minutes to half an hour (or longer). During this period, students read books they've selected themselves and the teacher confers with individuals (and sometimes small groups of readers pulled together for a particular purpose). At the end of the workshop, the class sometimes (but not always) comes back together for another meeting, during which the teacher may ask particular students to report. In most cases, these are students with whom the teacher has conferred that day and who she now wants to share something about how they are reading and responding with the rest of the class. Occasionally, kids can recommend texts to the class during this time. The structure is flexible; the only absolute ingredient is a block of time during which students read and the teacher confers with them.

Some elementary teachers start the day with independent reading, forgoing the initial whole-class meeting or minilesson, and then use a whole-class meeting at the end of independent reading as a way to segue into writing workshop or some other classroom structure. Others find later in the morning or after lunch a more harmonious time in light of their purposes and schedule. Some teachers, usually later in the year, have their students read their own books at the very end of the day as a way to prompt them to read more at home. Wherever it goes, it is a priority—one of the first things we schedule—because ongoing, everyday reading is so important if we are to grow as readers.

What do students read during this time? The main criterion is not what they are reading on a particular day but what they are reading over a period of time. They should be continually constructing an agenda, a plan for what book they will read next and next and next. Every powerful reader has a bedside table stacked with books she intends to get to sooner or later. We want students to have their own metaphorical nightstand stacked with books related to new or ongoing interests. The teacher cannot prescribe or assign what students read; the intellectual environment in which readers live must include choice. Over the last twenty years or so, *choice* or *ownership* has been something of a fetish for some teachers. But choice should be viewed as something that arises from the environment, not as the educational objective. What we are working toward is intention, the ability to plan and construct a reflective reading life. While it may occasionally be necessary for a student to abandon a book, that is always the exception. Teachers need to push students to be consciously aware of what they are after in their reading lives and to make and arrange selections that will further their projects. For some students, this means reading a particular genre or the works of a particular author; for others, it means reading many books related, even loosely, to one topic or theme; still others may be exploring a certain kind of feeling, a certain type of thinking.

While students are reading, the teacher confers with a few individuals one on one. Although a full discussion of all that goes on in conferences isn't necessary here, a sketch of the shape of a conference may be helpful. Conferences take place at the student's desk, not the teacher's—an "onsite" interruption of the student's reading, as it were. First, the teacher finds out what is going on in this child's reading, through observation and a brief interview: What, mainly, is this reader doing in this reading event? What and how is he thinking? The teacher listens and tries to fit this information into all the other things she knows about this student as a reader, a learner, a thinker, and a collaborator. She's not looking for a mistake to correct or something the reader is doing wrong. She may notice some thinking the reader has already begun and decide to help him name and extend it. Comparing what he talks about to her mental map of reading, she might decide to redirect his attention to some kind of thinking that doesn't yet seem evident. Her teaching consists of explaining to the student what needs to be learned and then helping him devise an activity that gets him thinking in the new way. The student then continues the activity after the teacher leaves the conference, extending his engagement with the teacher's objective beyond the moments she is physically present. Thus, a reading conference consists not merely of listening to a student read out loud (in fact, we do that infrequently) or making sure a student is getting her work done. Rather, a reading conference involves positioning students on the map of reading and helping them move further and more flexibly along it.

The writing, sketching, note-making, and other thinking-on-paper that students do as an extension of a reading conference may be housed in a reading journal. We discuss some of these response strategies below. But an independent reading workshop is not primarily concerned with writing or any other kind of external response. Mainly, it's about reading. Too often in school we think nothing happened if there is no commodity produced at the end of an experience. We think kids need to "do" something, not just read. But a big part of the message of independent reading is that reading itself is doing something. In life outside of school, readers do not make book covers or dioramas or give book reports. The only product of reading is experience, a reformulation of our past and the discovery of new questions for the future. Furthermore, when the objective involves motivation, intention, and energy for reading, inserting cumbersome projects into the process is like tying heavy weights to students' ankles. If we value reading as an aesthetic experience and as an intrinsically valuable activity in a learning life, the structures we establish in classrooms should say so.

Predictable Problems

Because independent reading affords students both choice and the time to carry out their intentions, relatively few problems arise. However, choosing, reading, and responding to texts independently all involve a level of self-confidence not shared equally by all students. Students who are used to doing only what they are told naturally have trouble believing that their decisions can be acceptable or sustainable. (This difficulty does not improve as children mature; college students suddenly given responsibility for their learning usually behave much more insecurely than primary-grade students do.) Nor is the trouble limited to students who struggle academically; kids used to getting high marks and other rewards are often the least willing to take a risk.

Most classes have a few students who are reluctant to make any choices without teacher guidance. They keep trying to hand responsibility back to the authority, and the teacher has to keep handing it right back. That is not to say that teachers can't offer any support, however. We make sure kids know themselves as readers and can remember successful reading experiences. We interview them about preferences and interests and get them to jot these realizations down. We make sure they know what their kind of book is, what level of difficulty they can tolerate about particular interests. And we get them to choose not just a single text but a reading agenda, a line of inquiry they can follow from book to book. If they need our approval, we give it to this larger agenda, even writing it down in their journals as an official assignment and signing it. What we are supporting, though, is the process of choosing, not thought content. The purpose is to let the student experience successful decisions so that future decisions will not be as painful.

Perhaps a thornier problem is that some students make dysfunctional decisions, and the teacher needs to redirect their choices while still keeping their energy high. A bad reading decision is one that undermines the reader's strength and purpose. Struggling readers, used to experiencing reading as confusion, can have such low expectations of the quality of reading experiences that they despair of meaning. They consistently choose books that are too hard, spend a great deal of time trying to get started, and abandon books daily. The productive teaching response, for the purpose of their developing wisdom and efficacy, is not simply to make the decision for them.

Rather, we need to guide them through the decision-making process, to set a long-term agenda, and discipline their work on that agenda. Often, with struggling readers, the most efficient way to solve this problem is to make the reading agenda more concrete by working with them to choose a set of texts they will read over a stretch of time. This keeps the decision making in their hands, but limits the choosing events so that they can sustain their engagement with print—the most important objective if they are to grow as readers.

In addition, some students, usually the same struggling readers we have been discussing, are distressed if they don't receive constant authoritative feedback on their reading, understanding, and response activity. It's almost as if only the teacher's attention makes the experience real. Thinking with a book is a wobbly and indefinite experience without the gaze of an authority figure saying *yes, that's good, that's right* all along the way. Much of the need for company in thinking can be satisfied by letting them discuss their book with a partner or a small group. That way, someone is listening to their thinking, sanctioning their internal processes, even if the approval is not authoritative. Most important, the teacher needs to resist being cast in a role that simply perpetuates dependency. The need for approval has been learned through relationships and experiences, and the ability to sustain independent work can only be encouraged in the same way. Frequent conversations about the importance of initiative and efficacy are also in order. With an insecure student, a one-on-one pep talk about her or his strong thinking in the past is essential.

Anyone who teaches in a reading workshop soon recognizes something that at first appears to be a management problem: Students suddenly looking up and talking when they are supposed to be reading. However, closer observation of these impulsive conversations reveals that they often spring from the reading. As we've said, readers always have others in mind when they read, people to whom they, internally, offer ideas and responses. It's hardly surprising that some students externalize this thinking. This social impulse is what drives the reading curriculum from independent reading toward partnerships and clubs. During independent reading, it's useful to provide opportunities for readers to talk across their nonshared texts. In a whole-class gathering or on a bulletin board especially reserved for this purpose, students may put out a call for conversations about topics like books by a certain author, how to find time to read, types of characters, genres, big ideas in books, response activities such as sketching or chart making, or kinds of thinking (envisionment, personal response, questioning, social critique) called forth in reading. Appointments such as these allow students to monitor their impulses to chat about their reading and make it not only possible but useful to cap the talking during independent reading time.

Social and Political Themes

In critical practice in education, so much attention is often given to anti-individualist values of community and collective action that we may risk ignoring the theme of freedom. Furthermore, critical educators can become so committed to ideas of social justice that we heap that content on students and restrict their freedom to inquire. For example, we might, in an effort to keep students focused on important social issues, assign everything they read as whole-class texts. That might intensify the language of justice while being poor practice of freedom. A goal of overturning processes of oppression is to increase people's freedom and self-determination. We want people to be able to pursue agendas they care about, to define their experiences with less intrusion from authority, to construct meaningful and pleasurable lives. Surely, that is the ultimate goal in reducing the unfairness in the world.

But it's not so obvious how to support people's ability to live freely, to avail themselves of the liberty to which they are entitled. Having guarantees of free speech, for instance, does not guarantee that people will be equally empowered to know what they want to say, equally disposed to speak, or equally listened to by others. We give students the freedom to choose what they read, but their choices are constrained by their histories, their personalities, their identities, their relationships, and their place in the world. Even though their teacher may not be telling them what to read and think, they may still choose texts that make them look cool to their friends or smart to their parents, remaining in line with cultural norms in place long before the teacher decided to allow "choice." The freedom to choose, combined with the demand that they develop meaningful intentions as readers, will resonate differently with students used to picking out toys in stores than it will with those who have never been able to choose anything they own. "Free choice" is never really free but is always conditioned by multiple conflicting pressures. For Freire and other critical educators, spaces of freedom and hope are opened only when people are consciously aware of and able to talk about these constraints on their lives and minds.

Creating freedom in independent reading, then, has to involve work on two fronts: providing the opportunity to make decisions and creating conversations about the pressures on students' choices. We can point out that several students are hot to read books based on the newest pop cultural fad and get kids talking about the ways their desires are sometimes constructed by corporate profit agendas. These conversations may not stop kids from reading badly written books about the next "in" thing, but they will at least make them aware of the pressures and do more to resist them. Our overall goal to reduce mass culture's power to make clones of us all doesn't mean we never participate in mass culture. We may also need to talk with students about the pressure to seem a better reader by picking books that are too hard, or about being so afraid of being seen as the uncool "schoolgirl" or "schoolboy" that they choose texts that are less rich than they are capable of understanding. Whatever the pressures, intentions are never simple and never isolated from social positions. We increase the possibility of freedom by getting our students to talk about the social processes by which their decisions are constructed, by making them aware of unexamined values so that they can make more wide-awake choices.

Relationship to the Wider World

A friend recently told us that a group of undergraduate future teachers had objected to the idea of giving students choices in school, asserting "they won't have choices in life, so they should be prepared for that." This statement is a significant claim about what life is like outside school. Do people have choices? What is it like to make a choice? How are our daily choices influenced by our ongoing intentions and projects? And how, from the perspective of social justice, should we think about individual freedoms?

Some educators dismiss the progressive emphasis on interest and choice, likening it to consumerism. Only in America, the argument goes, would the value system exemplified by a shopping mall be elevated to an educational good. This is an interesting challenge, and if students' choice of what they read and think about were as trivial as their choice of tennis shoes, then it would be valid. But no one said, when civil rights leaders staged sit-ins at lunch counters, that the ability to choose which restaurant to eat in was nothing more than consumerism. Well, probably someone did, but most of us wouldn't have taken such an argument seriously. At issue was much more than where African Americans ate lunch—it was being seen as fully human enough to choose one's daily life. When we are fighting for social justice, one of the values we are fighting for is the freedom of the vulnerable to choose, both the large decisions about the course of their lives and also the ordinary, everyday way they conduct life's business. The freedom to choose what one puts one's mind to is important—important enough to weigh against adults' desires to choose for children or against the belief that certain books are good for children or against adult anxiety that children's choices will be wrong.

Benjamin Barber has written:

> Participation as a political mode obviously presupposes citizens capable of meaningful and autonomous choice, as do all coherent theories of democracy. Consent without autonomy is not consent. But participation enhances volition in that it lends to choice the direct engagement of the deliberating mind and the choosing will. While clients or voters or constituents or masses may be characterized in ways that omit their free agency, participants cannot; individual volition is the heart of the idea of self-legislation through participation. (1984, 134)

Education for democratic participation has to help students develop agency. Future citizens have to be able to decide what interests them, what to think about, which journeys are worth the traveling. And they have to develop the efficacy to act on those choices. This is not the same kind of choice as deciding which kind of toothpaste to buy, and it is not simply a matter of "motivation." We are concerned, rather, with intention, volitional through-lines, what Dewey (1916) called aims. If reading really matters, if it is really thinking, then it must connect to projects rooted in the past and projected into the future. Such values make the obedient, exclusive reading of assigned texts, even good ones, seem shallow and dangerously trivial.

Whole-Class Shared Reading

For us, the purpose of the whole community reading a text together is so that everyone can share, in more detail than is possible in any other structure, some ways of thinking with text. When the whole class is reading the same thing, it's easier to talk in detail about how we envision scenes, how we make and revise interpretations, how we take textual evidence into account and change our understanding of what's going on in a story, how we apply a concept such as power to the details of a story or argument. With a shared text, it's easier to develop a shared language to describe the kinds of thinking we do. It's easier to help students write reflectively about their reading, sketch in response to text, role-play to get inside a scene, or use technology to collaborate with other readers at a distance. Therefore, our goals with shared texts focus on those things that are made most possible by mutual reading experiences: developing a shared discourse to describe our community's ways of reading and developing tools for thinking. We do these things not as ends in themselves, however, but in order to support students in their reading lives away from this mutual experience.

These goals are different from the ones that are more common in schools. Often, people read whole-class texts because they are anxious that without teacher help, students won't understand what they read. This concern, if it limits students' independent and small-group experiences, creates dependency and interferes with students' reading development. Some people assign most of the texts students read because they believe there are certain texts that everyone needs to read. But it is a delusion to think that anyone, even the smartest people in the world, could ever determine what everyone else should read. Sometimes, teachers may feel the need to control students' reading: to be certain that kids read enough, to make sure students read something "good for them," to see that they comply with demands for response activity, and to ensure they understand the text "properly."

To establish control, teachers may create a number of nonreading activities: quizzes, retellings, journals, reports, tests, and special forms of discussion. Each of these genres creates an unnecessary load of discourse learning and distorts the reading process toward accounting to authority rather than making meaning in dialogue. This control agenda also creates undemocratic habits in students: anxiety about complying with authority, lack of initiative, acceptance of authoritative interpretations. Readers who have all their reading assigned to them become apathetic, passive readers who get used to waiting for someone to tell them what to read and think about. This is not only dysfunctional; it's undemocratic. Just imagine a society in which all the citizens wait for authorities to tell them what to read.

Teachers are always looking for "good" books to share with a class, but there are perhaps more important decisions than the text to be shared that we must make. It is crucial to have some goals in mind about what we are using this whole-class experience to teach. Since we aren't teaching the book, what do we want out students to learn? For our purposes in this book, using shared texts to develop critical discourse is the most important objective we can name.

But we also have other goals for whole-class reading, purposes related to social justice, perhaps, but indirectly. Reading involves many kinds of thinking, and we might focus on a couple of them: envisioning, paying attention to sound and voice, exploring our relationships to characters, taking pleasure from language and design, entertaining multiple perspectives, developing questions and hunches, or applying intertextual thinking. We also might choose one or two response strategies to focus on for a particular book: drawing, drama, double-entry journals, thinking aloud ("say something"), or taking notes during oral reading and conversation. Sometimes, we choose these objectives from our assessment that something is missing from the class' work. Other times, students coconstruct what-we-are-working-on-with-this-book as a class, planning conversations, negotiating objectives among themselves and with us. It's not that we doggedly focus on particular kinds of thinking or particular response activities, to the exclusion of all else, but it is important that we know what we are trying to teach with a particular text. The goal is that students will have a clear-enough, rich-enough understanding of those objectives that they can employ them in their independent reading and in non-teacher-guided collaborations.

A shared text may be short (an article, picture book, poem, short story) or long (a whole book) and can be experienced by a whole class in two ways: having it read aloud or giving each student a copy. Some activities, like marking a text, are only possible when everyone has a book. Then, too, if each person has a copy, it can be taken home and read in a completely different context from the one in which it will be discussed; this highlights reading as preparation for conversation. Usually, however, we read most shared texts aloud, because the level of difficulty cannot be just right for all the readers in a class, and listening lets all of us share the thinking without the burden of decoding print. In addition, there is great benefit to having the sound of written language resonating in the classroom. Hearing sentences, the flow of logic, the structure of narrative, the intonation of phrasing, is crucial if students are to internalize written structures and use them to predict how texts might go when they read and write on their own. There is also no better way to create the felt sense of sharing a text, the concrete experience of togetherness around a story, than having everyone listen to the same voice. Finally, reading aloud allows us all to stay literally on the same page, to stop and think together, to watch together as the horizon of the textual world shifts before us.

Even though shared reading mainly involves the whole class reading, listening, or talking together, other, smaller, social structures also come into play. Within the shared experience, there are moments when everyone is doing something alone—writing about what they are thinking at a particular point, for example. Students may also have the same partner throughout the reading, the person to whom they turn to say something when appropriate or with whom they have a written conversation. Students can also meet in small groups to jump-start their thinking about the text and get a number of voices going at the same time. They may take notes or sketch and then compare how they approached it. They may even assign their own activity for the next couple of days' reading and meet later to compare strategies and negotiate meaning. To scaffold students' collaboration through shared experiences and help them develop habits and dispositions necessary to participate later in reading clubs, it is useful to give small groups gradual autonomy so that students get used to making decisions while still under a teacher's guidance. In other words, it behooves teachers to view whole-class shared reading not as a monolithic mass structure but as a fluid combination of smaller social structures.

Even though we have all these other goals for whole-class texts, the most significant outcome is, of course, community. It may be easy to lose sight of what is happening: the class is experiencing something together, feeling together, knowing that the others in the room are thinking and feeling similar things, understanding, too, that others are thinking slightly differently from oneself. Each participant knows that the others know the same story. That quality of *I-know-that-you-know* is called intersubjectivity, and it is a fundamental characteristic of human thinking. It's especially tricky to get intersubjectivity in reading, since it seems to happen inside the head. If we do not achieve it in a reading classroom, however, we cannot teach, because we have no shared understanding of "reading" to point to and affect. Shared experiences with text are crucial to creating such shared understanding. Reading a book together should be like taking a trip together. We have memories we feel confident in referring to in future conversations; our shared history permits us to build a richer network of communication and imagination. We can plan action together because we can refer to our shared sense of how the world goes and what matters in it.

There has been so much talk about *community* in professional literature over the past twenty years or so that the word may have become almost meaningless to some. We are mistaken in thinking of it just as a way of saying "be nice" or as a sort of naturalized warm fuzzy. A sense of *us*, of each individual belonging to a familiar group, is crucial to learning to think and to read. Shared texts, read purposefully, can help democratic classrooms full of individuals become communities.

Predictable Problems

Some of the risks in shared whole-class reading have to do with engagement. Sometimes students become passive and apathetic about experiences they have had no hand in setting up. Some students may feel the shared book is the teacher's and has nothing to do with them. Not seeing their own initiative as playing a role, they are not likely to spend any mental energy imagining new ways to think together or developing ideas to contribute. Whether they do what they are supposed to or resist, they do not see themselves as having a stake in or a responsibility for how conversations develop. Once their will is unplugged, they can choose only to obey or disobey, and which they do will usually be determined by the roles they have been constructed to play in school, the ways they have usually found, in school and at home, to take control of their lives.

The tendency to disengage is amplified because kids' classroom experience occurs in the context of the much wider experience of school. The norm in schooling is that the teacher (or the state or the district) selects a text and coerces those with less power into one of two possible positions: compliance or resistance. Even if we are trying to do something different with shared texts, students may perceive it as the same. The difference doesn't exist for them, either because they think it's a lie or because they never even perceive the teacher's intention that things are to go differently here. In elementary schools, they may be importing the norms of previous teachers and communities (or school-like experiences outside of this classroom). In secondary schools (and college), the possibility for this miscue is more intense because students are simultaneously participating in multiple ways of studenting; in their other classes, their passive attitude may be precisely what is demanded. Sometimes students' passivity can stem from the opposite circumstances. When their choices have always been honored, when they are used to determining their own activity, students may become willful and exceedingly self-directed and may view any shared agenda as an imposition. This can happen in progressive classrooms and in communities where children have much consumeristic autonomy, the resources and parental deference that allows them to buy whatever they want. The good intentions of their teachers (and perhaps parents) to create active, intentional learners may have become distorted in kids' individualistic drive for satisfaction. They may not value inquiry that is shared, public, and negotiated.

There is a need for much teaching in order to attempt to counter passivity. Students' conceptions of how to participate in this class are mediated by the discourse and activity set in motion by the teacher. If we want students to perceive this as a shared experience of thinking, as an opportunity to make up together some ways of responding to texts, of a journey we are taking together, we have to say those things again and again. We have to talk explicitly about what we are trying to do and what we want from them, how we want them to be actively engaged. We have to build structures in which they can be inventive and have their ideas taken up by the larger community. Though we plan objectives and activities, we have to make those plans open enough to be responsive to disruption and digression sponsored by all members of the community. We have to work hard to teach them to be open to shared community thinking, to public experiences and ideas, rather than being merely passive or willful about their engagement with others.

Another problem with selecting one text for a whole class is that some kids will say they don't like the book. That is the way the complaint comes out, and it is often the terms in which the teacher will worry about how things are going. Nevertheless, there is more going on in this seemingly simple statement than in a different statement of taste like "I don't like broccoli." First, we have to consider whether the text may indeed be inappropriate for the class. If we've chosen it for no reason other than it is "a classic" or is on a required list or is "good" for the students (like medicine), then resistance like this is to be expected. It's a sensible response to an authoritarian agenda. However, if we've chosen the book for these kids in good faith, as a product of some negotiation, with an informed expectation that it will introduce useful or important thinking to the community, that's a different problem. We need to focus on the kids' sense of why we are doing this together, of what is to be gained from openness to text and conversation. In a strong, thoughtful community, shared reading, even out loud, is not simply entertainment. It is an opportunity to think together, to negotiate meaning about the shared text and our shared world. Liking/hating, thumbs-up/thumbs-down are not the most important considerations and are not the main things we should be thinking and talking about. If we are taking the text as an object of inquiry and a point of departure for thinking critically about the world, then it is no more appropriate to say "I don't like it" than it is to say "I don't like it" when a sponge begins to sink in a science inquiry about buoyancy. It's a private preference that does not further public consideration and shared thought.

The statement "I don't like this book" is what Rorty (1999) calls a conversation-stopper. It's hard for anyone to say anything else once someone has staked a huge claim in a conversation on dismissing the object of shared attention, especially when we all know that we are going to be engaged with this text for some time to come. Once this loathing is on the floor, a few people will usually speak up sympathetically, saying that they agree the book isn't that good, and then everyone else feels foolish saying anything affirmative or trying to take up issues that might have been more productive of shared thinking. It's a killing consumerism that is worth resisting in our teaching because it not only interferes with aesthetic education, the disposition to remain open to a work of art and to collaborate with it. It's also a stance that is anathema to democratic participation. The fact that particular community concerns do not tickle us personally or do not affect our own pocket books should not keep us from engaging in public dialogue and social action. It is most useful to discuss these attitudes with students before someone creates an identity as "the one who hates this book." This is not silencing students' thoughts; rather, it is maintaining dialogue in the community. It's sometimes very hard work, changing this conception, and it's tricky trying to support student voices while perhaps seeming to censor certain kinds of comments, but it's important enough to keep trying.

Another problem that inevitably arises in whole-class discussion is the dominance of some voices and the silence of others. Chapter 3 suggests some strategies that help students become more aware of the need to share the floor and that help kids who would like to speak more find a way into the conversation. Still, no teacher can ever dust off his hands and say, "Okay, done. Fixed that." In any group, there are voices that are louder and more frequently heard, and there are voices that are softer and less often command attention. If we just think about ourselves talking in groups, we know that participation is always very complicated, that speakers and listeners are always making fluid, on-the-spot decisions about when to talk and where to put their energy. Researching conversation participants, we have found that students, even quiet ones, think constantly about whether they can, while simultaneously listening and thinking and monitoring, also compose something to say that will be taken as smart, interesting, helpful, relevant, and "right" (in that it fits with the values of the community). Sometimes, more silent students quietly despise the students who always talk, and they just don't want to become like those people who take up everyone's time with their blathering. Social norms, roles, personalities, and internalized pacing of turn-taking all play a role in determining who speaks when. It's not simply a matter of some people dominating others. It's certainly not all about intelligence or openness or willingness to be a participant. There are many ways of participating, and one cannot determine whether talk is democratic by counting the number of turns each individual takes.

It's hard for teachers to know whether a discussion has gone well, especially whether all members have participated equally. We always think, *it would have been better if so-and-so had talked.* Feeling like this and reflecting this way is a good thing up to a point, because it keeps us attempting to open up more participatory space, makes us attend to the unheard, and extends in us the ongoing process of democracy. Still, it might also be instructive to be realistic about it at the same time. In any community, some voices are heard more often than others, and often, leadership emerges from the more frequently heard voices. The concept of a leader—someone who speaks out more, who has a more frequent hand in setting agendas and deciding which topics get more attention than others—is not necessarily antidemocratic. Leaders can, however, become tyrants, imposing their views on group members without their consent. The key to keeping leaders in line is making them accountable to the larger group: they lead by consent of the group, not merely by force of their own will. In whole-class discussions, the teacher can create such accountability by regularly saying to the group, "Okay, we've heard these ideas from the people who've been speaking first. Are they the same as or different from the ideas of those who haven't talked yet?"

Social and Political Themes

Reading a book together as a class is a complex inquiry into how to live together, make decisions, and associate with others. More than any other classroom activity, whole-class shared reading takes place in a public space, a town square, as it were, and requires students to negotiate their individual preferences and habits within the collective will. Everybody has to come out of her or his own private house and engage with the big *us.*

For John Dewey, democracy is a mode of feeling, a way of living, a set of habits or predispositions that individuals share concerning each other. It involves each person being open to the ever-changing possibilities presented by the group. This attitude of openness is something we need to talk about explicitly with students, and they need to discuss it with each other. It is part of what we are teaching when we teach reading. What might the world be like if we succeeded in educating a generation of people so disposed?

At the same time, participation in whole-group activity and thinking needs to connect to the concerns, desires, and needs of individuals. People become alienated from public participation when it seems to have nothing to do with their "own" everyday lives. When we teach reading strategies through whole-class texts, we need to say more than "this is something you should do in your independent reading." We also need to say, "When we read and think together, whenever we participate in community activities, we are learning things to care about in our individual thoughts. We are sharing values, changing our minds, and developing other ways of seeing problems, all of which we can think about when we're alone and talk about with those closest to us. Without a public life, we have poor private lives." The social and political meaning of reading together cannot be implicit in the teacher's planning; it needs to be an articulated theme of class-room discussion.

Participating in a public conversation is not intrinsically good. It matters very much what the content of that public conversation is and what the content of our personal participation can be. One could argue that the last thing kids raised on Saturday-morning commercialism need is instruction in how to buy in to public thinking. By valuing the collective here, we are not suggest-ing that individuals uncritically internalize the values and perspectives of collective texts or con-versations. Our participation in groups must always involve weighing others' claims against our own commitments. We need to talk to kids about thinking for themselves even as we value think-ing with others.

In the midst of our thinking and writing here about the importance of collective, public dia-logue, we visited an exhibition at the Whitney Museum of American Art in New York. It was called The American Century, and it examined themes and trends in art in the United States during the twentieth century. One of the themes was "the cult of the individual," and it showed clearly how many artists have resisted the mass media and group-think that often generates a passive, conven-tional, and robotic public. Seeing this as clearly a critical theme and a desirable value for students to internalize, we were troubled anew by the complicated relationship of individuals to collectives. In attempting to correct individualistic values, we had been elevating the collective and depreciat-ing the individual, taking them as opposites rather than dialogical positions. Rethinking this posi-tion through the lens of art, we realized we needed to keep inquiring. We want students to resist conventional, easy thinking and to participate in changing the ways they view the world and the perspectives available to others around them, just as these artists had done. We began to see that engaging with "the public" does not mean merely receiving and internalizing what everyone else already accepts. Rather, it means seeing the public as multifarious and looking for the diversity of positions available in the conversation. It means also formulating an answer, sometimes in resistance to the direction of the tide of public opinion.

Whole-class discussions give us a chance to pursue the relationship of an individual to groups surrounding him or her. Talks on "the rug" are a manageable context for creating apprenticeships in thinking about significant social and political ideas. It is not unusual for a student in a discussion of a shared text to say, "Everybody seems to be thinking this thing, but I don't see it that way." What might be new is to talk about what this student just did as an instance of an individual's relation-ship to society. We can value, in so many words, the impulse to go against the grain. We might also talk about how being flexible enough to listen to others makes our own voices more trusted.

Whole-class discussions can also lead to powerful thinking about the ways people commu-nicate with each other in society. Communication, especially *talk*, is the primary means by which everyday public life is carried out. People negotiate, make mutual decisions, compromise, set agen-das, retell history, and dream futures together through talk. It is democracy's medium. Benjamin Barber writes:

> Because conversation responds to the endless variety of human experience and respects the initial legit-imacy of every human perspective, it is served by many voices rather than by one and achieves a rich ambiguity rather than a narrow clarity. It aims at creating a sense of commonality, not of unity, and the mutualism it aspires to weaves into one carpet the threads of a hundred viewpoints. Conversation does not reify metaphysical certainty as political unanimity; all it can hope to attain is a dynamic of interac-tion that permits transient convergences as well as ongoing differences and that makes moments of shared vision desirable oases in a never-ending conversational journey. (1984, 185)

People who are especially effective at democratic negotiation have capacities that if shared by everyone would create a social fabric that made sure more voices were heard, more justice shared, and more freedom won. Skill at talk could create more democracy. Burbules and Rice (1991) list the following "communicative virtues":

- Tolerance.
- Patience.
- Respect for differences.
- A willingness to listen.
- The inclination to admit that one may be mistaken.
- The ability to reinterpret or translate one's own concerns in a way that makes them comprehensible to others.
- Self-restraint in order that others may "have a turn" to speak.
- The disposition to express oneself honestly and sincerely. (41)

Scanning this list, our first reaction might be, "Hardly anyone has these virtues." Rice and Burbules point out, however, that many people do share them, under certain conditions—talking alone with a child, for instance, or with a parent or a friend. They are acquired by internalizing others' responses to us or by observing others' responses to third parties or by imitating people we admire. Every person who works on exhibiting these virtues replicates them in others—like a good virus. As with any instructional goal, however, demonstration should be accompanied by language that makes our political intentions as clear as possible.

Relationship to the Wider World

The culture of the United States increasingly becomes one of disunited individuals. Everything public is being privatized, and citizens retreat into gated communities and locked apartment buildings. Political mistrust of "big government" does away with public projects, social safety nets, and action in the name of justice. Everybody is an individual, first, last, and always, and if others can't get it together to make a good life for themselves, tough. Public dialogue is silenced by corporately owned media, by corporately purchased government favor, and by the consequent retreat of ordinary people from acting in the interests of any shared agenda.

At the same time, some conditions for democracy and public dialogue are growing, if imperfectly. Now more than ever before we are able to communicate—instantly, in the case of the Internet—with large numbers of other people in far-flung places. A great many people have the resources to produce, duplicate, and distribute printed material. Even though television is still controlled by corporate interests, cable television provides a little more access to diverse perspectives and information than we had in the days of the three national networks. Technology gives us the tools to reach one another, to create multiple new publics, if we have the intention, skill, and initiative to do so.

Our classrooms need to be open to the outside world, to become more involved in civic conversations and community service. However, it is inside the classroom community that we learn ways of dealing with others; dispositions to negotiate; and habits of listening and talking that will allow us to be effective, strategic, and sensitive participants in public discourse. Children in public school classrooms live in communities that contain more difference than most adults' lives afford. They go through every day side by side with people from many ethnic, political, and social backgrounds, with people whose interests and personalities are more varied than those of most adult coworkers. Schoolchildren are very much "in public," out in the community. Finding a voice here, developing the efficacy to speak and differ, attempting to create consensus, and building habits of civility are crucial steps in learning to create democracy moment by moment.

Reading Clubs

Reading clubs give readers the opportunity to think with others in ways they control themselves, to make collaborative decisions about what books to read and how to go about it, to carve out space for individual voices, and to deepen their habits of interpretation and critique. The members, usually three to five students, control the club from first to last, making decisions, learning from mistakes, and working out problems on their own. Because reading clubs stay together long enough to read a number of books (at least a couple of months), they are as much about collaboration and social negotiation as about reading and interpretation, and there is huge potential to learn in all these areas as they weave together over time. Reading clubs make it clearer than ever that reading and participating in communities are really the same thing.

When we, with colleagues at the Teacher College Reading Project, first started doing reading clubs, we introduced them right at the beginning of the school year. This was a big mistake. The kids didn't yet know each other—or themselves, for that matter—as readers, and they couldn't make wise choices about gathering around themselves the people who could best support their reading lives. Students need some months in which to define their reading lives, learn about each other, begin to share some values about reading, develop images of good conversations, and to participate in shorter-term groupings responding to their independent reading, whole-class texts, and short shared texts like poems and stories. Such an experiential base, with frequent reflection about what they were learning about reading together from the experiences, allowed students to make wiser decisions about the formation of more durable groups.

Now, we and other teachers employing reading clubs seem to follow a fairly predictable routine in forming them. Around the middle of the year (perhaps even a bit later), the teacher announces that reading clubs will be forming in a couple of weeks. The class then discusses the question, *What kinds of people will be the most supportive companions in your reading life?* After two or three brief conversations, students write a letter explaining their thinking but not naming names. In a follow-up conversation, the teacher reflects back to them the themes apparent in the letters, and the class again reflects on how they envision the clubs will operate. Then students write another letter naming the people they think would be good members of their reading club, stating the reasons each is the type of person they discussed in the first letter. The teacher then makes a sociogram (names spread over a sheet of paper with lines connecting students to their choices). Typically, the teacher has to tweak and manipulate a little here and there to make the groups come out even and to make sure every student belongs to a club. Then, on the day the clubs are to have their first organizational meeting, she announces them to the kids. (A less tidy way to do this is to have all the discussions, ask for the letters, and then just say, "Get into your reading clubs." At this point you have to throw yourself into the midst of the negotiations to make sure nothing comes out too badly. Doing it this way you interfere less with students' choices, but it makes many teachers nervous about some kids being left out and so forth. Randy actually prefers this way; Katherine prefers the former.)

Obviously, social negotiations are part of the work of reading clubs well before reading is. The first meeting goes very smoothly for about ten or fifteen minutes. By that time, what to name the club, whether to have officers, what book to read, or what reading procedures to follow has created conflict. That's okay; conflict is good, a necessary part of free and fair social life, even if it does not make everyone comfortable every minute. The only way to avoid conflict is to silence someone or everyone, and that does not permit the democratic community we're after. The goal is not to avoid conflict but to learn to work through it in ways that allow members of the clubs to remain committed to working together.

Anyone just beginning to work with small groups worries about where the books the clubs will read will come from. Ultimately, you need a big library of club books, multiple copies of texts likely to provoke good conversations. However, no one has this when they first begin. There are a number of strategies for getting started. Sometimes you can assemble the number of copies you need by borrowing from or trading with other teachers, consolidating single copies into sets and breaking up whole-class sets temporarily. (Often, kids themselves achieve this through a door-to-door campaign, but it's a good idea to explain the situation to colleagues beforehand.) Writing a proposal to administrators requesting five hundred dollars or so can make a shopping spree possible, and we have found it is best to believe there is always money around if you can shake it loose from other administrative agendas. If the principal does not have it, it's worth trying the district language arts coordinator and then the superintendent, since each office has some discretionary funds. In the longer term, you'll need to get your mind around your school's requisition process.

Again, written rationales and proposals for specific amounts are useful tools for this social action. Grants are available for teachers through many foundations and government agencies. All teachers use bonus points from book clubs to build these libraries, and most also buy some with their own money, even though it's so clearly unjust. And you'll be surprised how the students are able to use active resourcefulness to gather books from the school library, public libraries, the collections of friends and relatives, and through purchasing. We have seen this resourcefulness in poor neighborhoods as well as affluent ones. (Admittedly, the resources available to poor kids in cities are more ample than those in many rural communities.) When teachers turn difficulties over to kids, solutions present themselves through intricate relationships and channels no individual teacher could ever access. Teachers don't have to solve all the problems of getting books before beginning reading clubs.

During the first week or two, meeting almost every day during reading workshop allows the groups to consolidate, to develop a sense of "us." The group decides how to use this time: What decisions they need to make; whether to read while sitting together or to meet as a group only for discussion; what kinds of response activities will help them have better discussions. The structure of the reading period follows a basic workshop model of minilesson, work-time with the teacher conferring, and sharing. Once the clubs are rolling, meetings can be limited to twice a week; that way there's plenty to discuss each time. If they meet every day, the ten pages or so they may have read between meetings may not provide enough content for discussion, and the conversations have a tendency to degrade into procedural bickering. On days when the clubs don't meet, independent reading time can be devoted either to the club books or to independent books. Depending on how things go, some teachers find it necessary at some point to limit reading during this time to either independent or club books.

Minilessons and share sessions are a means for the teacher to introduce or revisit principles and structures for collaboration, reading, and response activity. Early on, minilessons and conferences tend to focus on clarifying and refining what a book club is. Suggesting an *agenda*—a predictable structure for all the club meetings—can be helpful if it's revised as the club develops new needs and ideas. If agendas are kept in a club portfolio, it is possible to see students' conceptions of what they can do together become more sophisticated over time. Teachers also give minilessons about rotating the role of a facilitator—not a boss, but someone to say "let's get started," help center the conversation, and decide the particulars of what happens when. Sometimes, teachers have found some other time of day to meet with facilitators in a "leadership council" in which they can support each other and receive advice about how to lead discussions from the teacher. It's often necessary to give a minilesson about doing almost all of the reading away from each other so that the meetings are mostly conversation. Teachers might also predict that they will have to remind students that response strategies, such as writing, drawing, using sticky notes, and making notes (strategies students will have learned during whole-class shared reading), are good homework in preparation for discussion. (If students don't take the hint, teachers eventually make reading at home and preparatory homework a requirement for club work.)

As time goes on, additional topics for minilessons and conferences are triggered by what is taking place in the groups. Most important, students will learn more about how to collaborate and have good conversations. We find it useful to watch for both needs and strengths along lines of growth like the following:

- Participants in good conversations really listen to each other and think together.
- In the beginnings of conversations, readers often entertain an open sort of wondering, casting about for possible things to talk about.
- Readers in conversation are willing to say first what's easiest to say.
- They can spot the more significant ideas on which to build their conversation.
- After the initial casting about, after they have recognized the more significant ideas, they name a topic as being "what's on the table."
- They keep the topic on the table for a good while, in order to build thinking.
- They refer frequently to things that are shared, such as the text, experiences, and shared notes.
- They are specifically aware of others in the group as particular readers and writers.
- They demonstrate a sensitivity to others being able to get into the conversation, especially quieter members who have trouble getting the floor.
- They ask each other follow-up questions to clarify that they have understood.
- They recognize the difference in their perspectives and interpretations.
- They are comfortable with disagreement but not addicted to it.
- They know how to go against the grain strategically, to stir up controversy in a conversation.
- They can change their minds on the basis of evidence and persuasion.
- They can compromise to reach consensus when necessary, as in decisions about what book to read or how to set up the agenda.
- They soften the edges of their disagreements by using phrases like "I see why you'd say that, but. . . ."
- They cycle back, returning to previous topics.
- They refer to past conversations.
- They see what the group needs and respond to those needs.
- They're comfortable just thinking quietly sometimes, not rushing to fill every pause.
- They're willing to speculate playfully about interpretations, to throw out ideas that may seem crazy.

- They pose problems about the text and about their conversation.
- They know how to formulate thoughtful questions for the group.
- They try to strike a balance between being faithful to a topic and being flexible enough to develop ideas.
- They are generous with their thinking, offering it freely.
- They are inventive about strategies for thinking, talking, preparing for discussion, and solving problems.
- Each member remains a participant, even in rough times.
- They demonstrate their trust that meaningful conversation is intrinsically beneficial.

Just as, during independent reading, the classroom is The Center for the Study of the People in This Room as Readers, during reading clubs, the classroom becomes The Center for the Study of Wonderful Conversation. Talk, as much as reading, is the object of study. To accomplish this, teachers have to make talk, usually fleeting and unobserved, visible and concrete. Adult demonstrations of good and bad conversations, fishbowl discussions, tapes and transcripts of groups, all are valuable tools. Some teachers find it helpful to gather all the tape recorders they can find in the building and set one up at each reading club, at least occasionally. Even if the teacher isn't going to listen to all these tapes, just having the tape running may help groups realize that their conversation is something they are *composing*. These teachers listen to portions of the tapes, sometimes on the drive home, sometimes to prepare for minilessons, sometimes to assess, sometimes to transcribe for teacher research. Sometimes, groups can replay their own tapes and reflect on their conversations; other times, groups can trade tapes and analyze the conversations of other clubs. Charts constructed by the whole class during shared reading stay up during reading clubs so that the class can revisit the discussion several times as they grow in their understanding of how to think together. (As always, the purpose of the chart is not to fix knowledge, but to revise it. The chart is an improvable object the class can use for thinking together [Wells 1999].) Rooted in whole-class shared reading, the class' inquiry into conversation extends throughout work in reading clubs, in which students have to take responsibility for creating good talk.

Predictable Problems

Teaching by way of reading clubs is all about problem solving. It might be possible to prepare instructions several pages long, to determine and delineate everything for students in advance. But this would short-circuit learning. Students first need to experience problems, even to endure some social pain in order to understand and buy into the wisdom of structures and procedures. They need to wrestle with the problems before they can really learn from their solutions, make strategic and intentional decisions about their ways of working together. That is why our approach to reading clubs is pretty open, especially at first, and we value a sense of ownership over the clubs even as we actively teach into them.

The problems begin with students' (and the teacher's) choices about who will be with whom. Sometimes, in the first few days, readers want to switch clubs or go off on their own. Almost always, we meet these requests with folded arms and forbidding or skeptical expressions. A big part of the learning involves staying together, working through problems with language, developing habits of resolving conflicts and compromising. Stomping off in a huff because you didn't get your way is not an option. On rare occasions, however, we do agree that the difficulty is not likely to go away, that there is a mistake in the club's constituency from the outset, and we allow, without fanfare, some slippage. On *very* rare occasions, we've started over from scratch after two or three weeks of trying to make it work, because the readers in all the clubs were so unevenly yoked, none of them could agree on a text.

We as teachers concerned with social justice may be disturbed by the groupings we see as we look across the room. Girls and boys may have chosen single-sex groups. Students of a particular race may all be together. These birds-of-a-feather trends seem to be a matter of social ease, and the early short-term groups may help. When students have had good experiences with a variety of people in the class, they seem more willing to diversify their choices, basing them on reading interests and conversation styles rather than automatic groupings scripted by the social world outside. (If the groups are still relatively segregated even after students have experienced diversified groups, maybe they know something we don't about their prospects for learning together.) If we are troubled by what appear to be ability-based groups, a better way to understand what brings these readers together might be to consider the kind of texts they will share. Reading club members do most of the reading on their own; the books need to be ones they can understand and think about, so it makes sense for students to get together with readers who are like them in terms of the difficulty of books they read. Joining a reading club with similar readers is not the same thing as having a teacher place you in the "low" reading group and deciding when you are ready to move "higher." Any reading club can choose any book, as long as they are continually monitoring for sense, so these sense-based groupings are not as oppressive as leveled groups. And of course, the class as a whole is still the basic community. That this community comprises people who affiliate with various subgroups shouldn't come as a shock to anyone.

How kids use the homework they've done to prepare for their book club discussions is another problem. Often, one student will read what he's written or show and talk about his drawing, the next will do likewise, and so on, right around the circle. After that they feel like they're done. There has been no collaboration, no thinking together, no negotiation of meaning, no discussion—it's just a patchwork quilt of everybody's separate thinking. The teacher has to interrupt this round-robin exercise, get everyone in the group to explore the first person's ideas. Only then should the group move on to another person's thoughts. Getting around to everyone in a single meeting is not necessarily the goal; over a number of conversations, everyone will have opportunities to share their work and initiate discussion. Getting students to wrap their minds around someone else's language, to think *along with* others, is an important way to teach listening. If nothing brought to the table is shared, the group fails to achieve an intersubjective conception of what they're talking about, and there has been no discussion.

Even without homework coming between discussants, readers sometimes act as if the other group members aren't there. One person says something, then somebody else says something completely unrelated. Here again, an interruption is in order, followed by some pretty heavy-handed assisted performance. We might say, "Wait a minute, let's go back to what Sammy just said, and everybody listen. Say it again, Sammy." Then, "So what does that make you think, Delores?" And, "How about you, Tony?" After a few students comment on Sammy's initial thoughts, we might say, "See what we just did? We took one person's ideas and we built on those. Before, you guys weren't even listening to each other. Now, keep on talking like this, and I'll listen." Sometimes we can achieve the same thing by just starting to participate in the conversation, asking a reader to clarify a remark, differing with someone, highlighting the importance of a point, in order to demonstrate conversational behavior rather than directing it. We circulate around the room, conferring in this way with different groups, in order to teach in detail habits of genuine listening.

Bickering usually occurs when members have different opinions about procedures: whether or not the meeting should include a brief time in which to write, how many pages to read, whether or not someone has been doing the reading and homework. These are layered problems. First, the group—or the stronger members in the group—may not be listening to everyone as plans are negotiated. The person who said she had play rehearsal and soccer practice the next few days so wouldn't be able to read a lot may have been ignored. Club members can't steam-roll over people; they have to listen and negotiate. When we intervene in disputes (and we don't always), we usually begin by asking the club to get out its agenda. Often, the answer is right there, already decided for them and by them; either they have forgotten the procedures they decided on or someone has impulsively or willfully ignored them. It's also possible that the consensus was imperfect in the first place and that the agenda needs to be renegotiated. The agenda, along with any other documents the group has agreed to live by, is the club's rule of law, a sort of constitution. It can be amended, but until then, the members have to do what it says.

Reading clubs look very different in different communities. In some schools club members may have fights, but they do not have vicious power struggles. In other kinds of communities, stronger children psychically crush those they perceive as weaker. In some the domination may be cheerful and good-natured, tastefully done in the name of getting things right and making the club really good. It's especially important for the teacher to monitor these situations, listening in and interrupting when necessary. Quieter members may need some specific sponsorship to get their voice heard in the group. It may even be necessary to impose temporary turn-taking procedures or written conversation strategies so that they can get the floor more often and find their voices. Taking the stronger students aside privately may also help, because the will to power can be such a part of their personalities that they are unable to see how they're behaving in the group and how that behavior fits into a larger pattern of difficulties they experience in other settings. These are usually kids intent on doing things well, and if the teacher can get them to understand a different standard—one of collaborating rather than winning—their will to please may become as strong as their will to power. But it's never easy; it's the hardest work imaginable.

Social pain goes with the reading club territory, and some teachers are personally disturbed by it. Kids are insulted and hurt sometimes. They cry. They get angry and pound the table. They feel rejected and abused, and the others feel guilty and defensive. We may begin to feel as if we've brought playground politics into the classroom, and we want it all just to stop. But kids can also choose to be kind, can take someone into their reading club in spite of his difficulties with the last one. Kids make up and help each other feel better. They give gifts, awards, and honors. They push each other to the breaking point but come back the next day ready to compromise. Reading clubs do permit kids to be cruel, but they also permit them to be kind. Both cruelty and kindness are intentional, moral, social action, and when kids have the freedom to make decisions about how to be together, they can choose either or both.

Just as in establishing the conditions for learning, teachers also establish the conditions for error: when we create contexts in which to make social decisions, we create both promise and risk. The teacher's role is to make sure that students recognize the results of their behavior toward one another, that they are confronted by the pain they cause and cannot ignore it. Reading clubs (and other collaborative structures in which students are in control of their social interactions) stand out from other aspects of school (except the playground) in that there are real social consequences to the kids' actions. Reading clubs are different from playground activities in that a teacher is ready to help kids reflect and learn to act in more functional, ethical ways, to help build habits of working together and enjoying each other, and to acculturate young citizens to democratic civility. What could be more important?

Social and Political Themes

Since different reading clubs are reading different books, related whole-class conversations are not about books. Sometimes, they're about reading, but most of the time they're about how to have a good reading club, how to have good conversations, how to solve social problems, how to collaborate. In other words, the whole-class conversations are full of social themes. The potential for conversations about social and political issues is enormous. Still, it's not hard to avoid the important conversations we should be having. It's easy to talk to kids about reading club relationships as if this is a special category of experience, as if the only question facing us is how to get by in this classroom structure. What themes might help us create the richest possible environment for social justice?

One difficult set of ideas comes up any time the teacher allows kids to make decisions about groupings. Sylvia wants to be in Tasha's group, but Tasha and the others don't want her there. These decisions involve themes of inclusion and exclusion, freedom of association, openness to others, empathy, and fairness. Recent literature about these ideas bespeaks a trend toward creating general rules that keep kids from excluding other kids. Vivian Gussin Paley's *You Can't Say You Can't Play* (1992) has been a rallying cry. Nancie Atwell says that in her school students cannot say no to one another (Henkin 1998). Roxanne Henkin (1998) suggests, as others have, that students be forbidden to form single-sex groups. Policies like this make us nervous. First, what principles of democracy are at stake? Second, what kinds of conversations, and therefore learning, are possible if teachers make other, different decisions?

The U.S. Constitution implicitly guarantees citizens freedom of association, which means the freedom to join with others by choice, the freedom to refuse to join with others, the freedom to include and to exclude. (The Supreme Court has abridged this freedom to exclude if and only if a large organization offers unique goods and privileges to members that are being systematically denied to particular classes of people, such as women.) The smaller and more intimate the group, the more important freedom of association is and the fiercer we would fight to defend it. Schools are an exception to this guarantee from the outset, since many students cannot choose their school and few students can choose the class to which they are assigned. This exception is probably for the best because it allows education to be nondiscriminatory and offers students the broadest exposure to the most varied ideas about what life is all about.

The question for a particular teacher is the degree to which freedom of association *within* a classroom is most educative for democratic participation. We are on very different ground here than if we merely ask which decision is likely to produce the fewest problems down the line and take the least time to address. Decisions about how to teach for social justice have to be more principled than that. Freedom of association is important because we construct our identities mostly through our affiliations with others; we not only express ourselves by choosing those with whom we associate, but we also *create* ourselves this way. Moreover, we create our learning lives by gathering particular others around us. Think of the powerful learners you know. What could be more important than their ability to choose well their collaborators, critics, and thought-collectives? No skill could be more important to gain in school. The trouble is, if Sylvia wants Tasha in her community of learners, and Tasha doesn't want Sylvia, someone is not going to get to choose. But freedom of association does not mean that everyone gets their way all the time; it means that people are free of authoritative interventions into associating as they please. From this perspective, it is neither desirable, nor even possible, to force Tasha to accept Sylvia. You may be able to make her quietly acquiesce to having Sylvia sit nearby, but you cannot make her *learn* with her.

Valuing freedom of association does not mean we say, "We don't care how you associate or how you treat each other," however. We still work to create shared values of openness, compassion, and fairness. We make students confront the social and emotional consequences of their decisions. We try to keep the issues open beyond the point when students may want to think everything is decided and over. We also work with students who may experience rejection and help them think of alternatives and maintain their personal dignity. We bring hypothetical issues as well as real cases to the whole class to reason through. None of this important teaching would be possible if we made the decisions about association in advance. In addition, we would lose this chance to talk about freedom of association in the world at large.

The fact that people have the freedom to associate in society does not mean that they take their ball and go home every time something in the group situation is uncomfortable or difficult. The possibilities of collective action and thinking keep people trying to stay together. (Think of churches, labor unions, charitable organizations, small political organizations, sports teams, and the like.) If individuals gave up on groups just because of social problems, much of the good in society would not get done, and many of the relationships that enrich individual lives would be unrealized. Of course, voluntary groups do sometimes splinter, and that is part of free association, but people of vision, commitment, and discipline work hard to maintain the group and not lose members. They compromise, postpone personal agendas, listen to the feelings of many members, and keep their eyes on the prize. They cultivate communicative virtues and develop more refined processes of decision making. Working with reading clubs, questions about how groups maintain themselves often arise, providing the opportunity to inquire about social groups in the outside world. Inviting adults to speak about the groups to which they belong, and bringing in books and articles about problems and solutions in current and historical groups, are useful resources.

Individuals within groups need to feel recognized and gain a sense of belonging from being a member. To the outside world, they need to be recognized as a member of the group. Some boundary has to exist, even if it's a thin one, between "us" and "the rest" or else the group has no identity. To help with group identity, groups almost always need a name, and they may have other symbols such as logos or flags. But it is the coconstructed, shared values and practices that help members separate life in the group from life outside. A set of groups with identical values and practices would be one group, not different groups. Asking reading clubs to think about the ways in which they differ helps solidify group identities. Talking about the varied groups to which individuals in the class belong is a way of honoring diversity and recognizing the ways each person constructs a personal identity partly through affiliation. Kids may also be interested in talking about the ways they, as individuals, are different in the different communities in which they participate. Jayla in her reading club is not exactly the same Jayla who sings in her church choir, and those Jaylas are different from the Jaylas who play on the soccer team, eat with her family, inquire in her science group, or run around with friends from down the street. Conversations about membership, about joining and leaving, adhering and resisting, can help students develop a perspective on being a contributing member of groups and negotiating roles within groups. Such lessons are valuable for participation in the social world.

Relationship to the Wider World

Democratic participation, after all, is not a matter of engaging with a huge mass of people, but rather about joining with local communities of people whose goals and interests are similar to one's own. (Local communities do not have to be geographically local. Transportation and communication across distances is easy enough now for geography to be only a minor concern with regard to group memberships.) Sometimes the goals may be specific and topical, such as stopping drunk driving or fighting Internet censorship. Other times, the goals may be more general, such as service to a local community. Members know each other, and implicit or explicit procedures develop for bringing new members into the group. A disposition to join and participate is the first step toward becoming an active citizen.

Democratic theorists, such as David Truman (1951) and Robert Dahl (1956, 1998), have written that the usual conception of American democracy as rule by the majority is mistaken. Law, policy, and elections are decided not by a majority but by overlapping small groups. These groups frame issues and agendas, agitate for change, apply pressure to institutions, and generate perspectives. In essence, they rule. Things get done in a democracy because small groups assemble around ideas, enlist others into the cause, and persistently make themselves heard by the government and the general public. Dahl refers to this process as "polyarchy," reflecting the reality that the public is really a set of publics. The process is uncertain, messy, sometimes contentious, often contradictory. As most adult Americans have figured out by now, by the time one gets to vote, alone in that shabby little booth, the possible options have been so radically narrowed that the notion that the majority's vote is "ruling" is rather silly. To participate in public life, then, to be a citizen, one must join groups or start them, continually thinking in dialogue and conceiving action *with others*.

CHAPTER 5

STRUGGLING AND DIFFICULTY IN READING
Managing Vulnerability

Working with struggling readers is not necessarily a separate aspect of a reading workshop, but creating ways in which to support the most vulnerable readers in a class does occupy much of a teacher's planning and thinking. We can't teach reading with an eye toward social justice if we don't address both the equity issues and some strategies for working with the students who need the most support. If we do not pay attention to how we work with these students, we run the risk of ignoring them entirely, thus setting up conditions in which only some students will benefit. The students already richest in reading capital will get richer while the poor get poorer. In so doing, we would reproduce the unjust callousness toward the vulnerable of the larger society— and of course, very often, they are the same people.

Who is a struggling reader? The term itself is suspect, since it implies that all struggling readers belong to a single category. Anyone can struggle, and no one struggles all the time. No two readers struggle in the same ways. A poor score on a test may mean simply that a reader struggles with tests, not with reading something she is interested in. Often the perception of struggling is not coming from the reader at all, but from grade-level expectations or similar setups of the system. However, even if we don't buy into these standards, there are still readers we would rightfully identify as "struggling."

People who, for one reason or another, misapprehended the reading process and have not put a reading system together that adds up to meaning; these are struggling readers. Looking at the words on the page, they feel as if they are trying to follow a conversation in a different language, and it does not add up to understanding. Perhaps they believe that reading is sounding out letters. Or they may spend all their mental energy recognizing words without internalizing the total sense of what the text is saying. They may put in time with text, their eyes going over every word and perhaps their lips uttering each one correctly, but never thinking the thoughts. When these problems occur in a text written in the reader's native tongue, about a topic of which the reader has some knowledge, we would say that reader is struggling. Struggling is not, however, the same thing as failing. Struggling implies *trying*, intentionally putting forth effort. When we watch readers in trouble, we *see* them struggle. Struggling implies that the effort expended is unnecessarily great, that reading should be easier and more energy efficient. It always involves a loss of meaning.

Teachers have classes in which some kids are struggling, in any number of ways, and others are not; this makes for instructional complexities (there are all these different kids and just one teacher). More than that, it turns a misunderstanding about reading into a social difficulty. The student looks around at his peers and realizes that their struggles are not like his. Certain tacit conclusions come to mind: I'm behind in some way; or I missed something; or I'm no good, but if I pretend, maybe no one will notice; or what can I do to avoid this?; or, the worst possibility, I'm not the kind of person who reads (Smith 1988). This measuring of self against others may be unavoidable in our society, but if reading is taught realistically, in all its diversity, the comparisons need not be this detrimental.

Investigating ourselves as readers (see Chapter 4) helps open a conversation about what makes reading hard for different people at different times. The point is for everyone to accept the reader she or he is and to develop an agenda for becoming the reader she or he wants to be. That we are all different as readers becomes very clear in this inquiry, and this realization is essential to a teacher's ability to talk honestly about difficulty and growth with individual struggling readers. If all the students bring in books they have found hard going, for example, talking about difficulties won't feel like "singling out" or tracking the students who need support. Understanding that anyone can struggle as a reader can awaken the whole community to the realization that these struggles are not a function of intelligence, ability, or age. Some teachers extend this inquiry through a brief whole-class study of difficulty, inviting students to read texts they find difficult, reading some short sections of texts that everyone in the room finds hard to make sense of, and talking together about how we handle difficulty and how it feels. This shared inquiry should be brief because reading at a "frustration level" makes everyone frustrated, and pretty soon, it becomes evident that readers aren't exactly enjoying themselves. Discipline problems sometimes become more pronounced, especially during extended reading sessions. (Adults asked to read material too difficult for them act up, get silly, go off-task, and generally misbehave in just the ways kids do, or worse.) Nevertheless, a little time spent looking closely at reading difficulty provides a set of shared experiences, a common vocabulary to use when working with individual students. It also helps teachers learn to recognize what difficulty in reading looks like from the outside.

Struggling readers need to choose books for independent reading very carefully (Bomer 1999). Because reading is so often confusing for them, they need to monitor closely whether they are experiencing understanding or confusion. If the book they are reading feels confusing, they need to find one that makes them have a feeling of understanding. The teacher needs to interrupt their reading frequently, reminding them to monitor for sense and helping them assess continually whether they have chosen wisely. It helps to narrow the selection process with these students, to make books they are likely to find friendly easily available, either in a special section of the classroom library or by developing independent reading agendas limited to texts they are likely to understand.

In many classrooms, in fact in many schools, books easy enough for struggling readers to get through successfully just aren't there. This is unfair, and it reproduces too-common injustice in the society at large. Money for books is one of the resources schools and teachers must allocate with an eye toward justice. If there is to be an imbalance, it should be in favor of the most vulnerable, not against them. It is hypocritical to attempt to teach for social justice and democracy without having enough easy books available to struggling readers.

A type of reading conference peculiar to struggling readers can be likened to running alongside a child learning to ride a bicycle (Tharp and Gallimore 1988). Teacher and student externalize the act of reading in conversation. The role of the teacher is to prop up the world of the text, to keep the reader's attention focused on what the text is *saying,* and to cue particular strategies for figuring out the words and meaning in the hard parts. Sometimes, the reader reads aloud, and the teacher coaches in response to long pauses and miscues. Most of the time, the teacher asks questions that encourage the reader to monitor for sense (*Does that make sense to you? What could it be?*). When a reader seems especially careless about the print on the page, the teacher might ask, *Does that look right?* When a reader seems unconcerned about whether a sentence sounds like language, the teacher asks, *Does that sound right? Is that the way we say it?* (Clay 1991, 1994; DeFord, Lyons, and Pinnell 1991). However, most often the problem is one of bad habits related to making meaning rather than with visual or syntactic cueing systems.

Very often, oral reading is not the issue: the reader utters most of the words written on the page, and the miscues they do make fit fairly well within the sentence and make some sense. Nevertheless, we know a reader is struggling because she is insecure or really wrong in her retelling of what she has read and her answers to questions about the text are unreasonable. In that case, the most useful kind of externalization is talking about meaning as it evolves. The student reads a bit, then reports on what she is thinking—what the text says and how she understands it. Then she reads a bit more and reports, and so on. Thinking aloud like this, in dialogue with the teacher's thinking and questioning, positions the reader actively and forces the reader to make something of what she is reading. When, as perhaps a follow-up to the conference, the reader is partnered with another to extend this work, there is a chance of rehabituating the student toward active meaning work rather than passively putting in time with eyes on print.

Reading with a partner, when it includes frequent interruptions to think aloud, is perhaps the most helpful structure for struggling readers. The two readers should plan ahead a few places to stop. At first, these stopping points will need to be frequent, perhaps every couple of paragraphs, but as time goes on, over weeks, the stops can be less frequent—every page, every couple of pages, every chapter. (This progression is too complex for a teacher to control; the detailed decisions should be in the readers' hands.) The social situation—having a partner waiting to hear what I think—requires a more active focus on meaning.

Scheduling conferences during reading workshop is a constant process of decision making for teachers. Clearly, struggling readers need more up-close assistance than others do, as well as more careful monitoring and more redirection from their avoidance behaviors. Direct attention is not the only way we educate, but it is an important way. Therefore, it is one of the resources distributed in the public of the classroom. As in the case of allocation of funds for texts, it is most fair that the balance be tipped in favor of the most vulnerable members of the population: teachers should give a little more time to those who need them most. Of course, the other children in the room mustn't be neglected—all children are members of a vulnerable class—but fairness does demand that we respond to need.

Spending a little time getting parents and other volunteers to read with kids who need support can free the teacher for other kinds of work. If volunteers are going to help, though, it is important that they understand how. Lester Laminack's *Volunteers Working with Young Readers* (1998) is a very valuable resource. Figure 5–1 lists a quick set of guidelines.

Along these same lines, it need not take anything away from the more powerful readers in a community for them to be helpful to the more vulnerable readers. The classroom community as a whole can provide a safe and supportive environment for struggling readers by:

- Launching a scavenger hunt in the school and community for easier and more interesting reading materials.
- Regularly checking up on one another to make sure the books we are reading feel like understanding in our minds.

- Speak softly, gently. Think of yourself as a voice inside the reader's head—because you will be.
- Interview first to find out what the reader is thinking and doing with this book. Find out how he is participating in the world of this book and how he is expecting it to go on from here.
- Aim through the reading for meaning. Act as if the child is telling you something that's supposed to make sense, rather than acting as if the student is performing "reading." Ask, *What did you say??* or *He did what??* as you would to yourself if you read something that didn't make sense to you.
- If the reader stops, wait. After humming something silently (maybe the *Jeopardy* song?) to yourself, ask what she is thinking.
- Ask, *What would make sense?* or *What could that be?* This asks the reader to make a sensible guess.
- If the reader seems not to be paying attention to the letters and words on the page, ask, *Does that look right?* This cues the reader to see whether the letters, based on the sounds they make, could represent the word they guessed from meaning. Then move on, get back to the story.
- If the reader guesses something that does not fit in the sentence grammatically, say, *Does that sound right?* or *Is that how we say it?* If it sounds okay to the reader, get back to the story.
- Occasionally talk about strategies for figuring out:
  - Reaching for more of the sentence, then trying the word again.
  - Going back to the start of the sentence and turning your mind on higher.
  - Make a guess that makes sense and go on to see if the sentence feels okay.
  - Try out the first sounds and see if it seems like a word you know.
  - See if you understand the whole sentence, and if you do, keep on reading.
- If the reader is skipping or miscuing senselessly one or more words in each sentence, then the conference has to be about honestly assessing what books are good for this reader. Visiting the bookshelves together and finding a book (or better yet, a set of books) the reader can make sense of is a good way to spend time.
- In addition to all this hard, close-in work, talk with the reader about bigger things, such as:
  - How this text is different from or the same as other things he has read or movies and television shows he's seen.
  - What kinds of times and places he is finding (or could find) for reading outside school.
  - How the two of you relate to particular characters.
  - Things you and the reader know about the book that aren't explicitly in the text.
  - What you and the reader are reminded of, from your own lives, and feelings you have in response to the text.
  - Important ideas you think the author is trying to say here.
  - Things that are fair or unfair in the book; times when people are or aren't free; ideas about people getting together and caring about one another.

Figure 5–1 *Figuring Out What It Says: Guidelines for Read-Along Conferences*

- Encouraging each other to find books that feel right and even being on the lookout for books for each other.
- Talking openly and often about experiences of difficulty and ways to handle it.
- Being willing, at least some of the time, to be a partner for someone else's reading choice—putting down my book to read with a friend for a while.

What we'd most like to avoid is creating a position analogous to that of a typical person in the United States public: ignoring the struggles of others, leaving it to the authorities to take care of as long as it doesn't reduce our comfort or privilege. A classroom concerned with social justice has to involve members in a continual inquiry into "what can we do in response to people who need help?"

Predictable Problems

We have so succumbed to the notion that ability tracking creates or reinforces injustice that we can't think about giving special attention to struggling students without becoming immediately anxious about creating a stigma. But if reading is one of the main things we do in the classroom and certain students are visibly less good at it, then those students are at risk of feeling embarrassed sometimes. A struggling reader may become visible in a number of ways: by virtue of the books he selects, by being overheard in conference with the teacher, or in situations where a number of readers are sharing a text. However, if everyone in the class understands that every person is different as a reader, with her own strengths and habits, there is no single "reading" standard that everyone is expected to "achieve." If difference is an assumption in the community, and if standardization is not required in order for a person to participate, then there is less pressure to blend in and make oneself invisible. In addition, if the whole class participates in finding easier texts, and anyone might be seen reading one of them, and the teacher occasionally reads an easy book aloud, the notion that we define ourselves as readers by particular levels of text is disrupted.

Difficulty and ability are not defined purely by some objective measure of text complexity. Difficulty is a function of the relationship between the reader's experience, identity, and knowledge and the assumed experience, identity, and knowledge in a text-world. A reader who seems to be struggling through a Katherine Patterson novel or a history text might seem to sail through an article about fishing, machines, anatomy, or baseball. When we lived in New York City and wanted to go out dancing, we would sometimes look at the "Clubs" listings in *Time Out New York*. We'd laugh as we read aloud to each other descriptions like:

> Ultraverbose DJs Two Lives . . . and Timeblind return to clubland aiming to "put the 'static' back in 'ecstatic' and 'open the realms of unfettered beauty to those who cannot or simply do not peer into it very often.' " Where we come from that's a gussied-up term for mooning, but these guys surely have something loftier in mind. Musically, it's an eclectic mix of abstract, minimal techno; underground hip-hop; funk and soul; "synapse-frying (gently-so) psychedelic stuff (rock and spacey sounds)"; heavy dub and more. (*Time Out New York*, April 13–20, 2000)

What the . . . ? Sure, we could read each of the individual words, but we lacked the experience, knowledge, and identity to make much meaning of it. Of course, the discourse was set up to exclude not-that-cool, middle-class teacher types from Queens. If discussion about such distances between particular texts and particular readers is a common part of the classroom conversation, then reading "improvement" is diversified, and there is less shame at having trouble understanding a particular text.

Shame is at the heart of another problem with teaching struggling readers. Often, by the time they get past third grade, they have developed complex abilities to hide and masquerade as more fluent readers. We see their low test scores, and even though we may not give those much credence, we do want to inquire into what is going on with these readers. When we ask them to retell something they have read, we may get verbose smoke screens and personal responses tangentially related to the text. Are these students inarticulate because they didn't comprehend what they read or because they're nervous about being put on the spot? And if they have successfully convinced other students of their pretended reading identity, they stand to lose face if we make them confront their need to work with easier text or any kind of text other than the one they've become famous for reading. These readers are living on credit, posturing beyond their means, and an intervention, a confrontation with where they really are and what they need to do to move forward, is crucial for them to grow. Readers can't grow by staring at text they cannot make sense of. Most of the time, it helps to get this reader together with a friend, have them choose a book together, and read as partners.

A completely different set of problems arises when struggling readers participate in shared reading. At any point in the curriculum, at least half of a particular student's reading experiences should involve print of which he can make sense, powerfully. The remaining half of the time (or less) he should be participating in conversations about literature and nonfiction, reading with others, and receiving full acceptance as a member of the community. If a teacher maintains a balance like that, she can feel confident that the student is becoming a better reader, while also knowing that he is participating in bigger kinds of interpretive, collaborative thinking. He has time to be the reader he is at present, while also acting like the reader he will become. He is reading his own book independently, while also participating in reading clubs and whole-group shared texts.

If shared texts are more difficult than a reader can handle alone, there are a number of options. If the teacher reads a text aloud to the whole class, difficulty with print is not an issue, and everybody has equal access to the conversation. When a reading club has chosen a book too difficult for one member, that student might listen to the book read aloud—by a parent, another adult, a willing friend, or on tape. Or the student might read with a partner: a group of four divides into two pairs, the partners reading together and reconvening as a foursome for discussions a couple of times a week. On occasion, one or two group members may struggle through a book on their own—read *at* the book without having it make too much sense—but still be able to participate in the club conversations once they catch on to what they missed. (A lot of students get through high school English this way!) While these aren't ideal ways to improve one's reading, they do permit a reader to participate actively as a full member of a dialogue group or class discussion without worrying too much about what is happening in her mind minute by minute as she reads. As long as the student also has occasions when she reads more successfully and independently, this kind of reading isn't harmful.

As much as possible, though, students should choose others who read like them when they form clubs and partnerships. Collaboration is most helpful when participants are working on close to the same thing, and book choice is less complicated when club members have both similar topic interests and similar levels of comfort with difficulty. We stress this when talking with students about how to make their clubs. This is significantly different from tracking. An authority is not dictating *where you belong* by some mysterious assessment and against some fixed standard. Rather, the learner himself, in relationship to other readers, reflects on, inquires into, investigates, and revises grouping decisions. This involves self-assessment and goal-setting and is therefore an inherently educative process, not an imposed judgment.

These practical problems and possible solutions center on identity: how will students wrestling with institutional expectations come to view themselves? "Struggling reader" is a role, and the institution of school has created it and will always fill it with someone. Those cast in that role will play it, often to perfection, adopting ways of behaving and thinking created by their interactions with significant others in the institution. Our task as educators is to make alternative identities available to these kids, to support them in their literacy growth even as we provide opportunities to perform differently, to "act smart," to feel entitled to membership in a democratic community.

We are told we live in a time of great literacy crisis. A bill introduced in the U.S. Congress in 2000 stated:

> America has a reading deficit. According to the National Adult Literacy Survey (NALS), conducted by the National Center for Education Statistics every ten years, 41,000,000 adults were unable to perform even the simplest literacy tasks. The 1998 National Assessment of Educational Progress (NAEP) found that 69 percent of fourth-grade students are reading below the proficient level. The 1998 NAEP found that minority students on average continue to lag far behind their nonminority counterparts in reading proficiency, even though many of the minority students are in programs authorized under title I of the Elementary and Secondary Education Act of 1965. . . . Reading scores continue to decline or remain stagnant, even though Congress has spent more than $120,000,000 over the past thirty years for such programs, a substantial portion of which has been dedicated to improving the reading skills of disadvantaged students.

Some adults in the United States cannot experience the enjoyment of reading novels and poetry. Some cannot read and understand a newspaper or a magazine. Some lack the skills to accomplish literate tasks such as voting, filling out tax returns, following directions, or completing job applications. They cannot read books to their children or write letters to their relatives.

There are also people who cannot read the bark and silhouette of trees when they stand in the middle of the woods. There are people who cannot make sense of the binary code that is the foundation on which their personal computer works. Some adults cannot hear the difference between the B section and the recapitulation in the allegro movement of a sonata. Some people cannot look at a river and know where the fish are, others are helpless at telling whether a wall is square or plumb. There are reports of people who cannot make meaning of a stock market ticker. You may know someone fairly well but be unaware of his inability to find anything to say about a painting by Rothko. Research has shown that some adults, and even some children, cannot open up their television set, their computer, or their automobile, read what is wrong with it, and repair it without getting specialized help from people with adequate skills. There are so many deficiencies in this society, one hardly knows where to begin.

Some of the nonprint types of "reading" mentioned here are every bit as functional and practical as reading stories or nonfiction text. Some are just as rich and rewarding aesthetically. They are not all that different from what you are doing right now. But only one kind of reading, which boils down to answering particular kinds of test questions, is considered a social deficit if we can't do it. This deficit is so limiting to one's life chances that it is worth diminishing children's life chances further, in response to it, by keeping them from proceeding through the school system. We do not have to think that the reading of print is *unimportant* to ask why it is *so* important. We can understand that making meaning of print is almost universally convenient in our culture and still ask, *Why bear down so hard on those who struggle with this one device for thinking and communicating?*

Print reading, especially when it structures claims about truth, rather conveniently separates people by race and culture and by economic advantage, especially in early childhood. Language, the primary tool by which communities identify and exclude outsiders, and glue themselves together, is surely the most vulnerable spot to target if one wants to privilege some and exclude others. Moreover, children with the most stable, trusting, orderly (but varied) environments are in the best position to have concepts and capacities add up. The children of those who struggle economically and socially are obviously more likely to be neglected or harmed, to risk having weaker bonds of trust, especially as generation after generation suffers the same traps.

To read, one has to pull together in the present moment all one knows about the world that is predictable and likely. One must have faith in meaning, believe that a word one day means the same thing it did the day before. A reader, a thinker, uses all that he is in bringing will and hope to the effort of taking the risk to guess at what a text is likely to say. Reading is an audacious act. Think about a child who has not been able to rely on adults in his life, who has even been harmed by them. How is he able to predict the rest of a sentence, to reconstruct an author's thoughts? Think about a child whose home language, the tongue in which she asked for more milk, spoke her first words, for which she was celebrated by those who love her, is not good enough for school. How is she able to make the thoughts on the page stand still and speak to her? For teachers watching the complicated struggles of many such children day after day, it is awe-inspiring that so *many* of them learn to read.

So why the overselling of literacy? Could it be that doing so privileges the privileged? Panicking about children who don't read at the same time and in the same way as others separates those children by ethnicity, language, and class. Maybe that's how it's supposed to work, maybe it's not done on purpose. Maybe people are looking out for their own, loving their children, wanting the best for them, assembling the resources and connections to make it all happen.

We have all bought into a metaphor for reading development. We think of it as a line on a graph that shows nothing but profit, continual improvement in a predetermined direction. When we see readers struggling, we imagine that they are at a lower point on the line than those who don't struggle. Similarly, imagine people standing in line to buy tickets to a concert. Some people are ahead of others, and being ahead is better than being behind, especially because it means that soon those people will not have to be in line any longer.

An improved metaphor, though still imperfect, would be a three-dimensional one that sees reading as a mountain. Readers could be high on it or low on it but in many different places. In that metaphor, assessing and helping a reader would involve knowing just where on the mountain he is, what the terrain is like, and what path upward would involve the least risk and effort for him. The topography would be complex enough that a reader could, at a particular moment, be losing elevation but still making progress up the mountain. The apex of this mountain is large and offers varied vistas from different perspectives. Shifting the metaphor like this helps us think about reading growth more realistically. We get rid of our notion that there is a single entity called "reading" and a single path to growth. It's still more limited than it should be, though, because the direction of progress still seems deceptively unified. In reality, there is no apex of reading that, once attained, is secured once and for all.

A better metaphor still would be to see reading as a country, a big one. There are varied landscapes, some mountainous, some marshy, some at the edges of oceans. Making progress through these varied terrains, and partaking of the pleasures they offer, involves different processes, depending on where one is located. When we start out with a reader, they might be anywhere in that country, and our job is to help her explore more of it and to notice more about the landscape in which she is at present. There is no single direction that everyone must go, and no one is ever finished with the journey. To thus diversify the possible locations in which we imagine all the readers in our classrooms would mean letting go of the binary notion of success/failure and the linear continuum between those two poles. We would let go of the language we use to describe—and think about—struggling readers, and we would gain a richer image of the progress they might make. A struggling reader in this metaphor would be someone paralyzed, frozen in place, immobile and unable to explore—a condition caused more by the linear metaphor for reading and our responses to it than by anything *in* the reader.

According to Hervé Varenne and Ray McDermott (1999), the linear metaphor of progress in which we now work is part of American culture:

> [S]chool success and failure are not simple consequences of the way the human world must be. It is a cultural mock-up, what we call a cultural fact. The success and failure system, as a cultural fact, is real in its connections to the political economy, exquisitely detailed in its connections with the everyday behavior of the people who make up the system, and in both these ways massively consequential in the lives of all. Yet it does not have to be this way, and if everyone stopped measuring, explaining, and remediating, school success and failure would in a significant sense disappear. Other ways to stratify would soon evolve, but this evolution would have the virtue of separating education from resource allocation. (xiii)

From this perspective, all linear gradations of reading achievement, all leveling of texts and readers, is harmful. It does not mean that readers should waste time with books they don't understand. It does not mean that we should neglect to support the students most vulnerable to the system's judgments and punishments. But it does mean that we should stop talking about some books and readers as higher and some as lower, that we should stop assuming that there are fourth-grade reading levels and second-grade books and eighth-grade readers. We should not think of a particular reading club as the low group and expect that their inquiry and conversation will be anything less than engaged, difficult, and intelligent.

Yes, the states will go on testing and the system will go on ranking and sorting. But our classrooms can be small, temporary (but still significant) disruptions in that system (Flannery 1990). The language we use there can be less hierarchical and more democratic, less competitive and more collaborative across differences. When we use language that way, we create a place where all young people can expand their potential as individuals within communities, and we invite every kid, without discrimination, to begin a lifelong exploration of the country of reading.

CHAPTER 6

A DEMOCRATIC ENVIRONMENT
A Place to Foster Public Voices

Let's face it; most of us are pretty laidback citizens. We mull over and talk with friends about lots of things going on in public forums, but we rarely do anything about them. It's not that we're mindless sheep: in our hearts, we often withhold our consent for the actions of our governments. But most of us have never been acculturated to think we can do something about the public world outside our private sphere; we don't have that kind of identity—we're just not that kind of person.

Our identities, though, come from the communities in which we have spent our lives thus far, the locations in which we've said, *I'm going to be like them,* and we can grow new identities—to a degree that would surprise us—by putting ourselves in new and different communities. If we desire to be more active citizens, we can find or create communities that bring out the citizen in us. We can also help our students develop more empowered identities by crafting a different kind of classroom community, one in which inventive initiative is expected—not in pursuit of wealth or personal aggrandizement, but in the interest of improving a shared reality, making life better for others.

To implement a critical curriculum, especially one that asks children to do something about the world, teachers must design a democratic classroom. John Dewey (1927) defines democracy as a *social idea,* which he distinguished from a *political system* of government. The two are interconnected, of course, but when we discuss the idea of a democratic classroom here, we mean the wider, broader definition of democracy that Dewey says "must affect all modes of human association, the family, the school, industry, religion" (143). Planning a classroom for citizenship, then, teachers must keep in mind this ideal of democracy as a mode of association: a place where people participate, where they act for the benefit of one another, where all perspectives are given audience, where difference is embraced and not shunned, where people make decisions and take on responsibilities for the good of the whole, and where members solve issues and problems in ways that have roots in the group's history. Sponsoring a democratic classroom means resisting, to the strongest extent possible, any practice that tends to sort children by race, ethnicity, and class—tests, tracking, report cards, centralized standards. It means adopting instead a critical and liberating pedagogy as part of a larger agenda of educational and social justice. It means teachers have to look critically at their bulletin boards and the books on their shelves; at the opportunities for social interaction among the classroom inhabitants; and at the curriculum itself, to be sure it represents multiple cultures and viewpoints. It means teachers must pay attention to the language they use to teach, avoiding what William Ayers (2000) calls "the toxic habit of labeling"—calling large groups of poor people "culturally deprived," for example. ("Being poor does not mean lacking culture," Ayers reminds us: "It means lacking money.")

A teacher must become more knowledgeable than ever about how issues of race, class, gender, and difference are being negotiated out in the world, and must "tie reading and writing to perpetuating or resisting" the status quo (Edelsky 1999, 15). Creating a more democratic classroom means risking topics of inquiry that might lead children to places not sanctioned by traditional education—school and community issues, issues of poverty, sexuality, and power, even the inequities present in their own home. It means the teacher and the students negotiate the curriculum: the students not only get to vote on what gets studied in the room but also have the opportunity to name and decide what they will vote about (Edelsky 1999, 10).

In order to nudge our students toward thinking, responding, and writing for social action, we need to rehearse them well in full, democratic *participation*. Children cannot think about, much less write for, social action in a classroom that is rule-bound, teacher-centered, and test-driven, with no room for them to follow their own interests and desires. A 1918 *English Journal* editorial said: "Training in a little autocracy is poor preparation for citizenship in a democracy" (quoted in Applebee 1974, 64). How can children learn how to reason socially and politically if they are never allowed to ask questions, explore thinking, make mistakes, proceed and digress? How, in a classroom that is entirely in the teacher's control, from where they sit, to when they can or cannot respond, to what and how fast and how much they should learn, can children ever practice self-control or understand tactics for social intercourse? In such classrooms, there is a veneer of control, of orderliness and peace. Follow those children out to the playground, however, and you will see nasty outbreaks of verbal and physical violence, of social ostracizing and scapegoating. All classrooms break loose at least a little bit when a substitute teacher visits for a day. But it appears that the most tightly controlled classrooms are the worst exemplars of the "when the cat's away, the mice will play" syndrome: the children have no internal sense of how to monitor their behavior.

In spite of all these cautions against teachers being too controlling, we are not saying education for participation comes about from a lack of control. The teacher does not create democracy by, either literally or figuratively, not showing up. In fact, it is the teacher's high expectations for ethical deliberation and social sensitivity that permit democratic participation. Democratic communities require skilled leadership. The sort of participation we have in mind, and the sort of democracy Dewey had in mind, arises from an individual's sense of responsibility to the group. Participation begins in the ability to think with others and about others, and in the awareness that others are listening and responding to one's words and actions. It is a way of living in conversation and under construction. The impulse to participate requires a belief that the world is still unfinished, that one's own actions might make a difference in the course of things one cares about. And impulses for citizenship, like all impulses, are born in the freedom to make decisions, to follow a trail of desire and interest, to think and work in chosen activity.

A classroom teacher, therefore, enables a greater sense of participation by employing, in all areas of the curriculum, some basic, guiding principles: intention, dialogue, collaboration, and inquiry. To many, these building blocks of democratic minds will be familiar, but let's discuss some practical examples.

Intention

Students will develop intention and a sense of purpose only if, much of the time, they are allowed to choose what to read and write and inquire into (Calkins 1994, 2001; Graves 1982; Smith 1988). Children who have not been allowed to choose, to carry out an intention, will not know inside that people can choose how to live. What is it that children can choose to do in the classroom, and how do their choices lead to longer-term projects that allow them to witness their actions making a difference in their growth as learners as well as in their social interactions?

- Most of the time, they choose what to write about in writing workshop. Much of the time, they also choose the form their writing will take and the particular nature of the process for a given piece.
- They are always reading something they have chosen, and they have time in school to do so, even if they are also reading shared texts with the class or a group.
- They usually make decisions about who should be in groups with them, and they are held accountable for the wisdom of those decisions.
- They carefully find their own way to productive topics of study in science and social studies inquiry, individually and in groups.
- They are often engaged in conversations about how to make wise choices in all these areas.
- Their choices are not just flashbulbs of intention, but develop into ongoing projects of learning, such as becoming an expert on poetry, reading everything by Eloise Greenfield, or understanding the connections of astronomy to human history.

Participants in a democracy must be able to examine their social environment and respond to it; otherwise, popular self-government is impossible. The ability to hook into something you want to accomplish and to pursue that desire across time is an essential attribute for a citizen to develop if she or he is to be capable of leading. Intention and the choices it entails are crucial aspects of classroom life if students are to learn the habits of active agents, become authors of their own social and political realities.

Dialogue

In order to participate in the classroom, children need to be able—and expected—to respond to one another and to the things they read or see. They need to feel that they are part of an ongoing conversation that has more than one side to it, and they need to learn how to remain open to multiple and diverse perspectives (Nystrand, Gamorand, Kachur, and Pendergrast 1997). The only way to learn these things is for children to talk back to the world and expect the world to talk back to them (Bakhtin 1981; Stock 1995). Dialogue is fostered by:

- Treating all texts, including textbooks, as one person's turn, not a final word. Students should always expect to answer back, through writing, talking, art, drama, and action, in all areas of inquiry, not just literary. And they expect other students to answer their answers.
- Using notebook or journal writing as a tool for thinking, across many curricular areas.

- Making joint decisions as often as possible. Even if the final decision will be the teacher's, conversations with the people affected should surround the decision.

- Discussing solutions after problems arise rather than solving problems in advance with preemptive rules.

- Expecting students to discuss the sources of their own ideas, the conversations, influences, and life experiences that have brought them to think the way they do.

- Seeing to it that student writing receives a meaningful *response* from peers and other audiences, not merely an evaluation from the teacher or evaluative comments from peers.

- Never asking students to write or read solely in order to practice or demonstrate skills, but rather always to do so for an appropriate social purpose, such as to get ready for a conversation, to interact with absent others through writing, or for publication.

The notion of citizen activists, people who can respond to social currents that are larger than the usual circle of their own life, requires that all people assume they are in dialogue with the world and the world with them. If something important happens in my country, *of course* I have a response. I'm supposed to, because I'm a part of this conversation. It would be less than honest for me to stay silent and not to act. I also expect, when I act or speak, to hear a response, sometimes affirming my view and sometimes rebutting it. But I certainly never expect to be taken as the final word. An understanding of dialogue, thus, is also at the heart of civic life.

Collaboration

Living, thinking, and working together constitute the kind of association that defines democracy. In traditional classrooms, children have few, if any, opportunities to learn how to work and think together. Picture children seated face forward in rows of desks. They spend their days reading sections of textbooks and answering questions on notebook paper to be graded by their teacher. They do not have the opportunity to plan what to study as a group or decide how to represent what the group learned. They do not know how to build on others' ideas or how to change their mind after hearing what someone else thinks. If they were given those opportunities, they would learn, over time, how to approach a situation, a new task, even a social conflict, by thinking through, with help from the group, ways of approaching the problem. The impulse to turn to others would be part of what it means to know, to understand, to learn (Short and Burke 1991).

Of course, being in small groups does not intrinsically make for collaboration. All teachers have seen students in groups simply stitch their individual work together like panels of a quilt, have seen students divide up tasks in such a way as to avoid working together at all, have heard voices rise in frustrated decibels over such critical issues as who does what, who owns what, who goes first, and so on. Collaboration only occurs when individuals are transformed by the work of the group, when everyone is changing her or his mind (Barnes and Todd 1995; Short, Harste, and Burke 1996). Examples of collaboration include:

- Homework partners who meet each morning to strategize how to get work done and fit school and other areas of life together.

- Reading clubs who think together about the meaning of the books they have read together.

- Science inquiry groups who define questions and research procedures and then modify them as they get new information.
- In whole-class discussions, being watchful of people who are trying to get into the conversation and acknowledging and connecting one's own comments to what others have said.
- Being civil and socially sensitive throughout the day.
- Talking frequently about the difficulties of collaboration and strategies to improve it.

Because democracy is about associated living, collaboration is obviously closely related. A concern for others, empathy, a habit of forming one's own thinking in anticipation of others' responses—these all are as much characteristics of democrats as they are of collaborative groups. Democracy is built on an awareness of how the individual being interacts with others.

Inquiry

Children who are presented with knowledge from the top down, as a body of facts to be absorbed, memorized, accepted, and later evaluated, will never know how to question, how to look critically at an issue to see who benefits from their knowing the information. Indeed, they may never *learn how to learn*. In an inquiry-based classroom, knowledge has to get down off its throne and play nice. Information is understood to be pliable, capable of being shaped to new purposes.

Learners' interests and experience lead them to work on a topic for a time (Whitmore and Norton-Meier 2000). They ask questions about the topic, find materials about the topic, read to find answers, develop more questions in light of new information, and decide how to record what they are learning. Their reading and questioning may lead them in new directions, or even to dead ends; they understand that learning is a journey that takes many interesting twists and turns (Kerr, Makuluni, and Nieves 2000). The concern is not for finding "answers" or for being "right," but for examining the topic from divergent perspectives and uncovering new questions and areas of interest (Short, Harste, and Burke 1996). Students can also decide on ways to represent what they learned to the rest of the classroom community, and that presentation may take a variety of forms from a "museum exhibit," to a mock trial, to a dramatic performance (Leland and Harste 1994).

Here are some examples of inquiry-based learning:

- Individual projects in which a student investigates a topic by reading, interviewing, watching videos, and other means and writes about how her ideas about the topic are changing.
- Group projects that flow from one topic into another as students learn the connections between particular elements in a domain. For instance, a group begins studying the Holocaust but in a couple of weeks is looking at pogroms in Russia and a few weeks later is trying to get multiple perspectives on Israeli/Palestinian conflicts.
- A class' systematic observations of bird feeders outside their classroom window lead them to inquire about the nature of different kinds of feathers.
- A teacher notices that, during writing workshop, one corner of the room starts to get noisy and jumpy at about the same time every day. She sets up a schedule for herself and two students to observe that corner and record what is happening there.

If the world is finished, if everything is known, then there is no room for ordinary people to construct knowledge and refine social life. For democracy to exist, there must be a resistance to closure, a tolerance of uncertainty, a willingness to investigate and try things out. A spirit of inquiry is not simply a separate educational innovation condoned by the experts who value democratic environments; inquiry and democracy are interrelated, complementary ideas.

When these principles are central to the life of the classroom, children have more practice with and achieve more fluency in the skills necessary for critique and social action. They know they can and should question and talk back to the things they read and see in the world. They understand how to work with others toward a common, negotiated goal (or if they haven't quite mastered seamless collaborating skills, they at least are prepared for diversity of opinion and multiple agendas). When the curriculum turns to social action, these students bring what they already know from everyday practice and participation in the democratic classroom to this new topic of inquiry.

Community

Democratic classrooms begin with the creation of community. Many teachers start the year with community-building activities. Along with their students, they draw, write, and talk about themselves, their families, their interests and passions. They share favorite books and authors or read last year's writing notebooks to one another and celebrate themselves as writers. They go on walks to the park and roll down a grassy hill; they play cooperative games and get to know one another. They also establish how they will be together. On the first day, instead of dictating a list of dos and don'ts, as if they are highest and only authority, these teachers ask children to draw and write about their ideal classroom environment for learning. They tell students they will share and compare and most of their visions will be realized, as long as everyone is in agreement. When students respond with environments that look and sound beautiful, peaceful, fun, full of friends and good times, teachers introduce the responsibilities that help make these environments happen. After all, students and teachers are required to live together for at least six hours, five days a week, 180 days a year. That's more time than most children spend with their own families.

If classroom communities are to live together peaceably and fulfill some of their visions for a good learning environment, they have to establish some guidelines. Nevertheless, when children are asked to write down some guidelines for living together, they usually draw on "rules" they've encountered at home, school, church, and swimming pools, a list of negatives:

- No hitting, spitting, pinching.
- No cursing.
- Don't steal.
- No horsing around.
- No talking back to the teacher.
- No copying or cheating.

The list goes on—no, no, no—the tedious chant of someone living with a rambunctious four-month-old puppy in the house. Lists like these are powerful, learned discourses. They are the rules children love to resist, are determined to break when the teacher is absent or when she turns her back for a moment.

Teachers need to construct new norms for living together, ones that reflect an explicit vision of how the class will live together rather than injunctions against particular, often trivial behavior. Instead of nos and don'ts, classes must develop alternative systems, such as guidelines, contracts, even constitutions. They must compose the words that say how they will be, hang them up in the room, and refer to these words often throughout the year.

One such constitution by Katherine's fourth and fifth graders reads:

> In Our Community:
> We listen to the person whose turn it is to talk.
> We take care of our materials and our classroom.
> We respect our differences.
> We love our similarities.

Katherine's K–2 multiage classrooms pledged to live out the statement: *To be a good friend.* Katherine talked with them about having empathy for another person so that you can *act* like a friend would act, even if you are not social friends. If you can put yourself in the other person's shoes, if you can feel the joy, the pain, the embarrassment, or the fear that the other person may be feeling, you will do what you can to celebrate or ease that feeling. Empathy and imagination are habits necessary for participating in a caring, cooperative, democratic life. You have to be able to feel or at least to imagine what it feels like to be the other person, or else you will not want to or will not be able to take action to help her.

Regardless of the age of their students, teachers concerned with social justice create curriculum at the beginning of the school year that helps children live their way into empathy for one another. Sometimes children find someone in the room who is very different from them (different gender, race, size, age) to interview. In the interviews, they find out each other's favorite TV shows, movies, food, and music. They ask about families and previous years in school. They draw each other, and then talk about what they notice about their partner's portrait of them. They spend a few days working with their partner, walking to lunch with them, reading with them, and assigning homework to each other—activities to get to know each other better. These partnerships are not intended to grow into special friendships, but they might. The most important goal is to open children's eyes to the world of another person, a world they may not have explored if they had not been asked to.

At the beginning of the school year, or whenever it seems useful, Katherine also asks children to role-play situations, real and pretend, that come up in their social interactions. It's a powerful exercise for children to pretend to be someone else, to have someone else's problem, especially someone very different socially, economically, physically, from themselves. The best time for this activity may be immediately after lunch or recess, when social ills have been played out on the playground and children's feelings are raw and exposed. When the children say yes, they are ready, they believe they have become that other person with that particular problem, Katherine asks, "What do you need now, in order to go on, in order to feel that you have been listened to and dealt with? Do you need someone just to listen to you? Do you need someone to hug you or bring you a glass of water or just to say, 'Are you all right?' " The children then begin to apply this idea in their actual daily interactions—John notices that Reuben needs help tying his shoes, Alicia helps Margot find her lost glove, Paul falls down and several classmates ask whether he is all right.

In her fourth- and fifth-grade classrooms, the list of do's Katherine's students create become benchmarks for behavior. If they all say they take care of materials and the classroom, for instance, would they then leave stuff strewn all over the floor at the end of the day? Would they rip pages out of books and write curse words on the walls? When students sometimes do these things, the class calls a community meeting to figure out what to do about it. When Isaiah wrote "Fuck you" on the closet wall, the class stopped doing their math work. Katherine called everyone to the meeting area, hugged Isaiah in the middle of the circle, and asked him what was wrong. His classmates asked him why he was so angry. Isaiah started crying. He had a whole lot to be angry about, things he couldn't talk about even in this safe community, but he never wrote on the walls after that day. One of the children went and got him a sponge and a spray bottle, and he cleaned it up.

Physical Space

A democratic classroom is shared by all who live in it. Children need to know that the classroom belongs to them, that they can make decisions about how it is set up and what goes on the walls. At the beginning of every year, before the children arrive, teachers may feel a bit embarrassed by the empty walls, bulletin boards, and bookshelves that children will face when they first come into class. After all, teachers usually begin the new school year with decorated bulletin boards full of wise sayings and pretty poems. They've assigned seats and laminated children's names onto desktops. By contrast, democratic classrooms are mostly empty. Bulletin boards are blank; books are still in boxes, with perhaps a few in baskets to use during the first week. The furniture stands in odd, impermanent arrangements, waiting for the occupants of this classroom to determine the traffic flow. When children walk into a democratic classroom, the first thing the teacher often says is, "Welcome! We're going to spend the next week building and organizing the classroom. How do you think it should look?"

The democratic classroom reflects the people who are living inside it during this particular school year, doing the work of this group, thinking what this group thinks. Charts or graphs or even useful and appropriate curriculum materials, like a list of the characteristics of a poem, are rarely kept from year to year, because these things represent the work and thinking of a particular group located in a particular moment in time. The power of each newly formed classroom community for starting fresh, for valuing what the current community thinks, is real and palpable. The lists and charts on the wall, much like the conversations the class members have, are loaded with words and phrases invented by this group. Children see their ideas and questions taken up by the teacher and their classmates, and they understand that in this place they are seen and heard. Their language, the words they choose to name the worlds they are constructing, fits them and they make use of it. For instance, when Katherine's kids needed to make a basket of books appropriate for a few struggling readers in the class, they discussed the implications of a label for the basket that might offend or embarrass anyone who took a book from it. Sarah, always wise and compassionate, remarked, "Everyone wants to read an easier book now and then. I mean, we need to take a break once in awhile!" The class loved the idea of taking a break, and so the label on the basket of easier books became "Take-a-Break Books." To another group of children, this label, or the charts about how this community works together, would carry little meaning, because they did not invent them; they did not live those words and ideas.

Curriculum

To enable students to have a vision of themselves as social/political beings, teachers must plan curriculum that takes up issues of power and justice as a matter of daily life. They need to add as many texts to their classroom library as they can find about persons working for justice. They can collect magazine articles, editorials, and news stories of children who are social activists. They can invite members of the community in to tell their stories of social action. And they might also reveal their own attempts to live socially and politically involved lives, something that admittedly feels risky to do in conservative times. Finally, they can allow the actual, lived experience of each classroom community to create much of the social studies curriculum. Writing a community pledge together at the beginning of the year is a way to study the ways that societies form and govern themselves.

Solving social difficulties and behavior issues as a class, rather than relying on her authority alone, allows Katherine's students to experience participatory democracy, decision making, problem solving, and conflict resolution firsthand. One year, when Katherine had some distinct behavior problems that affected the dynamic of the entire group, she brought the issue to the class to help solve. Every time someone suggested she try an extrinsic trick, such as filling a big jar of candy for good behavior, or writing individuals' names on the board for bad behavior, she refused, and explained why she did not believe rewards and punishments help people learn how to control their behavior (Kohn 1993). She asked them to try again to decide what they could do themselves to solve the problems. Over the course of several weeks, she let them tackle different solutions, and every day the class discussed how their solutions were working. This was tedious, painful work, but slowly her class gained some self-control. Eventually, this class was able to call its own community meetings and talk (or shout) its way through problems.

Because children need an empowered and active relationship to knowledge, critique must become a habit of the curriculum. Students need to ask: Who are the authors of the texts (whether novels, news articles, or advertisements) they read? How do these authors manipulate the texts to construct these realities? How are girls being portrayed in television shows? How are people of color written about in children's novels (or are they written about at all)? Readers need to look for what is missing in texts, for stories that are not told, for voices that are not heard. One year Katherine's fourth graders made an "ethnicity graph" of characters in the novels they were reading. They noticed that there was rarely a cast of mixed races acting as friends or families in the stories, as there was in their classroom and in their lives. There was rarely a black, Asian, Native American, East Indian, or Latino main character. There was rarely a story about kids like them living in a city like New York. Usually the books about people of color were what the students called "old stories"—myths, legends, and folktales. Such stories, while holding an important place in the history of world cultures, do not help children find themselves in text, nor do they help them see the world through the eyes of a character different from themselves.

It is a short leap from figuring out that an advertiser is targeting people of color or children in order to sell more products to writing a letter to that advertiser expressing consternation about the tactic. It is another short leap to decide to boycott that particular store or company and getting groups of people to do the same thing. The kind of thinking, observing, and inquiring necessary to lead a more critical and socially active life needs to permeate the classroom, all day, every day. These are not simply writing or even reading skills, but ways of looking at the world and responding to it. When we first met Patrick Shannon, we asked him how he had managed to turn one taxi ride from the airport in New York City into a story about a critical incident, complete with social/political analysis. He told us that he has an "ear" tuned to critical incidents; it is how he pays attention to the world (Shannon 1995).

We try to teach students to tune their ears to events, places, and incidents that are unfair and unjust. In gym, for instance, Katherine's girls noticed that the teacher always lined the class up with boys in one line, girls in the other. Leah asked him why he did that. He didn't know. It was just easier to organize, he said. He had always done it that way. Katherine's students had become very aware of issues of fairness in class discussions and pointed out to the science teacher that she always called on boys first. The specials teachers probably dreaded seeing that class walk down the hall—what new act of injustice and discrimination were they going to be called on the carpet for?

Much more of school learning should lead to action in the world, and activism is a much more authentic outcome of learning than many of the "projects" and assessments teachers traditionally use. If we usually think of writing workshop as a place for artistic writing, perhaps we should begin to expect other forms of writing in environmental studies, global studies, and political studies. When Edie Ziegler's third through fifth graders in Closter, New Jersey, studied the rain forest, what they learned triggered a number of activist projects: writing their representatives in Congress, posting warnings on the Internet, and mounting a whole-class "environmental expo" to inform the public about this crucial social issue. Kathy Doyle's fifth graders, for a science project, assembled terrariums of plants and small animals indigenous to various ecosystems. The more her students learned how the well-being of geckos and anoles depended on their interactions with plants, insects, climate, and soil, the more outraged they became at how the animals had been stored and treated in the pet shops where they bought them. They prepared pamphlets detailing the appropriate care of a number of species and distributed them to pet stores in their area. Other possibilities? Students might be on the lookout for inconsistencies and flat-out lies in their science and social studies texts. They might question the way science is taught and the ways they are expected to demonstrate understanding of that discipline. They might write to publishers asking why their textbooks don't include more women writers and multiethnic selections.

At other times, literate social action may rise from a class' life as a community, not rooted in any planned aspect of the curriculum but carrying at least as much potential punch for learning. Every year, Katherine's students become involved in spontaneous and authentic writing in response to some social issue, and they have witnessed their writing effect changes in circumstances. In a kindergarten class one year, when her children learned they had to leave the water faucet on for sixty seconds every morning to "get the lead out," they wanted to know how such a situation came to be. They wrote to the Board of Education, which simply reissued the memo suggesting the sixty-second flush. They purchased a water-testing kit to do their own informal testing of the water. The results convinced them they didn't want to drink that water. The students wrote a letter to their parents asking for a donation of a water filter, and the parents responded.

Those students felt powerful enough to look for other things that were not right or fair. With unshaking confidence in the potential power of literacy, they wrote their city councilman to request a ban on smoking in New York City restaurants, and when the law was passed soon after, they believed it was a result of their asking for it! Now the students were unstoppable. They wrote to a company in New Jersey to ask why those little milk cartons they sell for school lunches are so hard for children to open. "It is hard for us to be all by ourselves like grown-ups at lunch because we have to have help with our milk cartons." They wrote that even their "big, grown-up teacher" had trouble opening them.

Classrooms around the nation have been involved for decades in service projects to change problems in the environment, in school policies, in local and global societies. Kathleen Tolan's sixth graders wondered why they had to play in a schoolyard littered with crack vials and condoms. They wrote to their principal and school board. They tried to enlist parent support. They went to a school board meeting with a petition, organized clean-up teams, and took action in response to a problem many of the adults around them would have preferred to ignore. In an affluent, predominately white suburb in New Jersey, Maria Sweeney led her class in a yearlong study of the groundbreaking elections in South Africa in 1994. Throughout the study, she asked them to compare the political turmoil in South Africa to issues happening locally and historically in the United

States. At the end of the year, her class wrote and performed "No Easy Road to Freedom: A Play About South Africa." As Sweeney (1999) points out, the students "learned far more than most educated adults know about South Africa and the injustices of apartheid." Through the vehicle of the play, "every student, regardless of academic ability, played a critical role." Anything studied that deeply and for an entire year must surely leave footprints on children's lives and help them know what it feels like to make a difference in the world.

At Adam Clayton Powell Junior High in New York City, Michele Haiken led her adolescent students to critically examine the media and literature for how teenagers are portrayed, for what messages are being conveyed. She also teaches "healthy sexuality education," a course that informs students and helps them make choices without condemning them for having sexual feelings.

A whole-class inquiry can be an instructive model of the power in numbers. One year, Katherine's fourth graders wrote and collected dozens of signatures on a petition requesting more organized games and sports activities in the playground as a positive solution to the dangerous and violent games that were happening there. Everyone in the class was involved because everyone had to spend time out on the playground after lunch. Everyone was affected by what was happening outside, even the children who chose to sit quietly on the bench with a book. The power of collective action was brought home that year, and many of those children sponsored petitions in middle and high school for changing various aspects of their school environment. In a whole-class model of social action, responsibilities can be shared and resources multiplied. Children can take many different roles in the project and offer many talents and strengths besides leadership or literacy skills.

A potential disadvantage to the whole-class project is that perhaps not everyone would have chosen it on her own. Most often, the topic is introduced by a teacher with a strong, passionate concern for justice and social activism. Still, the children usually learn to care deeply about the "imposed" topic, whether it be a passion for mathematics or for saving rain forests. After all, we may not even know about or know to care about some injustice in the world until someone else opens our eyes and leads the way.

Another approach is to have several small groups of children research, think about, and ultimately choose a topic in which they want to become involved. However, as Edelsky (1999) points out, "it is naïve . . . to imagine that the teacher is a cipher—that the teacher's implicit (often unexamined) perspectives and issues are absent when she helps students pursue a topic" (4). Teachers need to remain active in the negotiations. They need to comment when a topic seems too broad or too narrow, offer resources to help direct the work, suggest ideas when students are clearly lost. Many children in Katherine's classes become obsessed with *her* obsessions: inequalities in funding for public schools; injustices to women and children; ways to "reduce, reuse, and recycle"; gun control. The tension between teacher-directed and child-centered activities and instruction is always present in a strong progressive classroom. Teachers must make decisions and choices about how this work will go, and they adjust and refine these decisions throughout their career. These decisions should be geared toward more student choice, more shared power and decision making, and more democracy in the classroom.

Embracing Difficulty in the Democratic Classroom

Once we invite participatory, interactive democracy into our classrooms, we also invite opposition, divergent thinking, and resistance. Our job is to embrace the difficulty, knowing that living through it provides the best learning for how to live together. The old saying *the cure for the ills of democracy is more democracy* is true. When there is a problem in the classroom, a community meeting may produce suggestions for how to solve it. Some meetings happen as the moment and the situation dictate. Students don't mind staying a few minutes after school or missing a few minutes of a scheduled class or their lunch period if a "hot" issue needs to be discussed. When Ben said that the mistreatment of Martin Luther King, Jr., reminded him of how the class treated him, Katherine stopped walking down the stairs to lunch, brought her students back up to the classroom, asked them to sit on the rug, and had Ben repeat what he had said to the whole class. In addition to such impromptu meetings, Katherine's classes have a weekly community meeting at which students discuss social issues. There is a sign-up sheet in the classroom on which students propose topics for that week's meeting. Topics have included the teasing of three Asian girls in class, the feeling that two boys were dominating all class discussions, behavior issues that interrupted people's thinking.

During these discussions, Katherine sits outside the circle and transcribes what is said. Sometimes she types up these transcriptions and analyzes them on the overhead. Other times, she just gives her opinion or helps the class see big ideas in the small details. Always, she solicits their ideas for solving the problem. She asks them to make an action plan. The solution to the issue of teasing the Asian girls was to ask the three girls to talk about their cultures. For two weeks, the girls made presentations, brought books to read, taught the class how to write some Chinese characters, took them through a tea ceremony. The girls said they felt much more comfortable in the class after those weeks, and many children chose books about Japanese, Chinese, and Korean cultures for their independent reading, asking the girls questions and making connections to what they had learned.

In a democratic classroom, students may voice opinions that are in social and political opposition to the teacher's. Aaron, Ivan, and Tommy, for instance, were very vocal about disliking the books Katherine read aloud. They had spent two years in her classroom, and they'd had a steady diet of stories about people (especially females, whenever she could find them) of color. They especially hated *Princess of the Press: The Story of Ida B. Wells-Barnett* (Medearis 1997). They claimed there were no big ideas to talk about. "What do you mean?" asked Leah, a brave young feminist. "Her parents died when she was fourteen. She had to raise five brothers and sisters all by herself. She got a job as a teacher when she was fourteen to support them. She owned her own newspaper, and wrote editorials against the lynchings of black people that were happening every day in her hometown. And she was threatened with death for that. How big do you have to get?"

Katherine's class worked through possible reasons these boys thought Ida B. Well's life was not big, not as big as, say, Martin Luther King, Jr.'s life. The girls argued that Wells was not able to become as big in history, first, because she was living in the 1880s and King lived in the 1960s, when blacks had more rights, and second, because she was a woman.

That issue settled, Aaron, in particular, seemed very angry as the biography continued. Normally a very active talker, he stopped contributing to the discussions, except to voice his opinion (a steady refrain) that (1) white people in books were always portrayed as "devils"; (2) there were also bad black people, like the ones who sold drugs on his street corner and harassed him on the way home from school; and (3) a lot of black people during slavery were treated very well in their master's house. As his anger and frustration grew, his responses to the Wells biography, usually out of context and off track, become ever more vitriolic. He postulated that blacks worked better in the sun because their skin didn't get "sun disease" like white skin can, and that people are probably just lying about slavery anyway. "These book writers weren't there, how do they know slavery really happened?" he wanted to know.

First, the class tried arguing that this is history, those white people were acting like "devils." Then they went to the texts on their bookshelves, to the biography of John Brown, to the stories of Quakers and other abolitionists, that tell another aspect of the story. Aaron wasn't convinced. They compared these books to earlier books they had read during their study of Native Americans, where all Native Americans are portrayed as good, spiritual people, protectors of the earth, and all whites are bad, especially Christopher Columbus.

One day Aaron's frustration finally built to the point that he said, "I'm just sick of reading about Native Americans, black people, and women. We've been studying Native Americans every year at this school since I was in kindergarten. Native American this, and Native American that. And they're always so nicey-nice in those picture books. I bet there were bad Indians too, but we never hear about them. Why can't we just read about a white *man* for once?"

In a democratic classroom, children need to feel free to speak and negotiate social difficulties when they arise. The teacher needs to recognize the potential for critique in the midst of a moment like this. Katherine fretted moment by moment about whether she should or should not allow Aaron to voice these grave misunderstandings and limited viewpoints in such a disturbing way. She countered her strong impulse to silence him or send him out of the room with her belief that he had as much right to air his ideas as someone who was speaking about the rights of the oppressed. She made a political decision to allow Aaron to vent his frustrations, despite the inaccuracies and the potential his words held to hurt others sitting in the classroom. She was physically sickened by his comments, and unsure about the appropriate way to handle them. Surprisingly and happily, in the course of Aaron's disturbing behavior, other students—African American and Latino, ones normally silenced by his dominant voice—argued with him using evidence from various books the class had read together through the years, historical events, and their own lives. They were appalled when Aaron attempted to co-opt "scientific data" to justify slave labor in cotton fields, and when he finally proposed the revisionist version of history that slavery never really happened, that African Americans were just making it up to make white people look like "devils." Leah turned to him and said, "Aaron, you're Jewish. Don't you know people try to say that the Holocaust didn't happen? Can you believe *that?* How does that make *you* feel?" Aaron stopped talking after that. His face took on a hardened look for the remainder of the year. Katherine still wonders if being in her classroom opened his heart and mind at all. She can only hope and believe she handled it the best way she could. By letting the three boys voice their unhappiness with her curriculum, by honoring all perspectives, she hoped the class would get to a better place as a community.

A scene like the preceding one does not happen in an environment where the teacher holds all the power and makes all the decisions, where children are all doing problem 13 on page 63, where the teacher micromanages the children's every move, including to and from the bathroom. A democratic classroom requires the teacher to let go of a great deal of authority, to create an environment that allows students to choose how to live together, and to hold out an expectation that every student will become powerful. Democracy demands our best selves. If a democratic society is to continue, its members must construct and maintain it.

CHAPTER 7

NOTICING THE WORLD
Writers Notebooks as Tools for Social Critique

Over the last thirty years or so, a lot of writing teachers have come to think of writing as having two faces. One face is directed outward toward others—it's the writing you do for readers. You think about the person or audience you're addressing, and you form your writing in anticipation of their response. You try to project your mind into their consciousnesses, to anticipate their objections, to connect to what matters to them. This other-directed writing, which is always some form of social action, is the focus of Chapter 8.

Here, we consider the other face of writing, the one that in some way is turned inward to the writer, the writing that is a tool for thinking rather than communicating. This is the writing you do to plan your life and activity, to think through your responses to your world, to claim your positions, to craft the self you want to be. It's as close as you can get to inner speech. It's like talking to yourself as you drive along in your car or striking poses in a mirror.

Keeping a writers notebook is writing to think. A writers notebook is similar to a journal; what makes it different is how it's used—as a well from which to draw writing projects directed at readers. It's like an artist's sketchbook, helping the writer notice and attend to what's around her. Writers use notebooks to gather and incubate ideas, to recycle material, to layer new thinking upon old. When they have a reason to speak out into the world, either because a situation calls for it or because the teacher says it's time, their notebooks provide a resource for topic, ideas, research, and planning or organizing drafts. Because the physical qualities of a notebook matter very much to a writer, everyone needn't have the same kind—to each his own (and her own). (Readers who need more of an introduction to writers notebooks may want to consult Randy's book *Time for Meaning* [1995] or the other references listed in Figure 7–1.)

Students need to learn what people who write in particular genres keep in their notebook. For example, poets collect images, sharp memories, phrases that sound good, lines they can't get out of their head. Entries like these get poets ready to make poems—it's a way of collecting raw material and doing the kind of thinking poetry requires. Making these kinds of entries draws students' attention to aspects of poetic writing like imagery and surprising juxtapositions of words. When they move on to write memoir, fiction, essays, or articles, the habits of thought gained in studying poetry stay with them.

The same is true when using writing as a tool for thinking about *social and political issues*. In their notebook, writers look at the world through various social and political lenses, creating the seeds for social and political action. Most important, they can rehearse and gradually internalize a habit of looking for trouble, of thinking critically about their social realities. The goal of education

Anderson, C. 2000. *How's It Going? A Practical Guide to Conferring with Student Writers*. Portsmouth, NH: Heinemann.

Bomer, R. 1995. *Time for Meaning: Crafting Literate Lives in Middle and High School*. Portsmouth, NH: Heinemann.

Calkins, L. 1991. *Living Between the Lines*. Portsmouth, NH: Heinemann.

Calkins, L. 1994. *The Art of Teaching Writing*, 2d ed. Portsmouth, NH: Heinemann.

Fletcher, R. 1996. *A Writers Notebook: Unlocking the Writer Within You*. New York: Avon.

Fletcher, R. 1996. *Breathing In, Breathing Out: Keeping a Writers Notebook*. Portsmouth, NH: Heinemann.

Hindley, J. 1996. *In the Company of Children*. York, ME: Stenhouse.

Murray, D. 1990. *Write to Learn*, 3d ed. New York: Holt, Rinehart, & Winston.

Figure 7–1   *Resources on Writers Notebooks*

is to enable students to do important thinking without teachers' assistance and sponsorship. Writers notebooks are one of the most useful tools for educating for social justice.

Valuing Social Responsiveness

Teachers cannot help but emphasize certain kinds of thinking over others. For instance, in *Time for Meaning*, Randy describes asking students to sit with one object they find in the room—a square of tile, a pencil, a shoe—for ten minutes and write about that one thing. Sustained attention like this usually produces detailed descriptions and may lead to associations. By teaching this lesson, a teacher shows he values observation and associative thinking. Other minilessons about ways to write in notebooks similarly underscore the value of particular ways of thinking: characterization, curiosity about people; dialogue, an ear for spoken language; reconstruction, plumbing deep lingering memories; interpretation, reflection; critique, responding to literature and other media. Of course, more thinking-with-writing possibilities are excluded than included, but our choices create and constrain the reservoirs from which students will draw, at least as long as they're in that classroom.

It's not surprising, then, that students rarely select topics related to social issues; everyday justice; power relationships; possibilities for collective interest and action; or other social, political, or critical topics. Sometimes there *could* be a critical angle to the material they choose, but because of the values teachers usually highlight, students' ways of thinking about their topic, their ways of "writing well," usually remain more personal, poetic, and descriptive.

For example, Sarai's entry, "The whole time I was little, my mother owned a candy store. I use to walk there after school. I could take a piece of candy and something to read. As long as it wasn't too much. Then a bigger nice store opened up on the same block. My mother didn't have any customers and she had to close the store. Now she works in an office, but I never saw it," could have become a piece about the ways people with little, struggling businesses are defeated by bigger, richer companies. It could have dealt with people trying to integrate their family and their work, sometimes possible in entrepeneurial venues, rarely possible in more bureaucratic contexts.

Instead, Sarai used this material as part of a larger memoir, a lovely, wistful description of those afternoons in her mother's store. The lens Sarai brought to her memory was not social, political, or economic, but private, personal, and aesthetic. Nothing was wrong with what she did. But might she have thought and written about it differently—asking different questions for different purposes—if her teacher had found a way to highlight more critical habits of mind in the writers notebook, the seedbed for her students' larger works?

To support more socially engaged, critical thought in student writing, teachers need to reframe the ways they direct their students' attention to the outside world. Writers notebooks are a tool for noticing the world, and how kids are taught to keep these notebooks influences the sorts of things they pay attention to. Many teachers show students how to attend to emotionally important memories and incidents, to areas of personal interest and expertise, to details of their environment, to the ordinarily unnoticed material inherent in the everyday. They want to teach them to value the ordinary, to see their own experience as important. That in itself is a political agenda. A teacher can broaden the categories by drawing students' attention to critical incidents and social issues—times when someone is treated unfairly; when someone abuses power; when the writer realizes that other people live very differently; times when the writer feels anger, pity, compassion, sympathy, toward individuals or for members of particular groups; when he has an idea for something he could do with others to make the world better. In other words, teachers can more often and more clearly support thinking that considers others in the writer's immediate environment and in the wider social world.

Our own notebooks are full of critical reflections. Flipping through the last week or so of entries, Randy sees notes taken during a workshop on feminist literature; in them, he wonders whether the professor's self-aggrandizing subtext was as oppressive to the middle and high school teachers she was addressing as the treatment the women in the story experienced was to them. He describes a fireman from the station down the street rudely ordering workmen at the house next door to ours to move their truck, which was blocking the fireman's personal car: a uniform automatically conveys authority. One short entry notices a little girl asking her big brother, "Can I watch you play?" While waiting to see a teacher in a school in a poor neighborhood, he describes in detail the physical appearance of the school's interior: nothing seems to be clean or in good condition. Then he reminds himself to make a similar entry the next time he's waiting to see a grants officer in a corporate office. Our critical thinking is often a kind of second act: we describe something that happens, then critique it, usually out of our concern for how we'd *like* our society to be. That same kind of second act needs to start appearing in the writers notebooks our students keep.

To get started, we teachers need to demonstrate thinking like this in our own notebooks. When we sit down to write, we need to cast our minds not just back to childhood, not just to the little pleasant details of our lives, not just to the things and people in our intimate circle, but also to the dozens of little outrages we experience as we walk to school or watch kids in the yard, as we engage with service workers, as we drive through the neighborhoods of our town, and as we watch the morning news. And some of these entries, when we wonder about our own conduct or express indignation at the conduct of others, should be shared with our students. Our conversations with children too often focus on the pleasant and pastoral (maybe we're still romantic about the world of childhood?); we need to make sure we demonstrate our own thinking about the wider world of struggle and conflict, to strengthen the foundation of students' critical thought and their writing for social action.

A useful technique is to ask students to look back through their notebook and catalog the kinds of entries they have made, in order to get a sense of their own strengths and to chart a course for new directions they might try. Being on the lookout for writing behavior is an important form of assessment and planning. If it doesn't come up on its own, we can encourage writers in our workshops to review their work with a social lens, looking for it's-not-fair entries, someone-should-do-something-about-this entries, how-to-make-the-world-better entries. Occasionally we may need to inflate the significance of even the faintest glimmerings of critical consciousness. Certainly, we need to pump up our talk about it in the classroom. By calling attention to this sort of thinking, we increase its value.

Katherine often begins a study of socially conscious writing by asking her students to look for entries in their writers notebooks that tackle social questions. She wants her students to see that they are, in fact, often aware of social issues, that she hasn't just designated a few weeks on the school calendar in which to get politically active. Perhaps they have written entries about people they know, incidents and events in their own lives and in the lives of people they love, that can be viewed in a political light by asking, *How did this come to be like this? Is this right?* In her initial minilessons Katherine says, "Spot the potential for socially engaged writing in your personal writing. Look at your entries through the lens of, *This is not fair. Something needs to be done about this!*"

Mercedes had arrived from the Dominican Republic only two years before she was in Katherine's class. She was still making sense of her new country, its unfamiliar language, its new people, new religions, new customs, and she wrote in her notebook about all the troubles she was encountering. She was often filled with surprise and disgust at the atrocities she saw in her new home:

Sept. 24

Yesterday I heard in the news a terrible and horrible thing. In New York here where I am some people were writing and drawing on the walls—burn Jewish on Yom Kippur. That is a terrible thing to do. Yom Kippur is on Sept 23. Yom Kippur is a Jewish holiday so yesterday those people took paints and wrote—burn Jewish. Those people are prejustice to Jewish. They don't like Jewish people. My fourth grade teacher is Jewish and I like her very much. She taught me and my fourth grade class how that holiday is celebrated. I don't remeber exactly what they are all I remeber is that the family come together in a reaunin and they sit down in the table they have drinks, like the kids drink grape juice and grown ups drink wine. I think everyones religen is great. I think what those people did was very rude. How will they like it if someone made fun of their religen. They will feel sad and horrible. They don't realize what they done until someone does the same to them. I am no saying revenge I am yust saying they don't realize what they've done.

It's very sad that people are doing this to each other. AMERICA is a free country. It doesn't mean you can do anything you want it means you have the right to come here. You have the right to have fun. It's a free country but it's not a country of hating one another.

Su Lee's notebook contained many entries about homelessness. When children are tuned in to the world around them, when they know that world is worth noticing and writing about, stories about homelessness almost always appear in their notebooks. Unfortunately, homelessness is a reality all over the United States, not just in New York City:

When I walk on the sidewalk, I see people, homeless people. I look at them sleeping on the street or freezing cold on the street. Things like that. I think about how lucky I am that I have a place to live, but they don't. I feel kind of sad that they have to live there night and day. Or maybe for the rest of their lives. Well, if I can change something in this world it will have to be that homeless people will live in a shelter home. They will sleep in a nice comfy bed to sleep in. With pillows, blankets and things like that. They will also have food to eat, I mean healthy, yummy, delicious kind of food to eat. They will have people there who will treat them as if they are your family, I mean in a good, happy way, not a bad way. They will be caring and helpful. If this happens, I will be kind of happy because I know that homeless people will be taken care of and be well treated. And I know that at least they don't have to live in the street sleeping in the cold with broken ragged clothes and without food. At least I know they will be taken care of.

   If I was them let me see for a minute let me picture how I will feel and how I would act about this. Okay, I will feel sad and mad because I would feel like that I won't be taken care of and I will be so hungry and I will have to be living on the street for the rest of my life like night and day. I would kind of act kind of mean, because I want my life to be a little better so I am kind of taking all my madness and sadness on someone who is trying to help me. But in general I don't really know how they live on like this, I mean like having no food, your broken clothes and sleeping on the sidewalks. I just don't know how you can do that. I can't even do this for a minute.

Ruth, who had filled at least eight notebooks in her two years in Katherine's classroom, was able to find several examples of this type of entry by looking back over all her old notebooks with this new lens. When she had written about her beloved babysitter, Althea, in fourth grade, she and Katherine both thought it was just another example of her curiosity, her sensitivity, and her ability to empathize and to live inside the skin and heart of another, all qualities that made Ruth such a magnificent writer of poetry, fiction, and nonfiction. Now, when she turned a critical eye to the story of how her babysitter left her family to come work in the United States, Ruth wondered all sorts of great social and political questions: What must life be like in Barbados that made it so hard to get a job or make enough money to live? Why did Althea become a babysitter and housecleaner instead of going to college or getting a better job?

With some nudging from Katherine, Ruth pursued these questions. She found other children in the class and in other classrooms in the school who also had babysitters from Caribbean islands, and then Ruth wondered why they all came from those places and not Italy or Israel? Althea came to Katherine's class to tell her story, and though it was very touching, Katherine was disappointed that she was not more openly critical of the systems in both her native country and her adopted home that kept her poor, separated from family, and working for white, middle-class families.

Noticing in School

School is no more immune to the issues of justice, power, and association than any other human institution. Follow any student around for the school day, and you will likely encounter:

- Questions of fairness about how people get picked for jobs, teams, or groups.
- Evidence of the low esteem in which school is held in society, including inadequate supplies and decrepit buildings.
- Oppression of younger people by elders.
- The power relations that surround "respect" and "disrespect."
- The complexities of getting along with a group of people.
- Decisions about how a group deals with an individual who will not conform.
- Issues of voice and silence.
- Abbreviated rights of free speech, free association, free press, and other constitutional "guarantees."
- The relations between individual choices (of topics, inquiries, reading material) and shared community pursuits.
- The power relations encoded in language (e.g., "correct" usage and pronunciation).

- The consequences of cruelty and kindness.
- Restrictions on being able to move freely among different groups (classes, study groups, friendships).

Every one of these issues is deeply political, and the circumstances surrounding them are opportunities for students to think about political themes, local and worldwide. These are the *same issues* for which people go to prison, endure torture, and die. We are not advocating a student revolution, anarchy in schools, or classrooms completely run by children's wishes, but since these topics are so close at hand, part of children's daily experience, teachers are making a political decision when they help—or don't help—students notice them.

In classrooms with ongoing writing workshops, writing-to-think also has a social purpose when community members write about their responses to one another. Writing in their notebook becomes a tool for thinking about, reflecting on, questioning, defending, and deconstructing the events that occur within the community and between its members. For instance, one year, Katherine's students wrote detailed, honest, personal responses to a serious racial incident that happened during recess. Another year, they explored how they exclude those in the classroom who differ from the rest in their emotional, physical, or learning needs. In both instances, the writing they produced inspired many subsequent class conversations; the conversations inspired more writing; and the class eventually produced some proposals for making things different and, perhaps, better for those who had suffered. Equally important, the persons who were being excluded, ridiculed, or threatened with violence felt strong and safe enough to present their perspectives as well, forcing everyone in the community to see how it feels to be the "other" and at the mercy of the group that holds the power. The inclusion of those formerly silenced voices changed the way Katherine's children interacted, as now they looked at one another in new ways. This was indeed writing for social action, although it didn't take the form of a letter to the mayor or protest placards outside the school. It was writing for, about, and to a specific community in which they spent so many hours together, and it changed how those hours were spent.

Teaching How to Look Through a Socially Critical Lens

It's one thing to be aware that writers notebooks can focus on social issues and questions; it's another to teach students to do this sort of thinking and writing. It helps if we examine a few aspects of that teaching—specifically, demonstration, assisted performance, and dialogic assessment (Bomer 1998)—separately.

Demonstration

It's hard for teachers to help students learn to write in a particular way, to lead discussions about strategies and lenses, unless we do some of the same sort of writing ourselves. Teachers can't buy examples of writers notebooks, shrink-wrapped with the lives from which they sprang: they have to use their own living, thinking, and writing. Using one's own writing not only lends credibility to teaching, it also provides the teacher with material for minilessons and conferences. Furthermore, since it is full of local references that are culturally familiar to the students, it helps them see that social action is not *out there* but right at hand. These writing demonstrations can be of two kinds: after the fact and in the midst.

In after-the-fact demonstrations, teachers read their own notebook entries written outside class, sometimes projecting them on transparencies or writing them on chart paper. The actual text, though, is only part of the story. Teachers situate the text within a narrative of when and how they wrote it: *Yesterday, I was driving home from school, and I saw [this or that], and I started wondering about it. I was thinking about [blah blah blah], and when I got home, here's what I wrote: [reading of text].* Depending on the actual content, the minilesson goes on to describe what the students can learn from this example.

In-the-midst demonstrations are perhaps even more useful because the noticing, thinking, and writing all happen on the spot, right there where the students can see them taking place. Choosing something they've just witnessed out the window or in the room, or perhaps in the hallway on their way to class, teachers wonder and reflect out loud for a minute or so, then decide aloud how to write this thinking, and begin composing in front of the students on an overhead or chart paper. It isn't, after all, self-evident how to start such an entry. Do I first write a description of what I saw, or do I begin with the larger critical issue that is beginning to take shape? How do I start writing about a big idea? There's no right answer, but the decision, one that some writers find paralyzing, has to be made, and no other mode of teaching can even get close to that level of detail.

Assisted Activity

To bridge their own doing with that of the students, teachers provide structured assistance—chances for the students to try out these strategies and lenses with teacher help. Even strong students may have trouble adopting a critical lens, sometimes because the very same compliant, uncomplaining nature that has made them successful in school also makes them reticent about detecting problems in their social worlds. Whole-class assisted performance allows the teacher to begin inducting students into the desired way of seeing. After a shared event, like yesterday's pep rally or assembly, a disturbance in the hall today, or a field trip, the teacher spends a few minutes of a minilesson orally constructing critical questions and perspectives, then asks students to extend their thinking in writing, and finally asks them to discuss with a partner the angle they adopted in their notebook entry. Taking a walk together around the neighborhood, or even just around the campus, provides a chance to focus everyone's attention on critical reflection if the walk is followed with writing and discussion. Photographs and videotapes bring the world into the classroom. Taped news broadcasts, short excerpts from movies or TV shows, and student- or teacher-produced images of provocative scenes happening in the world can help students tune in to areas of experience they might not have written about yet. Whole-class strategies like these, more detailed than a minilesson, help the group as a whole catch on to the intellectual frame we are setting in motion in the class.

Of course, in a writing workshop, a lot of assisted performance occurs in teacher conferences with individual students. Often, students summarize events in their writers notebook without doing much critical reflection. A helpful conference, in such a case, is a collaborative conversation that brings out the potential political themes in the event and leaves the student writing into that same sort of thinking. Early student attempts at being critical often tend to be oversimplified opinions or complaints rather than a more complex analysis of a social problem. In conferences with writers at that stage of development, the teacher helps the student consider the problem from a number of perspectives, not to crush the writer's own view but to allow more facets to develop. After a student is familiar with a wider range of social ills, a conference may involve imagining together possible alternatives or remedies, especially planning how one could unite other people around the concern and begin working to make it better. These same student writers, by sharing with the class what they have learned in these conferences, can provide demonstrations for others.

Dialogic Assessment

Regular appointments in which students are asked to give an account of how they have been working toward a heightened social awareness in their writing keep them focused on the goal. If a student knows that, at the end of today's writing workshop, she's going to have to write a note, talk to a partner, or report to the class about what she's been trying to do in her critical writing-to-think, she's more likely to make sure her work gives her something valuable to say. Simple questions can trigger complex discussions: *What kinds of topics do you notice yourself getting passionate about? What is giving you trouble about this kind of thinking? If you were going to teach someone to do the kind of writing we've been working on, what would be important to tell him? Which strategies have you tried so far in your notebook, and which ones do you need to work on? Who tried something new today? What topics you've already written about do you want to write more about? What are we learning at this point?* Such conversations are more than share sessions. They help the teacher monitor student thinking. They allow students to identify and assess their own thinking and learning. They represent the community's ongoing collaboration for social action.

When notebook entries don't immediately suggest social issues or spotlight injustices, teachers need to invite students to tune their ears and eyes to the world around them. Katherine asked one class to spend several weeks collecting social issues in their notebooks, exploring possibilities. (She's always careful about how long this stage lasts. Students need to move on to a specific topic while they're still excited.) Her minilessons posed these questions: *What do you want to speak publicly about? What things need to be addressed in your classroom, your school, your apartment building, your neighborhood, the city, the country, the world? How will you read and write differently— and reread differently—as you look for issues of fairness and inequity?* She wrote a number of notebook entries of her own that showed what turning one's eyes and ears to injustices in the social world meant and read them to her class. She also shared stories about political work with organizations like NCTE and local TAWL groups, showing the students pieces we had written opposing regressive federal reading legislation and standardized testing. And she asked them to watch the nightly news or read a daily paper and respond in their notebooks to any news item that made them say, *Someone should do something about this!*

Candace wrote in her notebook:

> I think it is unfair how those religis fanatics run around on the streat screaming things like Jeazes is the best or the sky will start falling if you belive in Jeses or youll die if you eat on romadon and other thins like that. So I think it should stop. I want to write to the groups of people who do that and explain how what they do is unfair because people can believe what they want to believe not what someone else believes. If everybody believd what everybody else believed, then we would all be stuck in a religes tornado and we would all die all together and let me say, who wants to die?
>
> Things I can do to stop the religus mix up
>
> Write a letter
> Protests
> Talk to people who agree with me
> Ask the people who do that to stop

Katherine asked her students to make a double-column entry in their writers notebooks. On one side of the page, they wrote the facts and the story of the news item they were interested in. On the other side of the page, they wrote how they felt about this issue, what questions they had, or ideas they might have for how to make things better. Here is one of Fred's notebook entries:

On the News	My Thoughts
From the radio, NPR	It is not right that some people (whites) should
In Georgia there have been droughts and floods destroying people's crops and many people were getting bans on growing from the goverment at low rates. But black farmers had to get loans from banks and getting no sympathy or help from anyone.	have the privilege to have bans while other people are going bankrupt. It's wrong especially because of discrimination. We should not have racism of black and white people. This issue makes me angry that the goverment is being unfair. And I didn't know there are issues as big as this.

Even though the writers were mainly thinking on paper during this period, Katherine continually reminded them that they were headed for social action, that they should be imagining responses not just as thoughts but as actual answers to people outside the classroom. Thus she was gearing writing-to-think toward potential audiences and public purposes early in the process.

Rereading for Themes and Possibilities

Once students have at least ten notebook entries focused on social issues, noticings, and questions, they should be able to reread their notebooks to see whether any important themes take shape: *What has been capturing my attention?* They may find that gender issues have been foremost in their minds, or they might realize they have tended to write about the struggles of the poor. Perhaps they have focused on the ways they and their friends are isolated from one another in school, or maybe they are concerned about the possibility of a war breaking out somewhere in the world. Environmental concerns, the media's preoccupation with physical appearance, or care for the elderly may have come up, directly or tangentially, in several entries. Some students may realize they have never written about the issues they care most about and so may need to turn their attention in a new direction now, making several entries about something that matters to them. By surveying their recent journeys of thought, writers allow a topic to choose them. Confronted with the evidence of their own attentive noticing, they may realize for the first time that there are political concerns they care about.

    Of course, students should not reread *only* the entries they have made since the class formally began turning its attention to social critique. Political issues—imbalances, silences, associations—are everywhere, constantly present in everyone's life. Therefore, earlier notebook entries that at first seem "personal" may also contain critical material. To spot the political potential in personal writing, students need to reread these entries using the same critical lenses they've been applying to the world:

- *Being fair and setting things right.* Very often, the impulse for students to write springs from the complaint that some adult action is unfair. In the margins or in a new entry, they can now develop their ideas about how things can be made fairer and about what fairness really means.

- *Trying on the perspectives of others.* Perhaps the student has written statements like, *Maybe she thought thus and so.* If not, she can look for opportunities to consider an event or situation from multiple points of view. This is the essence of being able to imagine taking social action.

- *What people need for happiness and well-being.* What is it that makes it possible to have a good life? Does everybody need the same things? Who has those things and who does not? How could it be possible for more people to have a happy, well-lived life?

- *Following the money.* Many of the events that excite or upset students have economic underpinnings. Thinking about where money comes from and where it goes can lead to important socially critical perspectives.

- *Questioning authority.* Fortunately, this is a habit of mind for many kids, and teachers can help students use their rebellious impulses productively in their political thinking. They may ask themselves: *Why is this so? Who benefits from this? Who says it has to be this way?* Often, the trick is to get them to think about these questions democratically, in the interests of a wider social group, rather than simply in terms of their individual desires.

- *Feelings of anger and indignation.* It is sometimes difficult, but always important, to help students differentiate anger that stems from their own sense of entitlement from a more righteous indignation in response to unfairness.

- *Feelings of empathy and compassion.* The affirmative face of social critique may be just as useful as indignation in helping students imagine themselves doing something to help someone else.

- *Identity and affiliation.* Every entry in a writers notebook can probably be read this way. Writers often wrestle with what sort of person they want to be, how they want to view themselves. Becoming a particular sort of person involves figuring out which other people one most wants to be like. Who one is partly a function of what team one is on.

- *Collective action.* Seeds of social action can be found in any entry that involves getting people together to do something, even if it is not especially political. Entries about doing things with others help students draw on familiar experiences in order to imagine coming together to explore and pursue more complex common social agendas. Entries about being on a winning baseball team may provide the vision for how to gather people together to improve the quality of the town's water.

- *Difference.* The realization that we are not all alike is the starting point for many of our affiliations, and also brings attention to many social inequalities that need addressing. Socially penetrating differences have to do with family, culture, race, sexuality, class, gender, or age. Of course, just noticing a difference, or even analyzing it, does not dictate what is to be done about it or how to think about it.

Going from Listening to the World to Talking Back

Students need to follow their socially critical thoughts with inquiry and action, both individually and collaboratively. Writing for social action is a conversation about how we all live together in the world. Socially conscious writers say to their readers, *Look at this! I've been noticing and questioning this thing that is happening in the world. I want you to notice it and question it, too. And I want us to work together to make it better.*

We want students to be able to continue their dialogues with the world beyond the time we know them, to carry what they learn in our classroom community with them into the other communities they become part of in their lives. In order to do so, they need to know how to identify problems and possibilities, to think about given realities while envisioning better potential worlds.

Maxine Greene (1998) has called for "teaching to the end of arousing a consciousness of membership, active and participant membership in a society of unfulfilled promises—teaching for . . . a wide-awakeness that might make injustice unendurable" (xxx). This consciousness, this wide-awakeness, can be born in writers notebooks, if students use the notebook to examine their world.

CHAPTER 8

WRITING FOR SOCIAL ACTION
Collaborating on Texts for Public Purposes

Education is constantly a form of action. If you know certain things, how will you act?

—Carol Gilligan

Find your own words.
Organize your own associates.
Propose your own solutions to the grievances you abhor.
Help write the next set of chapters on citizen activism.
If you are not ready to act, make room for those who are.

—Stephen Frantzich

Ten-year-old Elaine wrote the following reflection toward the end of her class' unit on writing for social action:

> Before we studied this project, when I first heard about it, I thought it would be kind of hard. Hard to work in a group, hard to write a letter or a speech or a note! It would be hard to even find someone to work with. But I accomplished all of it and managed to find something I liked. I learned to work in a group, to let new people in, to be the ruler of *my* world. It meant a lot to me. And to know how much my group appreciates me was the best of all. I learned how BIG I could possibly be.

Perhaps for anyone, the idea of trying to do something to make the world a better place is scary at first. We all feel small and weak and ill informed; we are sure no one will listen. And we don't really think, sitting there on our couch, that anything is compelling enough to draw us into a struggle. What Elaine found out was that by taking an interest *in conjunction with others,* we become bigger, we gain a sense of efficacy. We can't wait for efficacy to visit like an archangel, overcome us while we rest. It's a product of activity with others.

Writing for a better world takes two forms: first, writing that is primarily reflective, a tool for the writer's thinking about her socio-political environment, and second, writing that is intended to be read by people whose mind the writer intends to change. On the one hand, there are note-books; on the other, there are petitions, letters, press releases, posters, pamphlets, flyers, poems, songs, stories, and the rest of the genre-packed world of writing.

The latter follow the former. Students look back at what they've been writing about in their notebooks in order to decide what issue they'd like to pursue as a writing-for-social-action project. We did not dictate a topic for the whole class to take on, such as protesting dumping in a nearby lake or river or advocating for animal rights (although both of those topics became passions for a few students). We did not dictate what form the writing would take; we only saw to it that students did some kind of writing that left the classroom. It was up to the children to investigate what form made sense for their particular topics. They investigated, calculated, and negotiated in an authentic process of targeting their audience and deciding whether they wanted a specific action to be taken, or just wanted to raise consciousness about some issue.

After students have identified an issue they care about by rereading and layering their thoughts in their notebook, they need to research it in order to enrich the ways they talk about it with their classmates. The classroom becomes a sort of bazaar, where students try to market issues to one another and, in the process, form small groups around a common concern. They then build consensus with the members of their group, develop a common understanding of the issues, and decide on action goals. They identify forms of writing that could help them advance their vision and learn the craft of writing in those forms. They revise their strategies in light of how best to get their prospective readers to support them to act in the world. Finally, they send their writing out into the public space, monitor the response it elicits, and write again in order to create a dialogue: they wrestle with the world, encounter real opposition and real support.

The focus in this kind of curriculum (Figure 8–1 breaks down a writing-for-social-action study step by step) is on using *literacy* as a tool for change. (It's not about collecting cans for recy-cling!) Students can work on an issue in lots of ways, but as much of the daily classroom work as possible should focus on texts. If social critique and social action are to have a secure place in stu-dents' days, they had better be "academic." Nevertheless, social action is not a single genre or a single theme; it's a broad purpose and identity that writers need to try on in order open themselves to a lifetime of possibilities for democratic participation. Let's take a look at writing for social action in Katherine's classroom.

Getting Started: Grounding Social Action in Children's Lives

Katherine's students began by finding previous notebook entries connected to politically impor-tant topics. They also wrote additional notebook entries as they looked at the world through lenses related to social justice. Then they shared their notebook entries with partners during class meetings every day. The kids' strong feelings about what they had written about in their note-books led to lots of talk throughout the day. As they talked, they developed more and more topics in common, more shared perspectives, a closer-knit sense of the sorts of topics that were important to their community. The number of topics cooking in the notebooks began to reduce to fewer, bigger common concerns. Students also began to clip articles from various newspapers, building an ongoing "story" about certain hot topics. They quickly discovered that the same topic can be written about in very different styles and tones, and can present a different set of facts.

	Action	Description	Duration
1	Reviewing	Writers look back through their notebooks to find previous entries that connect to social issues and mark them.	A day or two
2	Collecting	Writers collect, in notebooks, their thinking in response to current events in the world around them, using lenses related to social justice.	Two to three weeks
3	Identifying topic	Writers reread notebooks to see what topic has most captured their interest and passion.	A day or two
4	Initial research	Writers find out enough about their topic to be able to describe it to potential allies among their classmates.	A few days
5	Creating coalitions	Students get one another interested in their topics, and decide, within newly formed groups, what they will work on.	A few days
6	Researching topic	Teams gather information about their topic, get their facts straight, and deepen their understanding, in order to plan action.	A week or so
7	Action plans	Groups plan what they are going to try to do, especially how they will use writing to do something about their issue.	A few days
8	Action	Groups carry out their plans, try things, encounter problems, reevaluate, revise, try something else, and so forth.	Three to four weeks
9	Shifts in focus	Some groups change their topic. Some individuals change groups.	Ongoing
10	Reflection and evaluation	Students reflect on and name what they have learned through their social action.	A few days

Figure 8–1   *Outline of a Study on Writing for Social Action*

As the children reread, wrote, and talked with partners about the issues that were coming alive in their notebooks, Katherine posed new questions or suggested new angles:

- *What is a major issue, and what do the people who think very differently from you think about it?* This involves taking perspectives and imagining other perspectives, including those of persons with whom you may disagree.

- *What political issues are interesting to your family?* Family concerns were fairly localized— Mayor Guiliani's proposal to issue jaywalking tickets; using pedestrian barriers to help direct city traffic; school uniforms; keeping real estate out of the hands of developers.

- *Is this issue a job for the government? What should not be taken care of by the government?* Some kids, focusing on the idea of fairness, wrote about more personal conflicts that might not lend themselves to obvious social action.

- *Could you support a project that others have already begun rather than start a new one?* Everyone concerned about an issue does not have to found his own organization; the crux of social action is many people joining in a shared endeavor. We are not trying to create mavericks.

Learning from Mentors

Over the next few weeks, the class invited parents, friends, and community members to talk about their experiences with political and social activism. These guest speakers were role models. These were people who had figured out how to move from response to real action in the world. The personal, specific details these living, breathing beings talked about went far in improving the performance of the children who were just beginning to uncover their own social awareness. Their stories were a frame on which Katherine's students could hang their own responses to the world.

One parent talked about his former work as a lobbyist. He was instrumental in helping the group think strategically, with political savvy, about how to be heard by the right people.

In the middle of the study, Martha's mother was arrested and jailed for twenty-four hours for participating in a rally in front of New York City Police Headquarters on behalf of Amadou Diallo, the African man who was shot forty-one times by four policemen. A black police officer had been the one to cuff Martha's mom. "That policeman was just doing his job," Martha explained, "but he probably felt terrible about it. Because of the Diallo case, people are saying that *all* police are bad, but maybe only those men who shot him were." Martha's mother stressed that her political work was a lifelong passion and goal, and that this latest protest was just one in a string of such encounters in a lifetime of democratic participation. She also made it clear that joining a protest rally is only one way to demonstrate activism. Behind the scenes of such a rally is a lot of work by lawyers, citizen advocates, journalists, and others working with paper and pen to demand justice.

A parent of a class member played in the band on the Rosie O'Donnell show. He told Katherine that Ms. O'Donnell often spoke openly and passionately on her show about issues such as gun control. He obtained a tape for the class to watch of the show she made the day after the murders at Columbine High School in Littleton, Colorado. That day, her guest was Congresswoman Carolyn McCarthy, who ran for office after her husband had been shot and murdered on a Long Island train, and who sponsored the Child Safety Protection Bill in Congress. Katherine's children were impressed with Ms. O'Donnell's strong commitment to end gun violence and with her conviction that children are not to blame but are too often the victims. They took pages of notes and talked for days about the statistics Ms. O'Donnell had cited, wondering if they could really be true: "sixteen kids killed every day from guns; one student killed in a classroom every two days." They quoted Ms. McCarthy in their notebook entries: "One voice can make a difference," and "E-mail your senator and congressman." And London, after learning that Ms. O'Donnell shared the concerns of her social action group, Students Against Student Violence, thought it couldn't hurt to try writing Ms. O'Donnell a letter requesting that her group come on the show:

> Dear Rosie O'Donnell:
>
> We are a group of 4th graders studying student violence. We have been focusing on Rudy Crew's (the New York City School Chancellor) school for 100 violent students.
>
> We are writing this letter because of what you said on your show the day after the Littleton shooting (we watched a tape of it in class). We have been talking about how scared, sad and angry it makes us all feel. We have also interviewed teachers about how they feel, and we wrote a letter to Rudy Crew on this subject.
>
> We would love it if we could come on your show to talk about this. We need an audience. We would like to make a difference. We believe since we're kids, we should be involved with this. We want other students to be able to enjoy what we have without violence. In addition, we would like to send a message to all children, especially young ones.

Anne Powers spoke to the class about her lifelong activism, dating back to peace marches and antisegregation marches in the 1960s. She had kept buttons from every rally and convention she had attended, and the children touched those buttons as if they were pieces of gold. Katherine's class was in the habit of writing thank-you notes to anyone who visited, and the letters her students sent to their activist guests sounded deeply inspired and full of dreams for a better world:

> Dear Anne Powers,
>
> I wish I was a Social Activist like you. I wish I can make the world safer and full of peace. I wish I can change the world and be proud of myself. And then I can make people feel safer and be happy living in this world, like you.
>
> I think you are very brave about marching in the Mumia protest. I don't think that he did anything wrong.
>
> It is a pleasure to know someone like you.
>
> You are like Martin Luther King, Jr.
>
> Sincerely,
> Miko

Anne's daughter, Liz Howort, and her friend Natasha Johnson also visited, and they described the high school organization they belonged to called Students Organizing Students (SOS). The group researches and negotiates the issues to which it will devote its time and energy and then plans what course of action to take. They had raised fifteen hundred dollars for Doctors Without Borders, taken a train to Philadelphia to join a rally for Mumia, and collected signatures on petitions they sent with letters to New York State legislators protesting the high-stakes test the students in their high school were required to take. The children loved talking with Liz and Natasha (their being only a few years older helped Katherine's students see themselves as activists) and begged them to stay for the whole morning to help them strategize. Liz's and Natasha's suggestions were authentic, things they had tried themselves. For instance, Liz explained they had learned the hard way that when you write a petition, each page has to have the mission statement on it in order to be considered valid. That bit of advice helped one group save days of extra work.

Katherine asked each guest, *What in your life made you become a concerned person?* For most, it was a moment in their childhood when they felt empathy for someone who had a more difficult life than their own. For many, it was also the influence of mentors: family members, members of religious organizations, freedom fighters, and members of resistance movements whose lives they had read about in school.

Using Critical Texts to Mentor Social Action Writing

During the social action study, Katherine read aloud biographies of persons who brought about important social change, particularly through writing or public speaking. She read *Peaceful Warrior,* Ed Clayton's biography of Martin Luther King, Jr. This book cited the writings of Thoreau, the teachings of Jesus Christ, and the nonviolent resistance of Ghandi as being instrumental in King's decision to fight injustice in a nonviolent way. Katherine's students referred to King's influences and mentors many times in the course of their own social action, and many used King as their mentor. Katherine also read aloud a biography called *Ida B. Wells, Princess of the Press,* and a biography of Harriet Beecher Stowe.

In conjunction with all three biographies, she read picture books like *Nettie's Trip South* (Turner 1987) and *The Story of Ruby Bridges* (Coles 1995). She read articles and bits from books written for adults to help flesh out the social/political context of the times in which the subjects of the biographies were living. In every case, the children understood and were in awe of the courage it took for these people to commit acts of resistance in such public ways as giving speeches and writing books. Katherine always emphasized the mentoring these freedom fighters had received and the collective aspects of their work, since we know that social/political action does not happen in a vacuum, nor by one person's hand, but by the collaboration and participation of many persons committed to the cause. Stowe benefited from the influence and encouragement of her liberal, politically active family, as well as from her quite liberated husband for that time and social context, who supported her decision to write. Wells and King were both part of larger activist groups who organized, marched, boycotted, and risked arrest and violence in order to effect change. All too often, people like King are presented to classrooms of children as heroes, men and women out of time almost, who bravely stood up to the rest of the world. They are that, indeed, but they also collaborated with many people to bring about the marches, protests, and speeches. This is a crucial idea for children to understand as they go about constructing themselves as social activists.

When teachers choose texts they think will be particularly evocative of critical conversations, they make it easier for themselves and their students to step into critique. All classroom conversations and teaching actions help create a culture that demonstrates what texts are for and how they work. Writers learn what themes are available, how the world becomes word, through their reading. In this, as in all aspects of literate craftwork, the reading–writing connection is crucial. Critique is a way of thinking, a habit of mind, and students will bring what they learn from the reading of texts to their writing—if teachers support it. Students will try to make their own texts do what they've seen other texts do. Teachers can help them see that writers thematically highlight issues of justice and fairness, that they sometimes take on the perspective of people whom society does not treat fairly, or that they focus on details of characters acting to help others or to change their world—that writing itself can sometimes be an action to effect transformations in readers.

For several weeks, Katherine asked her small reading groups to choose from among biographies of Susan B. Anthony, Frederick Douglass, Quanah Parker, Harriet Tubman, Cesar Chavez.

They tried to locate who had the power in these stories. They searched for ways in which power gets enacted in the world through policy and law. They looked at the part money plays in power. They looked for where the freedom fighters got their ideas and influences, and who their allies were in their fight against oppression. They discussed the obstacles faced by even those as courageous and successful at social activism as Ida B. Wells and Harriet Beecher Stowe, both of whom were limited in what they could achieve because they were women in a time when women's voices were silenced.

At one point in the study, the class even attempted to look at the idea of power from the perspective of those who had it. In the exhibits of ancient Greek, Egyptian, and Assyrian art housed in the Metropolitan Museum of Art, they noticed how power was communicated symbolically through size, costume, ornament, and physical stance. They looked at newspaper and magazine photographs of persons in power, and noticed how they were dressed, where they stood or sat in relation to others in the photo, and what symbols of office were arranged around them. From that time on, the children were able to spot the visual cues, especially in posed photographs in magazines, that caused some people to look "on top," others not. Analyzing what power "looks like" helps children grasp that power and oppression, through all of time and all around the world, are *systems* fed and maintained by everyone in the culture. This idea goes a long way toward helping them become critical consumers of products and information that maintain the status quo.

While they were reading these biographies, Katherine's students also analyzed different examples of political writings: Rachel Carson's essays about the environment; King's speeches; excerpts from Stowe's *Uncle Tom's Cabin;* poems by Philip Levine, Walt Whitman, Adrienne Rich, and Carolyn Forché. The class called these texts Writing That Changed the World. When they analyzed portions of King's "I Have a Dream" speech, they noticed how he crafted the text to enlist the support of all types of people. His words did not exclude white people, but instead were tremendously inclusive. King quoted the Bible, a text that holds a great deal of power and that for many lent credence to his ideas. The children even noticed that the speech repeated key lines and phrases and used beautiful imagery, tricks they had learned to make writing evocative when they were studying poetry. Min commented:

> He doesn't say, "Whites are bad." Instead, he encourages everyone to "join hands," "sit down at the table of brotherhood." He uses a lot of metaphors—"Cashing checks"—and repeats a lot to get the idea through to people. Sometimes—well actually a lot—when his repetition is beginning to grow annoying, he stops repeating. He uses other phrases or songs. He rhymes his words a lot.

Dylan wrote:

> I think he was really a very smart man. The thing is, Hitler's very smart, but he used it for bad, and so have many other leaders. But Martin was a very smart man. We should be happy he used it for good and not for bad like some people did. Martin's speech was great. I can't believe a couple of words put together can make something so powerful to change millions of people. I am also surprised that in all of this he did not use one act of violence, after people doing so much to him, like bombing him, killing those girls in church. I know I would at least get a gun to protect myself. But he didn't, and that shocks me.

In her analysis, Leah discussed the features of King's speech listed in Figure 8–2.

Finally, in filling her students up with inspirational stories and personal accounts from community activists, Katherine played tapes and made copies of lyrics from different songs about freedom and about freedom fighters. The children sang "We Shall Overcome" and "Follow the Drinking Gourd." They learned songs by Pete Seeger, Bob Dylan, James Taylor, Janis Ian, and Holly Near. Anita Hollander, a songwriter and performer, was so inspired by the issues her daughter

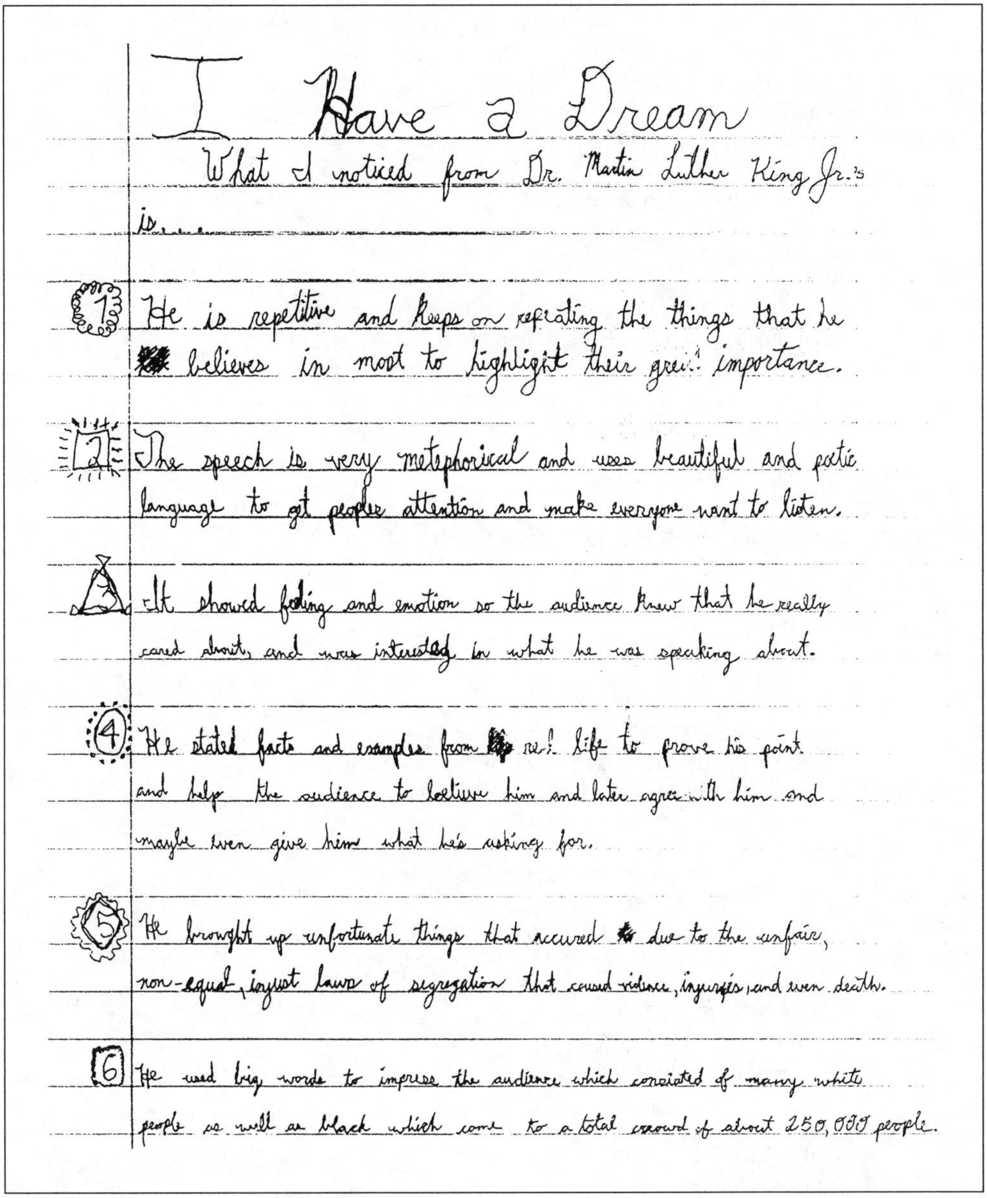

I Have a Dream

What I noticed from Dr. Martin Luther King Jr.'s is...

1. He is repetitive and keeps on repeating the things that he believes in most to highlight their great importance.

2. The speech is very metaphorical and uses beautiful and poetic language to get people's attention and make everyone want to listen.

3. It showed feeling and emotion so the audience knew that he really cared about and was interested in what he was speaking about.

4. He stated facts and examples from real life to prove his point and help the audience to believe him and later agree with him and maybe even give him what he's asking for.

5. He brought up unfortunate things that occurred due to the unfair, non-equal, unjust laws of segregation that caused violence, injuries, and even death.

6. He used big words to impress the audience which consisted of many white people as well as black which came to a total crowd of about 250,000 people.

Figure 8–2 *Leah's Analysis of King's Craft*

was learning and writing about, that she and London composed a song called "If We Sing Together" in response (see Figure 8–3). The class learned the song, and wrote a letter to Ms. O'Donnell asking if they could come on the show to perform it and to talk about their social action projects. The class was figuring out some powerful public avenues by which their voices could be heard.

IF WE SING TOGETHER

Anita Hollander

How can I make a better world?
    I'm so small.
Standing in crowds of people who
    seem so tall.
And how can I make these people hear
    what I say,
When all they do is interrupt
    and look away?

      But IF WE SING TOGETHER, hand in hand,
      We'll teach the world to see and understand.
      'Cause we were born to love and not to hate,
      And we can teach the world it's not too late.

How can I teach my friends at school
    not to fight,
When we go home and watch TV
    every night?
News shows and cop shows tell us to
    fight for good.
But, when does all the fighting stop?
    Man, I wish it would.

      But IF WE SING TOGETHER, voice with voice,
      We'll teach the world to know that there's a choice.
      'Cause we were born to love and not to hate,
      And we can teach the world it's not too late.

        Lately in dreams I get so frightened
        Feeling I'm all alone
        Going against the grain
        Watching a speeding train come towards me

Last night I heard my parents argue
    I was scared,
Thinking that I should do something
    if I dared.
But, maybe they won't hear me speak
    I'm not that loud.
If I could get them listening
    they'd be proud.

      But IF WE SING TOGETHER, hand in hand,
      We'll teach the world to see and understand.
      And IF WE SING TOGETHER, voice with voice,
      We'll teach the world to know that there's a choice.
      'Cause we were born to love and not to hate,
      And we can teach the world it's not too late.

Figure 8–3   *"If We Sing Together," Inspired by the Class' Social Action Study*

Choosing Causes and Building Coalitions

After two or three weeks of reading, talking, and writing responses, the children were "on fire" with social concerns. They rushed in every morning with news articles or stories that had aired on television news broadcasts the night before and discussed them in small groups. But how to move them from gathering information and becoming informed to actually taking action? This is an authentic and familiar moment of paralysis for adults as well. How many times have we become incensed about some injustice we hear about in the news, been sympathetic to and concerned about people suffering from poverty and abuse, or even come up against an issue that negatively affects our personal lives or property, and still done nothing about it? "What can I do?" we ask ourselves. "It probably won't change anything anyway." Or we may feel overwhelmed by the intricacies of the issue, or the danger involved in fighting it. Or we may be genuinely ignorant or confused about what the next step is. This awkward moment in the journey of social action reminded us of the move we help children make from daily notebook writing to committing to projects outside of the notebook that need to be shaped and imagined for a real audience. Sometimes the balloon of excitement for notebook writing deflates when kids find they have to stay with one topic for several weeks of revision and editing.

But in Katherine's classroom, the move from reflection to action did not feel like a lot of hard, boring revision. The drive and excitement for taking action was built in—perhaps because of the children's incredible naïveté about all that is involved in making social change or perhaps because of that sweet quality children have (and many adults have lost) of empathizing with others and wanting to right all wrongs. The difficulty in this social action writing study was not inciting a desire for action, but deciding how to organize and direct that energy and how to plan realizable goals.

From the first week of the study, several children were gathering informally to discuss a topic of common interest. Most, however, remained firmly entrenched in their own, individual interests. Perhaps this had somewhat to do with the fact that up to now the children had been choosing their own topics and writing to think in their own notebook. We understood that our students' writing had everything to do with the community of our classrooms and the social influences present from every discourse community our children participated in. But we had not thought, until this focused study of writing for social action, to ask children deliberately to collaborate with others on a writing and action agenda.

During the first year we tried this study in Katherine's classroom, Randy described it, over lunch, to his colleague Doug Dixon, a social studies educator and theorist of democracy. Feeling a little insecure about the whole thing, Randy commented that it was hard to imagine how they would make much difference, since they were only kids after all. And what could one child do? Doug responded that it might not matter that they are children, if they are writing. He said, that in fact, movements for social change do not happen as the result of individual effort. In democracies, power works through special-interest groups, not through individuals or the masses. Change happens when people work in collectives, joining their energy, skills, and intelligence toward a common cause. There was really no reason to think that children could not do this as well as adults. When Katherine introduced the idea of forming collectives for social change, the children's energy became instantly more focused and more optimistic. She asked the students to draw and write about their issue on poster board and then present the issue to the class and tell why they were interested in it. She kept a list of all the issues on chart paper. The original list of topics included animal rights, the mayor's proposal to issue jaywalking tickets, African American recognition, getting rid of nicotine, DEA (a pharmaceutical cream), unjust voting procedures, the environment, unfair labor practices, and the inability of female doctors to get part-time jobs.

As a class the students then realized that some of these topics were too personal, too vague, too huge, or complicated and eliminated some. Several children became interested in issues raised by their friends and wanted to switch. Others hung on to their particular passion and recruited others to join their cause. Eventually, everyone identified an issue they could and would become involved with and joined the group forming around that issue (groups usually had between four and six members). The first order of business was to establish an identity, give themselves a name. Katherine discussed in a minilesson what a name can and should signify: it can name point-blank the issue at stake (Against Student Violence); it can include words that depict what category of people make up the group (the above group became *Students* Against Student Violence), what type of activity is being performed (research, activism), or the type of group (task force or association, for example). A name needs to declare boldly what the group is agitating for or against.

Katherine gave each group a crate in which to store their artifacts, books, props, posters, and so on, and also gave them pocket folders in which to keep the numerous articles, memos, agendas, meeting minutes, letters, petitions, action plans, and sketches that they accumulated. Each group hung a banner on the classroom wall under a sign that read: Our Social Action Collectives: We Fight for What's Right. They decorated the crates and the folders with their group names and designed logos to represent their cause. Naming the group and designing activities helps set an exciting, unifying tone for collaboration in all kinds of group work. Making the names and logos public, along with some kind of title or explanation of the overall project, both informs the public of the work going on in the classroom and serves as a kind of contract for the class, a commitment to join this effort.

Once groups were established and named, the social difficulties of trying to organize a group effort surfaced. Who would be in charge of the collective? Did it make sense to elect a "president" of a group trying to right the injustices of the world? How would they distribute jobs? How would they go about getting other people interested and involved in their cause? How would they settle disagreements that arose about their action plan, their procedures, their belief systems? Why couldn't they get along when they were doing such good, important things in life?

Katherine deals with these social disputes as they arise. She begins with the assurance that dissonance like this is not at all uncommon in groups trying to organize for political and social action. Often people come together around a belief in or a passion for the same cause. Yet when they try to decide what to *do* about the issue, what course of action to take, all hell breaks loose as people try to imagine and predict the outcomes of various, specific activities. Group members soon discover who is more conservative than whom; who just wants to get out there and scream really loudly; who wants to infiltrate the channels of power slowly and strategically; who is able to devote most of her time, energy, and money to the cause; and who is able, for all kinds of viable reasons, to show solidarity only by adding his name to the membership roster. It is easy for teachers and students to feel frustrated at these points of civil unrest, yet these are some of the most important times for everyone to take risks, to problem solve, and to negotiate. There are powerful "social studies" lessons to be learned in the midst of this collaborative work.

In her conferences with different groups, Katherine uses the same structure that she uses in writing conferences. First, she watches, listens, and takes notes while the group proceeds. The children are used to this procedure, so they are able to carry on as if she's not sitting there. They know Katherine takes notes to help her "freeze" the conversation so she'll be able to talk about it later. They also know that she's probably *not* going to give them an answer to a problem they are experiencing but that she wants them to be able to articulate it and to generate possible solutions. It's quite difficult sometimes not to jump in and solve the conflicts, to give them jobs and assignments that she knows will make everything go more smoothly. Instead, she waits until she comes up with a question or suggestion that allows the group to solve the problem independently.

For instance, the Computers for Kids group ("we are going to try to get the kids in school who don't have computers at home, computers"), four very social boys, spent at least two work sessions arguing over who would get the really fun job of visiting other classrooms (thereby getting out of the classroom and wandering the halls) to take a survey of who had a computer at home and who did not. Katherine watched them almost come to fisticuffs over it, then asked simply, "How can you share that job?" They had been thinking each job had to be performed by only one person, and they each wanted to be the person who took the survey. Alerted to the possibility of a more flexible system, they decided to work in two teams of two, each team responsible for two floors of the school building.

The first day of taking surveys, the boys were gone for over an hour. (Katherine learned from a colleague that the boys had spent quite a bit of time playing in the downstairs bathroom.) In her next conference with them, Katherine asked them to describe what they'd done, saying they surely must have covered every class in the building. They reported that what took so long was waiting out in the hall in front of classrooms because maybe the class was not in the room, or teachers told them it wasn't a good time to interrupt, could they come back in fifteen minutes? This time, she said, "It seems to me that you have some very important work to get done here, and that this survey is just one step in a long, involved process. Can you come up with a more efficient way to conduct this survey that doesn't take so much travel time and doesn't interrupt the learning going on in other classrooms?" Eventually she had to tell the group to find a way to take the survey without going to each classroom. The boys finally asked Katherine to make copies of a written survey request, which they politely asked the school secretary to put in the teachers' mailboxes.

Most of the time, groups are able, after a conference with Katherine, to settle disputes and devise solutions to different problems. Most groups are happy to delegate roles and jobs to personalities most suited for them. The braver kids ask adults for things or make phone calls, the artistic kids draw posters and banners, and the more reticent ones work behind the scenes writing letters or doing research. What works for the dynamics of one group may not work for another, but at the end of each writing session, when children reflect on the work they did that day, the solutions they share become part of an image of how any group can work together. Ideas, such as writing an agenda before each group meeting or making a contract to sit together and not roam unproductively around the room or allowing each person a full uninterrupted three minutes to tell all of her or his ideas, provide the incentive for other groups to try similar procedures.

In the classroom, there is a large bulletin board where children post newspaper articles they run across about other groups' topics, as well as strategies for each other's action plans. On this same board, Katherine's students also had many opportunities to offer suggestions, resources, and solutions to the questions and problems being experienced by other groups. Although working in small groups sacrifices some of the intense group identity that can accompany whole-class inquiries and social action projects, Katherine was very pleased with the generosity and support her students showed for one another's efforts. In many ways, the atmosphere of sharing and "living through" one another's successes or setbacks felt more true and more earned than if Katherine had been orchestrating a whole-class project.

Zooming in on Groups at Work

In most cases, groups gravitate easily toward the news of the hour. One year a group of Katherine's students became obsessed with what was happening in Iraq. Every morning, huddled around a globe in the center of a round table, six boys studied news articles about Iraq, locating countries and continents involved in this drama. They checked out books about the two world wars to try to understand the history and agendas of war. Group member Dylan's father was in the FBI and stationed in Iraq, so they read news articles with a critical eye, looking for discrepancies with what Dylan's father told him. Their feelings and their focus shifted from a kind of rote, what-the-teacher-wants-us-to-say desire for peace, to a decision that war was the only solution, to anger about being lied to by our own government, and finally back to a heightened desire for peace. After studying the tiny countries of Iraq, Syria, and Iran, Colin pointed out that if we bombed Iraq, people in the neighboring countries, only a pencil-tip distance away on the globe, would be killed as well. These boys took their inquiry seriously, and even though they knew from the start that their actions were not going to affect the eventual outcome of the conflict, they decided they wanted to raise awareness about the horrors of war and the inadequacies of public information. They hung up posters and flyers around the school to get their consciousness-raising message out, including the twist on the idea of a board game shown in Figure 8–4.

Finally, the group decided to circulate a petition against the war in Iraq. They had heard somewhere in the course of their inquiry that if you get a hundred people to sign a petition, then it is official. Realizing the difficulty of finding a hundred children to sign, they wanted to set up a stand on the corner of Twenty-third Street and Sixth Avenue to get signatures. When their parents rejected this plan, they turned to the Internet. The father of a group member set up a web page on which they could put their petition online. They wrote a letter to the President to accompany their petition:

> Dear Mr. President,
>
> We don't want you to bomb Iraq. As you can see from our petecion, we (P.S. 11 kids) don't want you to have a war, etc. with Iraq. Think of it this way, you'll be harming millions of people, and killing them!
>
> You'll come out with better results. For example, we who live in New York, don't want to see a heat-seeking biological weapon cruising past our 4th/5th grade classroom window!
>
> So please consider what we say!

In the midst of the process of research and discovery, Ivan left the Peace in Iraq group to become a member of the Save the Starving Children of India group. He felt anything, even solving the problem of hunger in a country as vast as India, was easier than facing the fact that the government lies to us. His notebook shows some of the story of his intellectual and moral struggle:

Government Lying
2/26

I believe that the government lies to the people because they deny so many things. Like Area 51, not that there is proof that there is something going on there. Just that the whole government denies its existence, until finally Clinton signed something that said Area 51 was real. Why would the government cover it up unless there was something going on? Another thing. I believe in aliens. I believe aliens have landed here. And the government knows about it. People have sent in tapes. One tape was of nine stars, really, really bright ones. Each separated by a mile or more. Thousands of people in Phoenix, Arizona saw these stars. So it is no hoax. First, the government denies it. Then they admit it.

Figure 8–4 *Poster, Designed After a Board Game, by the Peace in Iraq Group*

Then they say that it's just U.S. Army testing. I am sorry but we can't have the technology to make a ship nine miles wide. Picture:

*- 1 mile - * - 1 mile - * - 1 mile - * - 1 mile -* - 1 mile -* - 1 mile-* - 1 mile -* - 1 mile -* - 1 mile

I believe they were aliens and most people in Phoenix do too. And going out of the subject of extra terrestrials. They lie about random things like the reason for a war with Iraq. It"s not because of the weapons inspection. And really, Kenneth Starr . . .

3/2

I think that the whole thing about government lying goes its own way. Some people know a lot, but they really don't. When I go into the government lying about extra terrestrials I don't have too much proof. So what about normal things. Like the fact that Bill Clinton wants a war with Iraq. I think it has a lot to do with all the oil that Iraq has in their country. And Clinton wants to get rid of Saddam Hussein, and it's all mixed together. And then Clinton just needed an excuse. So he was going to have the war, but Iraq agreed to let U.S. weapons inspectors to inspect Iraq's weapons. But Clinton still wants this war. And I don't want this war, because many will die. It will probably be biological war-fare which is all aimed at the citizens.

3/3

I think that the government is lying about Iraq. And I don't know the true reason. But I have some guesses. But that's what I'm complaining about the government lying. I choose the government lying (about Iraq) because I think it connects with so many other things that someone has to look into.

3/4

Yes I do want to stay with Iraq, because I think Clinton is making a big mistake, and if there will be a war, many people will die because of biological weapons and nuclear weapons, and I think you could get a good discussion going about rights and wrongs.

3/5

I am changing my topic to *Save starving children in the world* because it's not their fault and the government doesn't do anything about it, but I think someone should look into it.

When Leah and Sarah joined forces to write about women's rights, they remembered and appropriated strategies from the biographies read in class. They referred to the novel, *Elizabeth Blackwell, The First Woman Doctor* (Sabin 1990), they had read together, and how Blackwell had succeeded partly with the help of several men around her. They referred to the biography of Martin Luther King, Jr., remembering that there was mention of white people involved in the civil rights movement. Leah decided, "It's a good idea to include people of the opposite gender or color in your fight against oppression. That shows that not every man feels the same way about women or not every white person hates blacks." Within two days, they had recruited four boys to join their collective, The Women's Rights Association (WRA).

The WRA spent many days painting "consciousness raising" posters about things they had read about in their research: unequal pay for equal work, the slaughter of girl babies in China, a man pouring acid on his girlfriend's face because she would not go to bed with him. At some point, the group became fired up about one girl's claim that the Museum of Natural History did not have the same number of exhibits about females as it did about males. She remembered see-ing "hundreds of man statues," but not any of women "except that one of a naked cave woman." They designed new exhibits for the museum on the history of women that would include wax fig-ures of many famous females they had been reading biographies about. Then the group decided to visit the museum, bringing along their notebooks and cameras to document what they found. Discovering that in order to do this as a group they would need to go on a Saturday, Sarah com-posed a permission slip for parents to sign (see Figure 8–5).

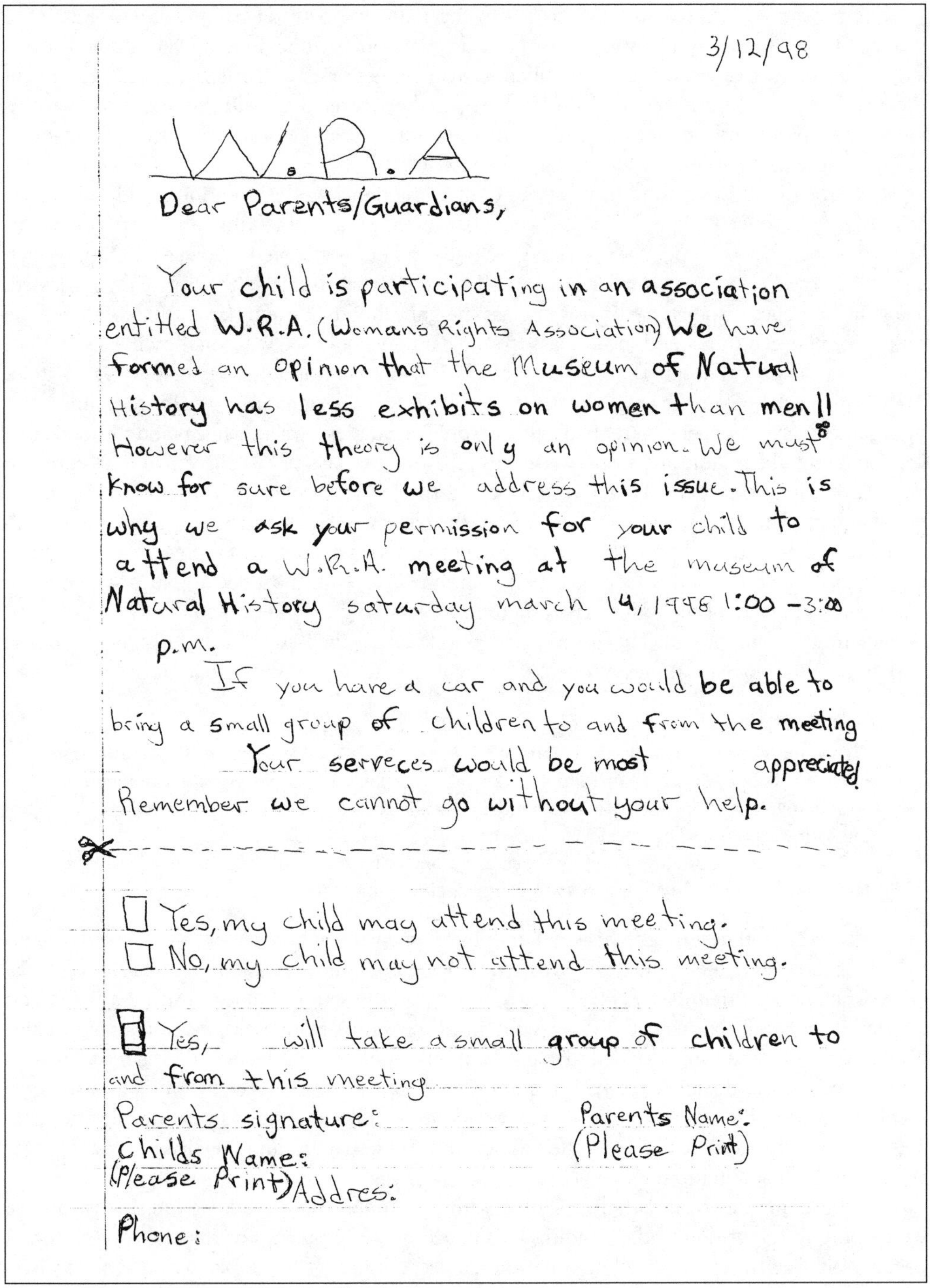

3/12/98

W.R.A

Dear Parents/Guardians,

Your child is participating in an association entitled **W.R.A.** (Womans Rights Association) We have formed an opinion that the Museum of Natural History has less exhibits on women than men !! However this theory is only an opinion. We must know for sure before we address this issue. This is why we ask your permission for your child to attend a W.R.A. meeting at the museum of Natural History saturday march 14, 1998 1:00 - 3:00 p.m.

If you have a car and you would be able to bring a small group of children to and from the meeting Your serveces would be most appreciated!
Remember we cannot go without your help.

✂ - - - - - - - - - - - - - - - - - - - -

☐ Yes, my child may attend this meeting.
☐ No, my child may not attend this meeting.

☑ Yes, will take a small group of children to and from this meeting

Parents signature: _____   Parents Name: _____
Childs Name: _____   (Please Print)
(Please Print)Addres: _____

Phone: _____

Figure 8–5   *Women's Rights Association Permission Slip*

A parent volunteered to take the group the following Saturday. On Monday, Katherine watched the members of the group enter her classroom one by one, looking very downhearted. When they had actually counted the number of "male statues" and "female statues," they found out there were an equal number. They also realized, as they traveled around the museum, that this particular museum had more to do with animals, continents, and cultures. A "history of women" did not particularly fit into its schema, it seemed to them.

Another group wanted to bring issues of class difference to the attention of children in the school. Karina noticed on her bus rides home that there was a distinct difference between neighborhoods she labeled "upper class" (see Figure 8–6) and her home on the Lower East Side, which she called "lower class." In particular, she was offended by what she feels she has actually witnessed, a lag time in police response to the "lower class" neighborhood. She and her group researched the difference between upper and lower class from what they could see with their own eyes.

They amassed a number of proofs of the class distinctions and discrepancies in Manhattan. They copied a map from the yellow pages of the phone book designating areas for recycling pickups. Quite clearly, areas of poverty had a pickup only one day per week, while neighborhoods that were known to be middle and upper class had pickups two days per week. When test scores for New York City public schools were published in the local newspapers, the group clipped the graphs, charts, and lists of scores, then compared the results, again using a map of Manhattan color-coded to indicate areas of poverty. The poor neighborhoods made lower scores on standardized tests than the middle- and upper-class neighborhoods. As with most social issues the children researched, the issue of economic class differences began to grow like some kind of monster and became hugely complicated. The group decided to focus on the issue of delayed police response in poor neighborhoods and they wrote to the mayor "just to let him know that this is happening":

> Dear Mayor Giuliani,
> This letter is concerned with the actions of the New York Police Department. We, as citizens of New York, are concerned that if police don't start responding people will stop calling them and try to take matters into their own hands. Which is good in some ways, but if you're fighting with weapons it's better to let a police man or woman deal with it.
>   You do not need to respond. Just consider putting or trying to put the same amount of the NYPD in "lower class" neiborhoods as in "higher class neiborhoods."

Katherine and her student teacher, Cindi Byun, spent a few hours after school one day reading all the drafts of letters children had written to persons in authority about their particular social issue. They noticed that the kids had clearly caught on to the importance of using a polite and respectful tone, but that repeatedly, the content of the letters made wild, passionate, and naïve claims. Katherine and Cindi decided to focus the minilessons and conferences for the next few days on how to find and document statistics, quotes, and citations as evidence to strengthen an argument. The "class differences" group was able to find several articles documenting specific cases and response times that had been written about in the newspapers, and they later sent a stronger version of the first letter to the mayor.

In other minilessons, Katherine shared with her students information from the writing we were doing in opposition to the Reading Excellence Act. She put up overheads, copied from a packet produced by NCTE, detailing ways to organize, outlines of action plans, and sample letters to legislators. The children took notes on these strategies, and then spent days working on action plans and outlines in their writing notebooks. During the social action study, most of the paperwork Katherine's students did was generated from within the real, ongoing decisions and revisions

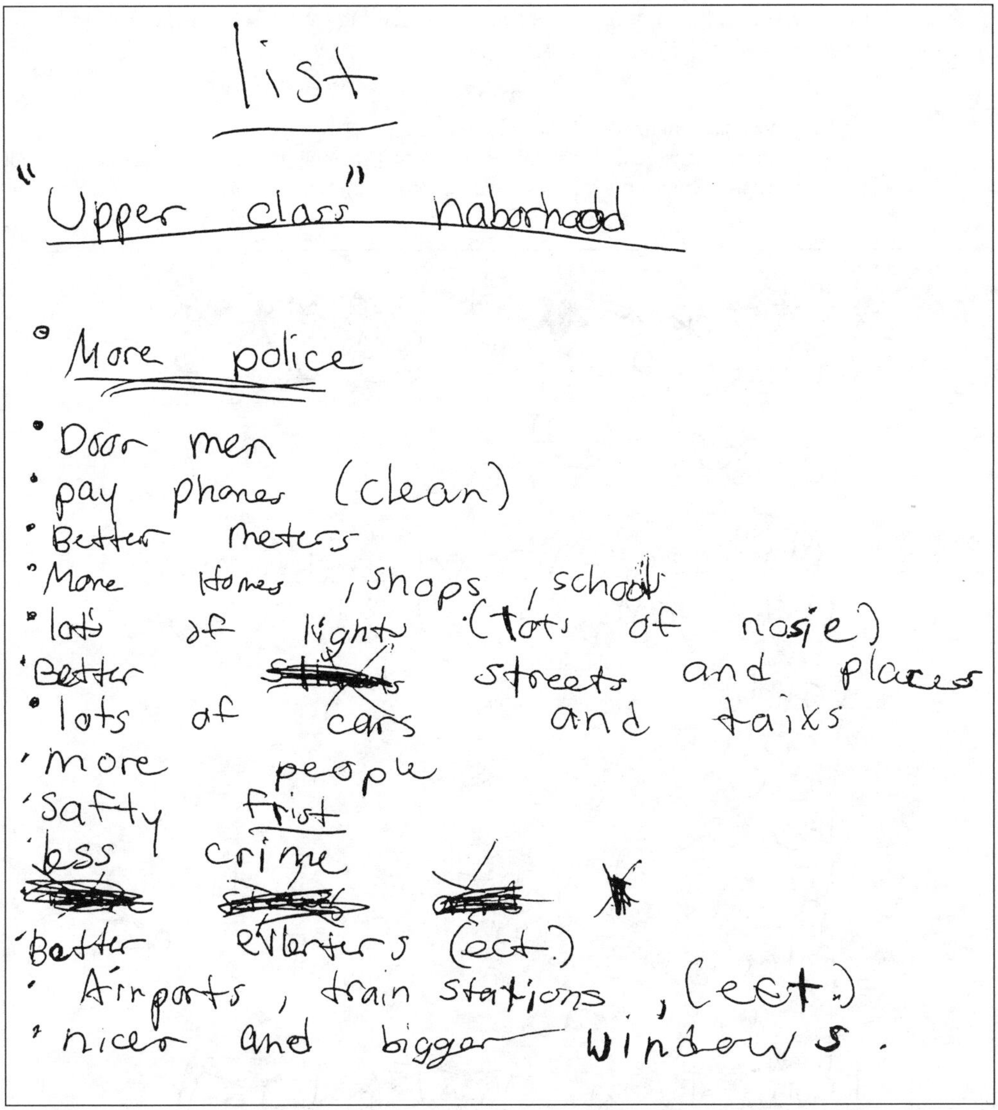

list

"Upper class" naborhood

- More police
- Door men
- pay phones (clean)
- Better meters
- More Homes, shops, school
- lots of lights (lots of nosie)
- Better ~~streets~~ streets and places
- lots of cars and taiks
- more people
- Safty frist
- less crime
  ~~xxx~~ ~~xxx~~ ~~xxx~~ ✗
- Better evfenters (ect.)
- Airports, train stations, (ect.)
- nicer and bigger windows.

Figure 8–6   *Karina's Notebook Observations of Rich Neighborhoods*

of each group's work. There were certain documents, and certain thinking devices, however, that Katherine felt would benefit all the children, so she had all the children create things like double-column entries, an action plan, a letter to a person in power, and nightly reflections on group progress. The homework assignments always related to each child's specific topic, and they were not graded but were meant to be useful to the group's progress and to be added into their files as working documents.

Here are excerpts and a copy of one of the pages (see Figure 8–7) from Candace's nightly notebook entries:

3/12

The thing I am most pashinnit about. What and why.

I want to do injustices in school systems because I feel strongly that it is very unfair that poor schools in poor neighborhoods don't get as much as people in rich schools. I mean, it's unfair how

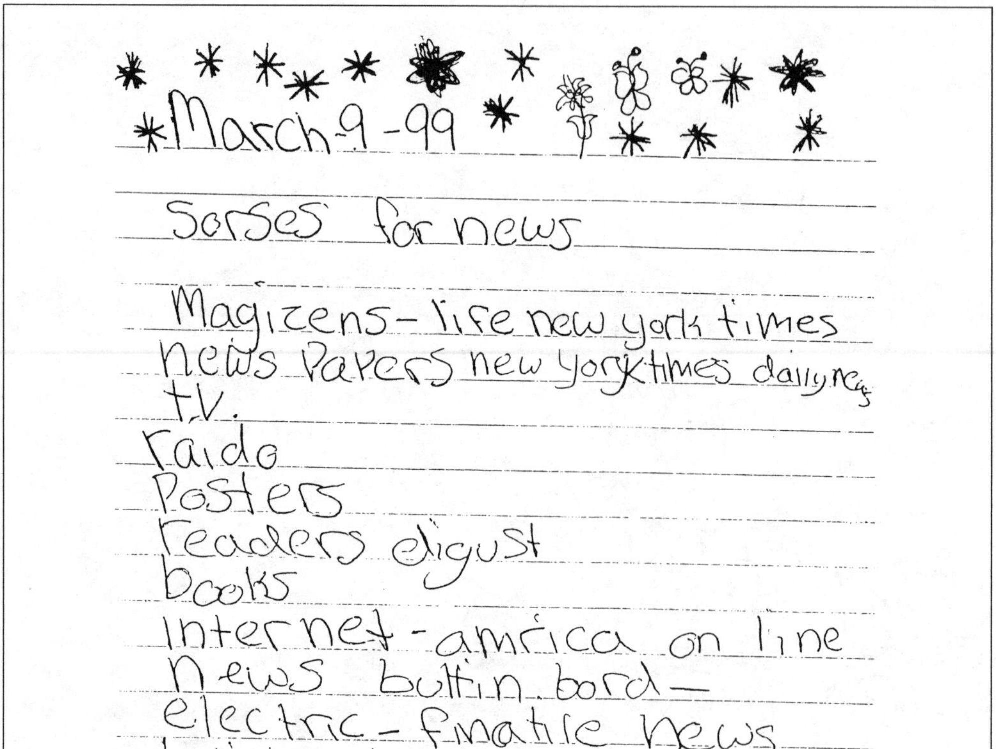

Figure 8–7 *Candace's Notebook Entry Brainstorming Sources of Information*

some people in rich schools say anybody is allowed to use it and then when they find out the person was from a poor school they say get away, we don't like you.

3/13

Social action plan for poor schools

Find out different schools that are poor and wealthy

Write to the poor schools, the government board of ed, and to wealthy schools

Make posters and letters

Phone calls for donating and to give them more supplies

How we are going to get more money: bake sales, junk sales, flower sales, candy sales, ect

Things to bye—

Pencils and pens

Paper

Books

Notebooks

Art supplies

Dictnireys

Chart

Baskets/storage

Clipboards

Staplers

Tape

3/16

I think it's very unfair how some schools get more things than other schools and nobody seems to notice because they think it's like picking up a piece of paper at someone else's house—to do it for them is waste of time—but Its not. Kids need all the help they can get and you never know, maybe the kids you help will be a president someday.

3/17

My social issue is poor and rich schools. I am interested in schools because I strongly believe that all schools should be equal because all kids should get the same quality in learning. Kids are our prise pustions. I also picked this because I feel really good when I help somebody or do something nice for someone. I feel very nice in the group I'm in and I have great plans to help the poor schools.

3/28

Dear Mayor of the United States

Dear ruty cruw [Rudy Crew]

Hi. My name is Candace and I am a kid from P.S. 11 and I really liked what you did when Rudy Juliana tried to take money from public schools and put it into private schools. (I think you did the right thing.) And that is why I am writing this letter to you because if you did not do that my school and many other schools that are public would have lost money, which I believe is not good. So I just wanted to say thank you, Mr. [Rudy Crew]. Keep up the good work. Also I would like to know if you ever wonder why some public schools are poor and some are rich or middle class. Well—if you do, I do too. I and a few girls in my class are trying to get schools to be more equal. Thank you for your time, concern, and thoughtfulness to read this letter.

Sincerely, Candace

Here is Ivan's action plan for "Save the Starving Children of India":

3/5

1. Find where the UNICEF headquarters are? Ms. Bomer knows.
2. Try to call up the United Nations.
3. Go around collecting charity money.

3/5

My group (which is helping starving kids around the world) is thinking of calling up the UN and saying that we were planning on starting a charity and find out where we would send it. I think that in America, alot of the poor people I think it is just their fault that they are starving or homeless because they don't try to get a job, they do try. But not hard enough. But in India and Africa and such areas, it is the government's fault, because the government is so poor in those countries that the germs are so big in the water that you can see them. The food is rotted so that if you eat or drink all that stuff you will get diseases. Most of them are fatal diseases too. And if they wanted to, it would be very hard to immigrate to America, because you don't have enough money. And they don't have apartments and if they do, they are very dirty and small because the government doesn't even have enough money to make apartments.

3/11

I think that our group shouldn't collect money for the U.N. because we probably will not get enough money to help more than 10 blocks. But I think we should convince other people to donate to UNICEF. We should use our writing, and maybe send it to the UN. Or maybe even print it in a newspaper. Because it seems like Ms. Bomer is trying to get our ideas past this classroom into the real world. We would write how they are important, even if they aren't part of our country. Because it's not their fault that they live in that country. And I think that writing is the best way to help them. Thomas Paine used his writing.

3/12

I think we should write our true feelings about children starving all over the world, and why it matters for us. And I think we need to decide between two different approaches. Very aggressive, like, we will do this, we should do this, or, the kids in India, and South Africa need your help, they are very poor. That is a more of make you cry approach. I think that our group should take a mix of Aggressive and Make you cry approach, because aggressive will get their attention, and make you cry will get you going. So when they see you telling them that people in India are dying and how it will effect the economy, and then you just go into facts about people dying, and then you switch into an emotional approach—so please, help the children, that's the best plan.

Here is Ruth's "Blankets With Love" action plan:

3/4

I'm going to do blankets with love. I have a lot of ideas to work with. Flyers, letters, having a box to collect the blankets of the school. I could find info to put in letters, signs, who could encourage other people. I need permission for some things, I know. All we want to accomplish is to encourage other people to help this. I want to be a part of those people who feel so good after helping someone without a home.

3/13

Our action plan is to write Ms. Steele asking her if we can have a box in the school to collect small essential household items. But we've done that.

   Optional:

   Maybe Nina could come to school and talk to the class about what this organization is about, in more depths than I can. If people in the class can get other people involved, they can encourage family members, or neighbors to volunteer or contribute too.

If Ms. Steele says yes, then maybe as well as the flyer going home, we can put an ad in the school newspaper asking others who read it outside of the school to help.

3/19

I don't know what to write with half my slate clear. My mind is still thinking of blankets with love for it still isn't finished. I still have time to make flyers, posters, ads in papers, ads in minds. Life is different, school especially, with this going on. I walk down the street seeing homeless people. I have learned to help, but are my hands made for it? I have no blankets, no couches, no rattles for the crying children, crying for what Nina gives, what she can't always carry either. All I have is my smile.

As groups began to require specific tools to enact their action plans, Katherine made copies of different kinds of documents from an excellent source called *The Kids' Guide to Social Action* by Barbara A. Lewis (1998). This book contains formats for every kind of political tool one can imagine: petition, survey, news release, letter, even scripts for how to interview and lobby. The book also includes strategies for taking action, and addresses for numerous established organizations that children might want to join, such as Earthwatch, Amnesty International, People for the Ethical Treatment of Animals (PETA), and Kids Voting USA. Cathy Fleischer's book, *Teachers Organizing for Change: Making Literacy Learning Everybody's Business* (2000), offers other real-world strategies for organizing and making change. When we read through the group folders from Katherine's class, we were moved and amused at the same time. The all-time favorite action plan was the petition. Class members wrote petitions about any topic they felt like sounding off about, including one addressed to Jerry Springer: "We, the undersighned are against Jerry Springer because of the violence he promotes, therefor we want him off the air."

Each group had at least three petitions against injustices related to their particular issue. There were more petitions with thirty and forty signatures (all the kids in the class plus anyone who happened to walk in that day) than any other type of document. That makes sense in terms of the instant gratification of having someone commit their signature in consensus with one's opinion. We found dozens of drafts of letters, many to persons who had nothing to do with the issue and could not possibly be of service. Many of the letters were unfinished, most were never sent. But the folders represented good work. They were full of related newspaper articles. There were letters children had received in response to their questions and opinions, and the kids asked Katherine to make copies they could send to their relatives. There were many revisions of poster drawings and letters; so much thought and care went into every document trying to make it sound and look just right.

We found a great deal of passion and energy in the children's concerns and their ideas for how to make things better. Sometimes they dreamed beyond the possible, as when the Students Against Student Violence demanded of then schools chancellor Rudy Crew that one hundred violent students currently housed together at a special school be granted one-on-one teaching. Their solutions to the world's problems were so kidlike, so naïve. Several groups wanted to sponsor bake sales to earn money for everything from pencils and paper for needy schools to saving starving children in India. They learned in the course of this work that the money they earn from such endeavors actually *can* help. They can send it along to UNICEF, or they can adopt an animal at a special zoo for injured wild animals, or they can buy enough supplies to send one box to one classroom at one school. Gestures like these mean everything. Many adults give up on charitable donations or on volunteerism because they think the problems are too huge. But the children in Katherine's classes learned that no gesture is too small if it is made in the direction of justice.

Writing to Power: Considering Audience and Purpose

As many groups reached the point where they needed to write to persons in power, Katherine put the collectives' action plans on hold for a week and provided some assisted performance and practice in letter writing. She began with a discussion about how writing can take different forms depending on whether it is meant to persuade, sell, inform, or redress grievances. The children thought about advertisements they saw every day in the subway trains, on bus kiosks, and on the walls of construction sites. Which were the messages that caught their eyes? "The ones that use big words, poetic words, so people will listen," Amalia said.

In one minilesson, Katherine asked the children to try out different voices. "What if you wanted to persuade your sibling or a younger child to give you something you wanted? How would you address a plea to someone younger than you?"

"I would whine and bribe."

"And how would you ask your parent or guardian? Would you speak in a different tone of voice than to the younger person?"

"I would act sick or flatter them, tell them how pretty they look and what a great mother they are."

"Now, how about the principal of the school or the President? Someone really high up and powerful?"

"Polite. Kind of shy. Not talk too long or too much because they are busy people."

Katherine had the children practice these three voices with a partner as they sat on the meeting rug. Then she sent them off to practice writing to someone in their notebook using each of these voices.

Heather's Three Practice Letters

Dear Molly (4 years old), (In a baby tone)

Molly, sweethart, I want to know if I could borow this thing you have. Its your little piano thingy. Maybe I could see it. I would teach you the old McDonald song on it!

Love your cousin, Heather

[Notice how Heather bargains "you show me yours, I'll show you mine" and promises to give something, a favorite song lesson, back.]

Dear Dad,

See their's this little thing I really want. I know your going to say no but you see I really want this thing and I'm on my knees begging. *PLEASE* can I. All I need is 1,500 dollars (in a small voice) plus it could help me on reports *and* keep me busy.

I know you are wondering what it could be ➜ a *comupeter*.

Love, (your datugher) Heather

[Notice Heather's awareness of what tone works with her father; she even gives stage directions in parentheses! Also, notice her savvy appeal to her parent's desire for her to do well in school and keep out of trouble.]

(My draft for letter to goverment):

Dear mayor:

I am doing a socil action studie on talk/standing up for animal rights and I think their should be a law against killing animals for fur espialy tigers and loins and racoons. I would love for you to do some sort of maybe a spech or a action or something like a fund.

Thank you for taking the time to read my letter and for thinking about it.

Sincerely,

Heather Gerhardt

P.S. 11 Distirct 2

4/5-406

P.S. You don't have to do this. Again thank you for your time.

[Notice the polite tone, the asking, then taking back, assuring the authority that this is in no way an order, but rather a simple appeal from a concerned child. She both understands and flatters by thanking him (twice) for giving attention to her letter, and she knows to sign off in a formal manner.]

In another minilesson, Katherine asked the children to think about the purposes behind different styles of writing. She asked members of some of the collectives to talk about their uses of writing and why they had chosen one form over another. Ruth said her group was wondering whether it would be better to send a flyer or a letter home to ask families to get involved in Blankets With Love. The group had made flyers with cute logos ("to grab kids' attention") to hang around the school and send home to bring in donations. But the group had another purpose too:

> We really don't *just* want people's blankets and coats and stuff. I mean, we want that too, later, but right now we want more people to get involved in this organization. Because there aren't even enough people to collect all the donations and nowhere to put them. So we need people's cars and their houses. We need to explain stuff, and we thought a letter would give us more time and space to explain things.

For several days, the children practiced writing letters. Katherine used sample letters provided by the task force from NCTE and from *The Kids' Guide to Social Action* as models. In a minilesson, the kids deconstructed a letter, paragraph by paragraph, and discussed why they thought it was set up the way it was. They noticed that the sample letters began in a direct manner, introducing the author of the letter, what group or organization he or she represented, and the purpose for writing the letter. Many of the kids' early drafts simply launched into a tirade about their issue, without ever mentioning who was writing the letter and why. The children noticed that the sample letters did not just complain about the problem but offered proof of the premise and some ideas for solutions as well. They saw that near the end there was often a plea for help or for some action to be taken. Figure 8–8 is an example.

The early drafts also contained many rude accusations (including calling the New York City Police Commissioner a "racist pig"), and so more lessons followed about what kinds of language and tone are appropriate for a letter to an official. Katherine wrote all the particularities of form and language the children brought up during discussions on a big chart, and that became the format most letters followed.

As an assignment, every individual in the class wrote at least one letter to a person or persons in power about their group's issue. This involved a lot of difficult problem solving: *who* is the best person to write? *what* should I say or ask? *how* should I say it? Each child had to decide what *type* of letter to write; depending on the needs of each group, the letter could register a complaint, solicit donations, or ask for help or information. The children exchanged letters with someone not in their group to see whether the letter made sense to an "objective" audience. They also watched for language that might offend or shut down communication. They wrote questions and comments on the letter and gave it back to the writer. Each child then had to revise according to the suggestions he or she received. In most cases, the groups then pooled the best chunks or most powerful turns of phrase from the individual letters to draft a joint letter signed by all members

To the U.N.

U.N Representatives:

Dear ~~The U.N.~~

I have heard that the children in India are becoming sick because of the parasites in the water ~~that~~ they drink. It makes many people go to hospitals and go see doctors for a check-up ~~on~~ their health, also to get ~~the prescription to get~~ medicine.

I think that we could start an organization to help support the children and ~~adults~~ elders in India. I think that with your help, we can save the people in India.

If we appreciate all that the world has given us, the people in India would appreciate our support and help. We need the world, and the world needs us. They need us to ~~guide~~ help them, and we need them to be ~~part of this world.~~ We are all in one world, and we are all there to help one another.

We could donate more healthy and money to India, just like ~~they do with~~ all the money we give to Israel. We could stand our ground and help others. If we do, they will help us later in the future. We could help our friends around the world, no matter how far they are, we would make the world strong, and a better place to live, because we want to make a difference.

[Because in India it isn't
the people's ~~fault~~ the goverment
is very corrupt and poor. And
it bearly can control such a big
population. But the population
continues to grow, and the
problem gets bigger. They need
help.

In the American goverment, it's usaully the people's fault
that they are poor. Because the government helps, But in
INdia they don't have that help. So Please spread our
leters.

Figure 8–8 *Draft and Revision of a Letter by Save the Starving Children of India*

of the group. In other cases, groups decided the stronger strategy would be to "flood" a legislator's office with as many letters on the topic as they could write. After Katherine's class watched the tape of Rosie O'Donnell's show the day after the murders in Littleton, Colorado, everyone in the class wrote letters to legislators requesting they pass gun control laws.

Any teacher of writing knows how difficult the concepts of "voice" and "audience" are for young or inexperienced writers. Writing, like thinking, is such an internal process: what comes out on the page is full of codes, references, even language that has meaning only for the writer. One of the major jobs of revision is making language work for the intended audience. It is difficult for students to know first of all who their readers will be and then how to rearrange the words to speak precisely to those readers. When we help our students publish a piece of writing out of their writers notebook that tries to carry meaning to someone other than themselves, we tell them they are responsible for making the writing clear and appropriate for the intended audience. The lessons Katherine taught about writing in different voices to persons at different levels of familiarity and authority demonstrated the concepts of voice and audience clearly to her students.

Of course, it takes practice and many drafts before the class can agree that the tone and language are appropriate for the audience. Salim, who always addressed everyone, children and adults, with extreme politeness, had difficulty varying the tone of voice in his practice letters. He wrote to his best friend in the class: "Dear Tommy, I regret to inform you that there is a big problem in our United States, and I ask you for your aid in what I am doing. I am trying to address President Bill Clinton to discuss with him this problem. Sincerely, Salim." In her conference with him, Katherine asked him to pretend that she was his best friend, Tommy, and to talk to her face to face about his question. After some practice with a more casual, conversational tone, Salim revised his letter to read: "Dear Tommy, Hi! I would really like to do something about this big problem we are having in the U.S., and I would like you to help."

Most children, though, had trouble creating the kind of letter that would invite its reader to take the time to listen and perhaps respond. A letter of complaint needs to sound firm yet not close down communication with insults or unsubstantiated claims. This is an authentic problem even for professional writers. As we compose our writing, we are in constant dialogue with our thoughts and the questions and concerns we anticipate from our readers. The children worked hard at negotiating their own interests and the reader's feelings and understandings. The group that called itself Violence by Police had the hardest time with this. The group was diverse: three African Americans, two Latinos, one Japanese, and one Anglo. The children of color took the issue of possible racist feelings among police officers in New York City personally. After the much-publicized murder of Amadou Diallo by four police officers, many similar stories of police profiling appeared in the media, and each story fed their anger even more. Their letters hurled insults (the "racist pig" remark); mentioned statistics from the newspaper accusing the police forces in New York and New Jersey of profiling; insisted that the four officers involved in the Diallo case were "crazy" ("But before I jump to conclusions," that student wrote, "I would like to ask if Diallo was killed on purpose or by accident? Because I mean it only takes one shot to kill someone, not 41 shots! I want the truth and I am really serious. Please think carefully!"); demanded that any policeman who shoots "innocent" people have his right to carry guns suspended ("and I'm saying police*man* because it looks like there are usually men police not women"); and asked that someone explain how officers were trained to use weapons in the first place.

Every time that group brought its letter drafts to the whole-class discussions, the class vetoed them as being too offensive or too unsubstantiated. "Where are your facts, your evidence?" was a common question. "Who would want to open the envelope and read *that*?" Finally, one wise classmate suggested they just write a letter saying they were not taking sides but they wanted to know the truth about how officers are trained to respond to threatening situations. Ivan said, "The police like to talk to kids. Why don't you ask them to come visit our class? Whenever I talk to the police on my street, they're always real friendly." So that was the letter that finally went out to Police Commissioner Howard Safir:

> Dear Mr. Safir:
>
> We are fourth graders at P.S. 11. We have been reading and watching T.V. about the Diallo case for our social action project. We know there are different sides of the story
>
> We are not interested in taking sides, but we are interested in understanding how police are trained to use their weapons. We would be very interested in learning from an actual police officer.
>
> PS Would it be possible for an actual Police Officer to come and see us? And please write back.

And this is the letter that the group finally sent to Mayor Giuliani:

> 4/29/99
>
> Mayor Rudolph Giuliani
> City Hall
> New York, NY 10007
>
> Dear Mr. Mayor:
>
> We are fourth grade students writing to you because we have heard different points of view on police brutality. We are writing to you because we know you have the power to change the way police are using their utilities against people who have rights.
>
> The students at P.S. 11 had the great opportunity to meet Martin Luther King III at our school; we know he believes in non-violence, just like his father did, and just like we do. We have an idea that we could ask Martin Luther King III to talk non-violently to the police. We are sure you meant the police to do no harm, but it has happened.
>
> Thank you for your time and support and for reading our letter.

One of the most powerful lessons in tone, tact, and audience occurred the year Min, a fifth grader, had the words to an editorial she had submitted to the school newspaper (a medium written by and for the parents and children of P.S. 11) edited by several parents and faculty members. Min gave Katherine permission to put the editorial on a transparency and to open a class discussion about why it had been heavily "edited" and ultimately rejected by the adults who had final authority over the production of the newspaper. (See Figure 8–9.)

The class discussions about this editorial were a real exercise in perspective. The issues were complicated, and the class had to ask some of the adults involved to explain their reasoning. They tried to understand what the editors had objected to: the issue itself or the wording. They wondered if the problem was that the words of the editorial might offend its intended audience. Min stood by her wording, noting that editorials she read in the *New York Times* would probably offend whoever disagreed with them. "I thought that's kind of the point," she said. The students wondered if the wording was not right because it painted an unflattering portrait of the persons who pay to produce this paper. The teacher who had edited Min's original version pointed out that some of Min's complaints were shortsighted in their portrayal of the person who was responsible for 160 children at recess. This teacher felt that her revisions offered positive solutions rather than issuing idle complaints and insults. The story became more complicated for Katherine when Min's parents, very gracious, unassuming people, expressed their unhappiness with how their daughter's original words had been rejected. "We left Korea because of oppression and political

What Happened in the Yard

This is what happened in the yard. Some kids, while playing the game known as *tag*, were hurt slightly. The teacher on lunch duty, ████████, took tag away. I think that taking tag away was a good idea, but it should be only for a short time, not permanently.

████████ said that he would wait about a week, then talk to us about tag. ~~but he didn't mention it again.~~

I think that if ████████ gives tag back to the children, ~~he should~~ *we could* have a special spot for the kids to play tag in, such as the little area near the three silver poles. It was wrong of the kids playing near the scaffolding and getting hurt, but tag itself is a simple game, not like street soccer, where you fight to get the ball. I think *Could* ████████ ~~should~~ introduce *some* new games ~~for us~~ *we* to play, maybe set up a group of kids who race together, play games, and things like that. The school should install new equipment, and since so many balls have gone *perhaps* and disappeared over walls, the school should send somebody to get them, because now there are only ~~two~~ *a few* balls. ~~a basketball and a blue rubber ball.~~ Many children want to use the balls, but everyone wants to do something different, so that causes many problems, and kids fight over them sometimes.

~~And if~~ It's so important to the teachers that the kids don't get hurt. *what could we* ~~and so on, why don't they~~ do ~~something~~ about it? ~~I don't think they have ever done anything about what is happening in the schoolyard. They hard-~~ *kids Teachers should talk about playground problems with so we can come up with solutions.* ~~ly ever talk about it with the kids, and then suddenly, very abruptly, they take away a game.~~ So many times children get hurt playing tag, and they also get hit by balls, but the school hasn't ever done anything about it. As long as I can remember, as long as I was allowed to play in the "big yard", everybody has had the same problem. Since the teachers are in charge, they should change something, but the teachers don't talk the kids *person to person,* they just give punishment, take away privileges, and in that manner, we keep returning to the same spot. (In my classroom, Ms. Bomer's class, we have occasional discussions about our problems. Most of our problems had to do with the yard, that fights had aroused, people had been hurt.) ~~And if the~~ ~~adults won't~~ *Let's all* ~~try hard enough to~~ make the yard a friendly environment where children can learn, play and have fun, and *it will be* ~~a~~ *one* safe place where kids can play without getting hurt, *or* we shouldn't go out into the yard at all.

Figure 8–9 *Min's Editorial, with Edits by the Adults in Charge of the School Newspaper*

silencing," Min's father explained. Min's mother said she had taught her daughter that writing was an important tool to express anger and dissatisfaction. She wanted Min to have avenues, through her writing, her artwork, and her music, for positive and nonviolent means for making change.

The story of Min's editorial was an open textbook and source of dialogue for several weeks. Katherine did not wish to step in and solve the problem on her own; she wanted to include her students in a very real problem of censorship, information, and freedom of speech. This discussion was similar to many others Katherine's class had when there were no ready answers or when the answers left some unsatisfied: they were always occasions for serious thinking and meaning making. Ruth noticed that Min's choice of the word *should* is pointing a finger at someone, while using *could* opens the possibility of compromise. Aaron had a rebuttal: "If we say 'You could, perhaps, if you really want to,' who's going to listen to that?" He pointed out that in the text from the flyers that were distributed in the African American community of Montgomery, Alabama, in 1955, calling for a bus boycott, the language was direct, imperative. "Don't ride. Take a cab. Walk." "There's no 'maybe you could think about the possibility of not getting on the bus today.'"

Overall, the children's experiences with writing letters requesting help and information were powerful and extremely exciting and satisfying. Most of the groups who were able to strategize and pinpoint the proper avenues and authorities received responses to their queries. Whenever a piece of mail from "outside" arrived in their classroom, all work stopped so that the recipients could read the letter out loud to the class. The Students Against Student Violence group received two letters from Rudy Crew. The children were disappointed with his first response, because he wrote that they were right to want to feel safe in their own school and that he would send his deputy to come speak to them about how to ensure safety in their school. The kids immediately wrote back that they felt very safe in their school, but that, again, what they had trouble with was his decision to place one hundred violent students all together in a school in Queens. The revised version was worded more strongly, and the kids remembered to use metaphors, like Martin Luther King, Jr.:

> Dear Mr. Crew,
>
> We would like to hear your side of the story about violent kids and we really don't think you should send 100 of them to be in a school together. We think that it would cause even *more* violence. It's like sending a worm to deliver a message to a bird. Please tell us your side on this issue. We only read what they say in the papers.

In this letter, they also wrote a much more detailed outline of why they thought he should try to provide one-on-one teaching for children who have violent tendencies—that what they needed was personal attention, not to be lumped together with a bunch of other violent kids.

> We think it would be much better if you did 1 on 1 teaching, for a few reasons:
>
> 1. They might build a trusting relationship.
> 2. They might forget about being "cool" or killing somebody to be noticed because there will be no one else in the room.
> 3. Also maybe it would make them learn more.

Crew wrote back again, again offering to send his deputy to come talk to them, this time about why the group's proposal was too difficult, financially, to arrange.

The Violence by Police group also felt that Mayor Giuliani had not really read their letters, that he just repeated what he said on the news, that "recently graduated police cadets had received special training on how to respectfully interact with people of different backgrounds." But they believed that at least he had actually responded to them because his signature was on the letter. (They hadn't yet heard of signature stamps!)

Most of the responses from individuals and from corporations, however, were generous and serious in tone. PETA sent packets of information and a box of books about animal care and tips for activism. UNICEF also sent many packets of information about worldwide hunger and child labor in third-world countries. Scholastic responded to the Unequal Public Schools group with a letter praising their efforts to share supplies with more needy children and with five boxes of books for them to pass along to their adopted school. No doubt the children could have kept up a running correspondence with various outside entities if they had had more time. Katherine received several letters of response from computer companies, City Council members, senators, and others after the school year ended.

Many of the children's letters did not receive any response. While that was usually disappointing to them (as it is to anyone whose letter goes unanswered), the class used those opportunities to ask if they had written to the right person, at the right time, with the correct return address information, and with properly worded appeals. In other words, the class took these nonresponses as learning opportunities and moved on. There were enough responses overall to help the class feel that their letters were reaching real audiences and that their words and ideas were being taken seriously.

Reflecting on Learning and Transformation

In a study like this, in which children are venturing beyond the boundaries of the classroom and state-mandated curriculum and getting "caught up" in real endeavors, what are they learning? What do they learn if all their excitement and effort come to naught? How do they feel when they are faced, once again, with their smallness, their naïveté about how the world works, and their ultimate lack of power? Like most teachers, Katherine initially wanted to protect her students from the disappointments that are inevitable in this type of inquiry. The stakes felt somehow much larger than those usually associated with "schoolwork." Whenever Katherine wants to know how things feel for kids, she asks them. She kept up a running dialogue with her students throughout the study, checking in, processing, discussing pros and cons of the work they were doing. Over and over, her students said this was the most fun, the most interesting and important work they had ever done in school. The successes were the greatest they had ever had, and the disappointments struck them as challenges that mattered, unlike the confusing mazes of much of the schoolwork they are required to perform.

The stories of social action ended with the imposed end of the school year on June 28. By that point several of Katherine's students felt great about what they had accomplished. The Unequal Public Schools group had collected several boxes of supplies and books to deliver to a nearby school. The Blankets With Love group received so many donations, the front lobby of the school became a fire hazard from all the boxes of coats, blankets, children's clothing. There were even donations of furniture and appliances that Ruth's stepmother had to pick up in a special truck. Ruth hoped to interview some people who received donations of suits and household items. She thought that hearing from them how the donations helped would make more kids want to get involved. When she moved on to a middle school in New York City, she planned to continue her work with the organization, and she wrote letters to her new school administration for permission to pursue her project.

For Katherine, the celebrations were more subtle. The Computers for Kids group she had had such difficulty taming had taken very meaningful turns in their purpose and intention. Originally, the boys were "pissed off" that their access to certain "adult-oriented" areas was denied when they signed on to the Internet at home. They flailed about, wanting to write to then President Clinton to complain, wanting to "nuke" the computer companies who had, in their minds, locked up the keys to the universe. It took many conferences, many invitations to ask experts (the computer teacher, for example) for information, to help those boys understand that their parents had made the decision and bought special software that closed certain areas to them. In conversations with the rest of the class, the boys learned that not everyone had the good fortune to have this problem, because not everyone had a computer at home. The Unequal Public Schools group told the class that in some neighborhoods, almost all children had computers in their homes, and at those local schools, each classroom was equipped with enough computers for every student in the class. In other neighborhoods, neither the schools nor the homes had computers. In light of this information, the Computers for Kids group's focus changed from censorship to equal access. The boys began to survey the population of their own school and discovered that more than 90 percent of their fellow students did not own computers. That was when they began to brainstorm how they could get computers donated to those homes that did not have them and to maneuver the words of their letters to demonstrate what the benefit of such donations would be to big computer companies.

> Dear Gateway,
> We are 4th grade students studying kids that don't have computers.
> Can you help us? Please donate the computers that you don't need to school PS 11 on 21st between 8th and 9th. We are going to have a lotto in our school for kids that don't have computers. Also, while you help us, your taxes will be lowered and people will be thankful that you helped.

Katherine asked her students to write reflections at the end of the study about what they had learned, what surprised them, what they might take away with them into their next project. Their responses were touching. Every child in the class wrote differently about what she or he had learned and how the study had affected her or him. Some children learned how complicated the world is, especially when you open your eyes and look at it critically. Fixing that can never be easy, as Leah points out:

> What am I learning from the social action writing study?
> When we went to the museum of natural history on Saturday, we had been planning to make a presentation and speech on the exhibit we had planned for the museum, to the curator on that same day. After looking at some of the museum's exhibits, we realized that our exhibit would not fit in with the atmosphere of the museum. Our exhibits had no artifacts or tribes from South Africa or Asia. And we could not just barge in the curator who probably didn't go to work on Saturdays anyway. That particular action plan didn't quite seem to work out too well. Ms. Bomer said that what we're doing is almost exactly like real life, in the real world. We said, "It IS the real world." Maybe the real world is a little bit harder than we thought.
> What I am learning is that you can't just sit around and wait for someone to come up to you and say "Hey kid, see that museum over there, there are not equal exhibits on men and women. Do you want to do something about it? Because if you do, I do too and I'll pay for it all! I'll get it done!" Because it ain't gonna happen. You have to go out and do things on your own. Nobody's gonna live your life for you, you have to live life for yourself. Not everything will go just the way you want it to, but you'll just have to deal with it, that's life.

Others learned things about the world we wish they didn't have to, yet this is why we teach the way we do:

> I have learned a lot about welfare, and about the homeless and needy. Nina drew a graph to show me what a mother and daughter would get from the goverment. It was so shoking to see that it doesn't pay for the rent of a house all together. How is a mother going to get a job if she doesn't have desent clothes for even an interview and doesn't have a safe place to keep her child? Nina fills the "gap in service." She finds homes—donations furnish them. Soon she is lent a suit to go to a job interview. And social workers help the familys with knowing where to go next. This study has made me realize how important "Blankets With Love" is. Not only does it furnish homes, it furnishes lives. (Ruth)

Still other children cited the nuts-and-bolts learning they gained about how to use writing to get attention and make changes:

> I feel I'm learning how to say and write how I feel in a way that won't insult anybody. What I mean is that now I'm writing to Mayor Giuliani and I'm writing about how the cops respond to people of New York City. I wrote to him because he is the one that is really in charge of the cops and I feel that they are not doing a good job and I don't want to insult him by saying he's not doing a good job with them. I just want him to consider it and maybe help them. I am learning how to make a difference in a way that is appropriate for people to consider it. Because if I don't do it in a way that is appropriate they will probably say "Why should we listen, this person can't even be nice!" I'm learning how to discuss things better. (Galina)

> I think that I am learning that kids can stand up for what they believe in. I have learned how to work better in a group and how to use my writing to tell people in power what I want. This study has helped me to write longer, richer things that really express how I feel. I think that I can now look at the world with a different pair of eyes, because I used to only look at things on the surface, but now I think I go a little deeper. I think that my entire class is becoming braver, like the Iraq group. They're trying to help the president say "No!" to bombing Iraq. My group (women's rights) is a HUGE group. So we have a hard time working together and staying with a topic. So I am trying (along with the other kids in my group) to change that. All in all, I think I learned a lot of good stuff. (Maya)

For many, the benefits were primarily social and had to do with how they learned they could work with someone else on a project bigger than they were, and how that made them feel good.

> I am learning to care for the world and what to do to make it a better place. Also how to make a difference and somehow I talk more! Somehow I know how to feel, how to care for the things beyond me. It opens me into more family caring like. I came out of the Spawn which haunted me. Anyway it taught me how to have better relationships with friends and enemies. (Tomas)

> I am learning how women are treated differently than men and that most of the things are unfair. I'm also learning how to participate in something I stand for and demolish what I don't. I learned how to write letters to people in power. I have learned that working in a group of people I never work with, on an issue I respect is better and sometimes more fun than working with my friends with an issue I don't respect. (Colin)

In the midst of learning how to write for social action, the children in Katherine's classes experienced having their voices heard by persons in authority, by persons with more power than they had. They learned good lessons about how to approach the people who could get them closer and closer to their goal. They learned that targeting candidates in an election year is a good strategy. They learned about the power of numbers and about working together, splitting up the tasks, pooling talents and skills.

The kids had begun learning how to look at the world with a critical lens, with an eye and ear tuned to inequities and injustices. Not a day went by that someone in the WRA didn't notice an inequity toward women. Colin came in one spring morning, and announced, "There are a lot of cold medicine commercials on right now, and you know what? The man always gets the *right* medicine! The woman keeps having a clogged-up nose, but the man goes out and treats it! That's sexist!" The WRA decided to set up a site on the Internet that listed all the examples of how women are not treated the same way as men. The girls in this group witnessed with their own eyes and ears the transformations that consciousness-raising had on the boys in the class. This fed their eagerness to get the message to boys and girls around the world.

The work of social action isn't easy. It involves grappling with serious questions about power and authority, about rights and oppressions, about violence and peace, about democracy. We were surprised by the willingness of these students to take on this work and to put such intense energy and effort into it. We were amazed at how the projects took on lives of their own and how much of what the children learned during this study carried on into the rest of their reading and writing and living together in the classroom. But we also realized that this energy and commitment was not a sudden thing. There wasn't a "first day of social action writing." It was not a matter of saying, "Turn to a fresh page in your writers notebook and start caring about the world." The caring about others, the seeds of social action, had always been there. They were planted in all of Katherine's teaching, from the moment her students entered her classroom on the first day of school. The whole of her teaching, along with that of many other teachers across the country, is angled toward making a better world. Her students look at the world with critical eyes, and they talk back to it in their writing. Many of Katherine's students continued to follow the nightly news with insider interest. The work they had done to make the world a better place changed how they read books, how they wrote poetry, how they made their art. They had begun to look at the world with an eye toward changing what is not fair and just. We hope this becomes how they live their whole lives.

CHAPTER 9

TEACHERS AS POLITICAL AGENTS

When we teachers attend writing institutes, we write. When we participate in reading initiatives or literature projects, we read. Attending workshops by science educators, we observe physical phenomena and form hypotheses. Constructivist math workshops get us to solve problems using multiple strategies and concrete and creative reasoning. To prepare ourselves as teachers, we must engage in interesting intellectual and practical challenges while attending to our own processes of thinking and acting.

Many teachers now view education as being mainly about processes rather than static bodies of knowledge. That fundamental shift in purpose changes what it means to be prepared. Rather than having piles of information banked in the mind, it is essential to be well acquainted, from the inside, with the processes and practices into which we are acculturating our students. (Knowledge is still relevant, of course, but the issue is how to use it and manage it rather than simply dumping it and measuring it.) To be able to teach students how to do something, we need to be doing it or have previous strong experiences doing it. In John Dewey's terms, it is not enough to have a map in hand; we need to have made the journey.

As teachers we participate in an adult community, then function as brokers in bringing the practices of that community into our own classrooms. A broker, in this sense, is someone who stands at the boundary between two different communities or systems of activity and who actively imports the ways of being and doing of one community into the other (Wenger 1998). Unless we work very deliberately at doing something else, we broker our own experiences as students in the banking model of education (Freire 1970)—about 16,000 hours' worth—into our classroom. To counter this powerful trend, we need powerful new learning experiences, we need to be fully aware of and constantly reflect on the real processes of that learning, and we need actively to imagine how to broker such learning into our classroom communities. We need to put ourselves in the position of being enculturated differently.

To create classrooms as spaces where people participate in democracy and take up social action as part of their processes of thinking, we need to be involved in activist communities outside of school. This does not mean just sending checks to the Sierra Club but also working actively with others to affect specific cultural and political changes in local communities and institutions, the state, the nation. From such involvement, we can learn strategies for action, specific skills for affecting public opinion and leaders' decisions. We learn how to write a press release and where and when to send it. We learn how to set up computers to print trifold leaflets. We learn where to find the addresses of legislators and the best ways to communicate with them. We internalize the process by which a bill becomes law in ways we never did in our high school government classes.

Activists develop habits and impulses that are latent in most citizens' lives. Writing a letter to the editor of the local paper no longer seems like a big once-in-a-lifetime deal but a regular, immediate response. Checking in with others working toward shared goals becomes part of the daily routine. Scanning news and legislative communications for information about pet issues becomes part of a reading life. E-mailing copies of letters for others to use as templates becomes part of a writing life.

Activists learn what to expect from collaborations with others working together toward political ends. They learn to look past irrelevant differences in the interest of sharing goals for action, understanding that coalitions are built around very specific positions. They learn to broaden idiosyncratic perspectives in order to find the largest acceptable common ground with others. They learn to disagree civilly about strategy in the interests of maintaining community in the group. They learn what kinds of action are useful in the various stages of a group's evolution, when to attempt small, winnable agendas, and when to emphasize the patient, long haul.

As activist teachers, we appropriate emotional and intellectual ways of being that we can then externalize in our classrooms. We learn how to have a strong sense of purpose but to keep the people we are working beside most prominently in our minds, since it is togetherness, not merely being right, that sustains long work toward real change. We learn when and how to inspire friends to action and when to lay back. We learn how to make meetings and events joyful, interesting, and fun while maintaining a strong sense of purpose and a commitment to business.

Like most things that matter in teaching, these dispositions are not easily available in curriculum guides, workshops, or books. Only those who act ever really develop a sense of efficacy, and without a sense of efficacy, how can we teach students that they can make a difference?

Expanding the Meaning of Teaching

Committed teachers will do almost anything to become better teachers, so we have couched our argument in those terms as a beginning, as if the reason to take social action were only to inform teaching. A little perspective might be in order, however. We are, after all, talking about changing the world.

The teaching profession has come to understand that teaching literacy does not mean simply installing the ability to read and write into students' heads once and for all. It means something more complex, something along the lines of teaching students to adapt flexibly to linguistic and literate practices in various communities as they move through life. Literacy means different things in different communities and situations, and teachers work to help students become strategic inquirers and inspired participants as they interact with diverse groups of others. As teachers we create environments that bring out various properties of literate participation common to situations outside school. In other words, we create social worlds in which students live and work with language.

As teachers we try to make those worlds receptive to student voices, even the smallest of them. We try to construct social systems that are as just and democratic as possible. We actively attempt to enculturate individuals to an ethic of associated living and never-ending inquiry into the world around them. Yet we know too well that the world we create in our classroom does not align neatly with the world outside. The most typical response to this disjuncture is to say, *When children get out into the world, they're going to have to be competitive and individualistic, and they'll face the reality of failure and success and unfairness. School ought to prepare them for that world by re-creating it inside classrooms.* Here's another possibility. Let's try to make our classrooms and the world fit together better by changing more of the world. Okay, so it will take longer. Still, it's a more worthwhile project, and a more logical extension of our purposes in teaching.

Teaching must be advocacy: for kids, for democracy, for a better world. If it is not advocacy for those ideals, then it is advocacy for something else. We spend most of our days in our classrooms, so most of our advocacy will occur there. But our ambitions need not stop at the threshold. We might also teach the world to accept a new kind of person.

To educate for public participation must mean, in addition to supporting students' acquisition of strategies and dispositions, also to contribute to the construction of public spaces receptive to their voices. If we are teaching kids to write letters to politicians, we need also to work for a political system that listens to citizens' voices. If we are sponsoring the practice of producing flyers, tracts, pamphlets, and other texts designed to educate and mobilize fellow community members, we ought also work to develop communities capable of uniting around shared interests and values. Otherwise, we are just teaching kids to talk to walls.

Working with our communities to empower citizens may also help parents and other community members better understand why we teach for social justice. When every adult is isolated in her own job, her own enrichment, and her own family's entertainment, it seems only reasonable to expect school to prepare children for the marketplace, for competition, and for sport. Consequently, political conversations are thought to be "controversial," while school programs designed to educate students to be businesspeople are thought to be "practical" in the interest of "achievement" and "excellence." Teachers make up a substantial percentage of the workforce of most communities. Our participation in a different kind of adulthood might help shift some of those specious definitions.

Furthermore, the development of empowered citizens is not something that can occur within the walls of a school. Children who are abused or silenced in their homes or communities will not likely become strong as a result of the assignments they complete in school. Children face an uphill struggle toward democratic participation (or literacy or mathematical understanding or you name it) when they grow up in desperate families in which parents scramble hopelessly for life's necessities. If we really want to improve the life chances of children, it's no good staying in our rooms.

Choosing Where to Become Involved

We can't do everything; we have to make choices about where we put our time and energy. Teachers are inclined to care about everything, though, so it is hard for us to make decisions about where we will become most involved. The danger is in not choosing, in trying to do so much that all our commitments remain marginal. It may help to keep in mind that whatever issue we choose to work on, whether high-stakes testing or child abuse or preserving forests or workers' rights to a living wage, by engaging with others to transform the world, we create more democracy. When we work with groups for change, we participate in public life, we make the people more self-governing, we engage in the process. In that sense, even the most hopeless cause is transformative and emancipatory. Moreover, action begets action, so even a "wrong" initial decision is better than frozen inaction.

Some options for involvement center on education, and they may, for some, be the most logical places to become active. Many teachers have, over the past few years, become political agents in response to government intrusions into classroom practice. The federal Reading Excellence Act, introduced in 1998, attempted, in effect, to impose on the entire country a particular, limited perspective on reading. A number of states have passed, or attempted to pass, legislation pertaining to the teaching of phonics and phonemic awareness, even well into secondary school. Even in cases where the phonics laws apply only to early reading instruction, many upper-grade literacy teachers recognize the threat to student comprehension and critical thinking such limited practices represent. The standards movement has dominated much of the public conversation about teaching and learning for nearly two decades, and the way that movement insists on specifying and centralizing what is to be learned in school naturally leads to social conflict, whether the focus is writing, mathematics, or history. This movement toward standardizing student learning has fed the historical backlash against multicultural initiatives based on difference, such as bilingual education.

The standards ideology that all students should know how to do the same things at the same high levels of attainment, and that no lemons should get out of the factory, has led inevitably to high-stakes testing. Tests with high stakes are those with serious consequences for students, teachers, and schools, such as graduation and promotion, funding, and employment. Tying important decisions to a single test has serious effects on students' and teachers' emotional health; on school community life; on curriculum; on the life chances of members of society's most vulnerable groups; and, ironically, on standards, since everyone's efforts are focused so sharply on the form and content of the tests.

Accompanying these political developments, surely not accidentally, is the movement to privatize public education and to drive reform via market forces. The promise of billions of dollars of the people's money has attracted the attention of corporate entities, and this prospect has awakened a renewed debate about the nature and role of public education in a democracy. As the marketplace recognizes the disposable cash in the hands of children and adolescents, businesses with products to sell to the young, from soft drinks to software, have begun buying a presence in schools. Because all of these developments confront teachers in our daily workspace, many of us have begun rising up and speaking out in response, taking as our teaching space a larger public that includes adults and peers.

As important as it is that we teachers add our voices to these public educational debates, there is something almost sad about the fact that it has taken threats to our ways of doing our job to activate our political will. While it is probably noble that we think so much of our work, there are also larger issues that affect children's lives and learning and the quality of our shared world more powerfully than schooling ever can. It's sometimes embarrassing after spending the day worried about phonics legislation to read an article about the death penalty, global warming, economic globalization and its risks, the control of the media in the hands of a few, or the mockery campaign financing makes of democracy. Certainly, for teachers not interested in political action regarding education, there are plenty of big issues to engage and actions to pursue. Citizens may want to browse some of the following web sites listing issues and the organizations working to support or defeat them:

> *http://www.rethinkingschools.org/Links/Links.htm*
> *http://www.inequality.org/resourcesfr.html*
> *http://www.socio.demon.co.uk/magazine/5/issue5.html*
> *http://www.speakout.com/activism/voxcap/*
> *http://www.webactive.com/directory/topic-index.html*

http://witnesstothefuture.com/links/index.html#online
http://www.fairtest.org/arn/parents.html

Getting to Work: The Process of Social Action

Having identified something we're interested in working on, what do you do now? If someone isn't coming right up to you and twisting your arm to attend a rally, how do you work for change? What do you do first, and how do you plan future activity? It is this initial moment of frozen helplessness that most reveals how essential it is that we as teachers engage in social action. If we don't know how to begin acting on our own passions, how can we teach students to be participants in a democracy, which is our main obligation as public schoolteachers? We need a process.

Based on her research about how community organizers (professional social activists) do their work and her reflections on how teachers might learn from these more experienced others, Cathy Fleischer (2000) describes the organizing process as having five broad, recursive stages:

1. Building community.
2. Identifying purpose.
3. Developing leaders.
4. Taking action.
5. Evaluating progress.

This outline may serve as a map of the process and a way to organize our thinking about how to go about social action.

As we described children doing in the previous chapter, the first step is to get together with other people. Social action *is* organizing. As Marge Piercy (1986) writes:

> Alone, you can fight,
> you can refuse, you can
> take what revenge you can
> but they roll over you. (44)

It is politically crucial to connect our actions with others' because democracies work through the efforts of groups, as power is negotiated among their competing interests (Dahl 1956; Dixon 1999; Truman 1951). Joining our efforts to others' is also psychologically necessary, since the group motivates, energizes, and disciplines individual activity. In our busy, distracted lives, we are more likely to get that pamphlet written if the group meets tomorrow than if we are accountable to no one but ourselves. When we need to go to the state capitol to meet with a legislator, we are more likely to find the necessary courage if others are driving there with us.

Cathy Fleischer points out that building community is work we teachers are specially equipped to perform, since it is our daily practice in the classroom. Furthermore, we have deep and powerful connections to the communities in which we work, so we are uniquely situated to gather others around shared agendas. The fact that Fleischer names the first step building community rather than getting a group together helps us realize that we are not just talking about signing people up. A more carefully sustained project is involved, of forging relationships, bonding, creating trust, listening to one another's stories, and becoming comfortable with each other. The group also needs to set up a communication system, such as e-mail, a web-based conference system, or telephone tree, and a schedule for getting together in the flesh. For the purpose of action, the group will need a good name, and creating the name can also help members assume a group identity.

Fleischer's second stage, identifying purpose, is too often skipped by people eager to get on with changing the world. Just as a piece of writing is out of focus until the writer has clarified her purpose and audience, so too is social action diffuse, uncoordinated, and ineffective until a group has determined what they are trying to accomplish. An issue, such as high-stakes testing, child abuse, or a living wage, may have brought the group together, but this is analogous to an author having found a topic; it is not, in and of itself, a social purpose. What are we trying to do about high-stakes testing? Who are we talking to about child abuse, and what do we want them to do? Having a focus, however, has to be balanced against being broad enough to appeal to people with different specific passions and outlasting a particular action plan. The conversations among group members about how broadly or narrowly to define their purpose help everyone develop shared definitions and intersubjective thinking about the issue. Individuals are forced to revise their idiosyncratic responses to the world into the kinds of arguments and narratives that other people find persuasive.

When Fleischer lists developing leaders as the third stage of the organizing process, she is referring mostly to community organizers developing indigenous leaders in a community, or else to teachers helping parent groups develop leaders. In her discussions, however, it's clear that we could just as well think of this stage as being about the development of roles and identities for all participants, not just the people who emerge as leaders. When one or two teachers gather a group of other educators and parents together around an issue, the leadership often rests with the people who called the meeting in the first place. Sometimes, however, the people who called the meeting may not want to speak out in public, or might be unable to get to a phone during the day to call legislators, or might not be confident enough about their writing to send letters and press releases to the newspaper. There are roles that call for chutzpah, for speed at writing, for gentleness and tact with people, for outspokenness, organization, passion, diligence, and persistence, for skill at recruiting others, for a willingness to run errands. Helping everyone identify his or her role within the group is perhaps more crucial than figuring out who is going to preside. In some groups, these roles evolve without having to assign them; however, with all the pressure and everyday disorder that accompanies this kind of part-time work, it is wise to be as deliberate and conscious about such things as possible.

Taking action is, of course, what the previous steps are leading up to. Everything else is essential, but only if the group gets around to doing something. It is so easy for people in education to think that something has occurred just because we have had a discussion in a room. We give our time lavishly to talk with colleagues about issues, and we display an almost limitless tolerance for deliberation. Much of this book has been about the great importance of critical conversations, but there comes a time to stop talking to people inside our own communities and to affect the world outside our usual circles. Fleischer lists the following types of tactics:

- *Create and offer information.* Make flyers, posters, phone trees, and fact sheets; set up petitions in public places; chat informally with neighbors at spontaneous moments.
- *Combine entertainment and information.* Stage workshops, rallies, gatherings, concerts, readings, demonstrations, contests.

- *Work with the media:*
  a. *Contact reporters.* Get in touch with the local editor and reporter whose beat is closest to your issue and make your concern known so that they might contact your group when they write about it.
  b. *Set up events that look like "news" and invite reporters.* Stage demonstrations related to some seasonal news cycle (beginning and end of school, winter holidays, spring break, snow, heat) or other action-oriented, visual events that call on viewers to get up and do something. Write press releases as short news stories with the date and the words "for immediate release" at the top of the page, and assume they are exactly what will appear in the paper. Follow up the press release with repeated phone calls to the paper or station right up until the event begins.
  c. *Write letters to the editor.* Most newspaper readers read them. Get your group together for a couple of hours and have a writing workshop in which everyone composes letters to news organizations. Write letters supporting recent stories, letters, and editorials with which the group agrees. Write to express your concern about issues not receiving the coverage you think they should. Write to rebut others' letters, and when you do, avoid restating their case; get out your own perspective.
  d. *Set up a media watch.* Divide the media up among members of the group. When there are inaccuracies in the way newspeople report your issue, call up the editor or segment producer and give her the facts. (You'll need fact sheets.)
- *Make legislative contacts.* Invite legislators to events that will have fairly large numbers of people at them, since those are the ones they are more likely to attend. Always invite the media as well: it's important for friendly legislators to get good press coverage when they show up. When you write to legislators, say you are writing on behalf of the group, and provide facts about the group, including numbers when they are large. Get individual members of the group to write at the same time about the same issue, since many letters affect legislators more than single ones. Follow up with phone calls, in which you will get to talk briefly to a member of the legislator's staff about your views on the issue. Concentrate on the focus issue.

Implicit in every stage of Fleischer's description of the organizing process but listed as a discreet stage is the reflective and empirical evaluation of progress. Good teachers are used to thinking of evaluation as an ongoing process, and that habit serves us well in social action. Basically, it's a chance to reflect on where the group wanted to go and whether they are on track in getting there, to reset direction if they're not, and to renew energy. As with educational assessment, the best practices involve asking the people most affected by the action how things are going, observing interactions, gathering relevant evidence, and thinking hard about it.

Action as Inquiry

Connected with the ongoing assessment of social action is an attitude that takes action as a form of inquiry. Just as teaching is more powerful when it includes research, integrating inquiry into action makes us more aware of what we are doing, allows us to use the action more deliberately in our teaching, and allows us to communicate with other educators about what we are doing. Questions like *How does this work?* and *What happens when we try this?* are interesting to pursue when we organize parents, affect legislators, or mobilize community.

By taking an inquiring stance, we allow issues to remain complicated even as we achieve enough closure to act on them. Our understanding becomes richer and more intricate. We are able to deliberate in public, to engage in collaborative thinking rather than polarized debate. We are able to maintain more productive relationships with those whose views do not match our own or who may be as yet undecided on the issue. In fighting high-stakes testing, for example, it is important to hear the voices saying that the schools do not belong to the teachers who work in them but to the people. When the public calls for accountability, we may be able to hear behind these words a desire to understand what kind of world schools are making. We may then be able to do more than merely resist high-stakes testing: we can attempt to create more adequate structures for conversation among educators and interested members of the community, where education and democracy work both ways, where values and goals can be more communally negotiated. Without that kind of complex understanding of student assessment, we can fight, but our position will be indefensible in the public eye. When we listen and inquire, our definition of the issue, our sense of what we are working on, remains flexible, broad, and deep enough to respond to changes in the environment and may allow us to open third, fourth, and fifth ways beyond the typical binary positions so often constructed in the press.

Strategies for inquiring into our social action are similar to the strategies we use in teacher research. When we have town meetings or conversations with policymakers, we should take careful notes and tape-record our oral recollections of the details immediately afterward. Randy has used the drive home from the state capitol as an opportunity to reassemble what occurred in meetings, since taping the actual conversations would seem politically adversarial. In our social action, we produce documents, as do those who oppose us, and collecting those artifacts, organizing and filing them with some discipline, allows them to be available for later reflection and storytelling. News reports can sometimes track (or perhaps create) the changing public perception of an issue, so clipping and filing them lets us look across time at whether our actions have affected the shape of the discussion. Interviewing key players, whether legislators, policymakers, business leaders, community activists, parents, students, or other teachers, permits the voices of participants to be heard at more length than public dialogue will bear, and a deeper understanding of what is really going on, what people are really fighting for, can emerge as a result. Keeping a journal can help us develop interpretations, record changing perceptions, and remember events that might otherwise be lost.

Though inquiry can inform the entire process of social action, one of the best reasons to do it is so that we can talk with one another across contexts. Just as inquiry into our practices as teachers and our students' learning has produced unprecedented sophistication about how classrooms work, deliberate investigations of our practices of social action will allow our profession to understand the accompanying strategies, ethics, and predictable interactions. It will also make the whole business more interesting to those of us who have become hooked on thoughtfulness. Just as new kinds of articles, journals, and books were born from teacher research, so might new publications emerge from our work in policy and politics. Already, professional conferences have begun to include sessions dealing with this kind of activity. Developing the audience for these conversations and publications will permit new voices to enter our professional conversation and further turn our field's attention toward democracy, social justice, and critical literacy.

Bringing What We Learn into the Classroom

Informing our own understanding about social action prepares us for Monday morning, provides material for teaching, becomes the stuff of minilessons and conferences. The following questions can spark a whole curriculum:

- What genres have you and others used in writing about this issue (e.g., letters, fact sheets, bumper stickers, posters and signs, websites, pamphlets, articles, editorials)?
- How have you written differently about this for different audiences (politicians, the public, news reporters, children, others on your side, parents)?
- What kinds of revisions have you made to your writing?
- How does talk with others affect your writing? What kinds of talk occur before, during, and after you work on a draft?
- How does thinking and caring about this issue make you read differently?
- What specific technical things have you needed to learn in order to write for social action (e.g., addressing legislators, compressing your thoughts into a short message, deleting extra words in very short texts, researching state laws, sharpening the clarity and focus of your message, using HTML to create a web page)?
- How is your correspondence with others involved with the same issues part of your reading and writing life?
- What is the role of literature (stories, poems) in helping others to care about this issue?
- How do your social commitments lead you to choose particular books?
- How does reading nonbook material (Internet sites, magazine and newspaper articles, pamphlets put out by organizations) about your favorite issues fit into your reading life?

Even though this chapter is primarily about actions we take outside the classroom, it is important to think about how we make our participation in democracy visible to our students. Any one item that comes to light in your responses to the above questions (economy of words on buttons and bumper stickers, say) could be the subject of a minilesson. If one minilesson is about the range of genres available for writing about this issue, also plan to go back through each genre, one by one, then return to specific features of craft in each genre. Teaching "genres for social action" involves scores of lessons, not one. There are also many different types of minilessons. Sometimes, it helps just to tell the story of something you did in your own work for social action. Other times, showing your drafts and revisions is useful. Often it's a good idea to have the whole class practice a particular thing (writing an inside address on a letter, using an Internet search engine, distributing particular tasks to members of their group) while you watch and help. Figure 9–1 lists and describes types of minilessons for brokering adult practices into the classroom and making them as visible as possible to learners.

Our Professional Language and Values

We have stressed throughout this book the importance of using the language of democracy and justice in our classrooms, and we want to make a similar point about the ways we professionals talk with one another. Our profession, like the general public, remains trapped in the discourses

Presenting an Artifact
Bring in your own relevant writing or reading and show your students one thing you have done at home: your revisions, your notes, the way you've marked up a text you're reading, the project you are working on, or something you have written or made in the past.

Writing in Front of the Class
Draft or revise something you are working on in front of the kids while you think aloud about the decisions you are making. Use either chart paper or a projected transparency. What part of the process you highlight will be determined by what you want them to learn.

Reading and Thinking Aloud
Take something someone else has written and read it out loud, stopping to think aloud about the content or craft of the writing, depending on your specific purpose in reading it.

Directly Explaining Technique
Just tell them, as explicitly as you can, one thing you want them to know or do, using your own experience as an example.

Assisting Performance
After explaining some strategy, get everyone to try it with your guidance before getting back to ongoing work.

Anecdotal Troubleshooting
When you see a particular kind of problem in students' work, talk about the ways you and others in your social action community have solved a similar problem. Alternatively, have a particular preselected student or group talk about how they have approached a similar problem.

Introducing a Guest
Bring in an outsider, having told them exactly what you'd like him to talk about. A community organizer, for example, might be able to talk about a specific strategy. You may also want to use a guest as a sort of hero or someone to identify with.

Adding an Item to an Ongoing List
Many people post charts in the room about things like

- "Actions we are taking"
- "Useful kinds of writing"
- "Future ideas for service"
- "How our reading is changing"

Adding a single item to a chart helps students see a lesson in context with other things the class has taken up. The list is not a checklist or limitation of activity but is seen as an improvable object, something we all expect to outgrow continually.

Correcting a Misconception
Students working on social action will be full of misconceptions. Rather than being overwhelmed or discouraged, it's just as well to focus on these misconceptions one at a time.

Describing a Resource
Showing the class a particular book, newspaper, web page, or other resource is an important lesson for helping them work more independently.

Holding a Class Policy Meeting
The fact that a lot of people are trying to do complicated things in a small space means that issues in management are going to come up. Sometimes, these may have to be decisions you make as the teacher; more often, they are useful opportunities for democratic problem solving.

Sharing a Strategy
Speaking from either your own experience or the work of someone you know or something you have read about, tell the story of a particular strategy some activist or organizer has tried.

Figure 9–1 *Twelve Kinds of Minilessons for Brokering Political Practices into Classrooms*

of psychology and scientific management that captured education early in the twentieth century. Very likely, we will all spend much of our careers having to speak those languages in many contexts, using words and phrases like *achievement, standards, research tells us,* and *what works.* Still, we need as often as possible to reframe our conversation to claim a language of democracy, social action, and justice, to speak very specifically about what those ideas mean to us, and to justify our practice in those terms. Too often, we advocate or oppose practice because of its supposed effectiveness rather than its relationship to important principles of public life. We talk about *authenticity* and *natural processes* and *research-based practice* in ways that mask our real ideological commitments.

To take one example from our own work, in *Time for Meaning* (Bomer 1995) Randy used as an example a notebook entry in which a student started off writing about a television show:

> I'm watching this tv show about Vietnam. It goes through the war with this one group of soldiers. It shows how cruel and messy the war was. I don't watch it for all the violence and blood. I'm watching because it show the war throught the eyes of the soldiers not the government's eyes. There's alot of killing. But killing is wierd to me. To animals it's a part of life, a way of survival. But to people it is bad. For animals it is a way of population control. Disease is too. But people fight them every step of the way. It was meant to be a perfect balance. Maybe that's why the world is going to hell. Are we screwed up or is life screwed up. Something must be wrong or else everything would be perfect. Why do people have to be so nosy. Everything that comes along we have to figure out and conqure. Thus causing invension, putting ourselves on a pedastle. Do we really have to be superior. They persicuted Hitler for trying to create the so-called "perfect race." But isn't that what we are trying to do as people. Putting ourselves above all else. Putting ourselves before the perfect balance. Screw evolution. Let's get back to the way it was supposed to be. Putting ourselves on the same level as all else. Trying to solve the problems we created. How stupid can anything be. Why make all of these problems that make life so hard. Are we that board with life that we have to make problems to solve. Or don't we know the point of solving a problem is so there isn't a problem anymore. Why don't we get down to the whole point of life which is survival. Get back to real life which is the unwritten part of Life, liberty, and pursuit of happiness. We have to be showered with luxuries. But the only real luxury there is is survival. We messed the world up past the point of fixing. So we might as well end the world and hope and pray that the next people don't screw up like we did when we upset the perfect balance. (55–56)

This student is writing about human beings and their relationship to nature, interrogating what is justifiable and what is not, taking a stand against critics of hunting as morally indefensible in an ecological view of human/earth relationships. He is also valuing a perspective that views war (and presumably other areas of experience) through the eyes of common people, locating moral authority and intellectual credibility not in power structures but in ordinary people's everyday life.

The point Randy made about this entry was that it was an example of writing as a tool for thinking, writing that takes the writer to a new mental place. There was no discussion in *Time for Meaning* of the political thinking the student engaged in on that day and many subsequent days. The ongoing conversation in Randy's classroom made that kind of writing fairly common in students' notebooks and projects, but there is little sense of that political conversation in the book. It's repressed in favor of comments about craft and tools and community, all of which may be important things to discuss. But there is something rather hollow about all that talk about method and technique with so little attention to the explicitly political themes of the class's shared values.

In *Time for Meaning,* Randy also discusses another student whose notebook was filled with her passions about her family's farm, the outdoors, and the environment:

> Today on the farm we finished off a field of corn that we picked. I've always liked to help unload a wagon of shelled corn. I climb up in and keep pushing the corn out at the bottom where my brother

is and [he] keeps the corn from falling on the ground. Today on this nice fall day I stood on all the corn and looked around at the farm, house, woods, and the world in general and I realized how lucky I was. I really can't picture my life without the farm. Everything would be so different. I would hate to live like all my friends. Such an awful life. People act like I'm held back from activities and my social life because of the farm. If that's what it would take to keep the farm in the family and to keep it as it is, I would sacrifice anything, and I mean it. Farm life is so wonderful, I love it dearly. I really don't [know] how I'd survive if I didn't have my cows and my "homey farm" kind of attitude surrounding me. But of course the farms in this country are dropping like flies, and there's not many of my kind left. I'm not sure how long our own farm will exist even though we are out of debt. If people only knew what we are going through. But nobody knows or cares. It's damn sad!! (58–59)

All year long, these obsessions threaded through her entries and through her pieces of writing in different genres. When she wrote nonfiction, it was about the greenhouse effect. One memoir was about her special place, a tree bent over a creek, where she retreated when she needed to get away by herself and think. Her poems too grew from these same passions:

Fearing Myself

Behind my house there lays a woods.
And in that woods is a magical land.
It's nothing technical or anything big.
I go there for the Peace.
Peace.
I see the deer run into the woods,
And it reminds me of what this world is
Supposed to be.
The deer are free and unharmful.
If only the world were like deer.
Everything would be so much better.
War.
Enemies.
Hatred.
Selfishness.
Pollution.
Crime.
The list goes on and on.
I go to the woods to sit by the creek.
To look around and see myself.
I think about the wrongs,
And look for the rights.
The way everything is now,
I wonder.
I'm so young and it scares me to no end
To think about what it will be like when
I'm older.
I'd rather sit in the woods, by the creek
And watch myself and the world fade to
Darkness. (130)

Here is another poem, untitled, this student wrote in the same genre study:

> As I tasted the polluted air of the meadow,
> I realized how far away I was from the cruel,
>   vicious society.
> I stood there in the waist high weeds and grass
>   with a breeze slightly blowing my blonde hair.
> A single bird cried out a precious tune.
> Where was this god-like whimper coming from?
> There were no trees for it to perch on.
> No sky for it to crash through.
> No earth for it to bury itself in from this
> Sweet World.
>
> I see a future yet unknown
> A past I'll always cherish
> A present I'm unsure to say
> And a world about to Perish
> The sun shall rise no more again
> I hear my distant cries
> But when this places crashes to the ground
> I can at least say
> I tried (139)

This student takes up a sequence of related issues that are grounded in her daily life: from disappearing spots in which to be alone in peace to the disappearance of family farms to the greenhouse effect. Taken together, these pieces of writing represent a sophisticated analysis of corporate, industrial effects on the earth and people's ways of living with it. Far from taking a simplistic, blaming view of the situation, however, the writer worries about her own complicity in the process and about how her own development as a person interacts with these environmental issues. She wants to choose herself as someone who can at least try to make a difference in this tidal wave of change.

The point Randy made here was that this student returned to the same material again and again and wrote about it in different genres. Again, he repressed the explicitly political content of the student's work, even in a book about nurturing student voice, in order to make a point about the writing process. The point itself was worth making, and we both still believe it's useful to think about students returning to the same life material and recasting it in different genres at different times. But there's something so receptive to technique, to method, in our culture as educators that it seems nearly inevitable, exclusively useful, to talk about the strategy without discussing the ideological content of students'—or their teachers'—thinking.

We would like to call for a different set of lenses for "what counts" in teaching. It's not that it does not matter whether or not kids learn to read but that the "learning to read" needs to be connected to a set of social conditions and relationships inside and outside the classroom. When we listen to one another, we ought to be able to hear those conditions in the story. We need to ask questions about the compromises to freedom, justice, and connectedness that occur when teaching methods "work." We need to value the attempts other teachers make to work for democracy even if their narratives do not always end with the students "loving it," as so many of our narratives seem compelled to do. We need to stop searching for tidy solutions to ethical and political problems, such as "classroom management," and embrace these problems as the complex, human, social processes they really are.

We need to justify our thinking about reading not just in terms of "our theory of literacy learning," as if the theory built itself inside our skulls, but in terms of practices and discourses we have learned as part of a specific historical, political, sociocultural trend and particular commitments to political ideals. Justifying our practice in terms of "cueing systems" and "transactional theory" is just as vacant a legitimization as trying to justify practice by "the nature of an alphabetic writing system" or "what the brain tells us about how kids learn." None of these things are ideals or justifications, none of them are principles. Our shared political life, a long tradition of inching toward democracy, a struggle for a more humane, more meaningful, more just world—if we can't justify our practice in these terms, we had better keep thinking.

CHAPTER 10

BREAKING THE SILENCE
The Politics of Children's Personal Writing

Lollipop

I remember climbing on the chair she was sitting in and hugging her. I was just old enough to know what pregnant meant, to know I had been part of her once too. The smell in the office was sterile, like the adhesive on bandages, like the tiny tubes with color-coded tops, like the vinyl covering the chairs where my mom sat as I gushed with happiness.

Sometimes I think it was my fault the baby died. I was too little to walk great distances, so my mom would carry me to school and from it. She keeps telling me, "No, it's not your fault; no, not your fault," but I wonder then, what else made the baby choose to leave this world?

One day we drove again to somewhere in Flushing to that same sterile place, and I looked at pictures of tiny Asian children pinned to the bulletin board, all glossy and laminated. I looked for my face every time I went there, every time becoming more and more frustrated. I wanted to see me. I wanted to see me more than anything else. I wanted to know I was discernible from the others, that I was able to know myself. That I was original. That I had my own mind and face and habits and background. But my face wasn't there. It was here, the place where I touch every day, the place where all my words come from.

I waited while my mom went, I think upstairs. Then we were standing in front of a sort of counter, or a booth. I saw red in a jar. I saw hatred, life, a ruby in a jar. I offered my mother a lollipop. She was tired, very tired, could hardly walk from being tired. She declined. I ate it. I felt as though I needed to appease her for something that wasn't my fault, that I didn't fully understand. I remember it was green . . . apple, or lime, something sweet, something delicious, something that melted away in my mouth and left only bitterness on my tongue. (Min, age 10)

Min wrote this memoir excerpt when she was a fifth grader in my classroom. Aside from it being one of the most sophisticated and beautifully written pieces by a student of mine, I recognized how political Min's personal story is. True, it doesn't sound like something from *The Nation* or *The New Republic*. It would not incite riots or get Min arrested. This writing is political because it is by a child in a public school about a subject that involves the decisions and actions of the adults who are responsible for her. It is political because no one asks children to narrate their life experiences; no one asks them to try to make sense of what is happening to them or of how events in their lives shape who they are and how they feel about themselves. In all the current policymaking having to do with how American children should be educated, with standards and standardized testing, world-class competition, back-to-basics, and character education programs, who is asking children what kind of a classroom they would prefer to learn in and how they would like to be treated?

Several decades ago, Carol Gilligan realized that in the story of human development, the voices, the relationships, and the lives of women were absent. It was a massive, cultural not-knowing. Making that discovery, she has said, she "felt an immense loss" (Gilligan 1997). Most of her work since then has sought to fill that absence with the voices, perceptions, and life stories of women and girls. Also largely absent in the research on human development have been the voices of people of color, gays, and children. In order to write her brilliant novel *Beloved*, Toni Morrison researched narratives by slaves, and she found them reticent, silent about their interior lives. Over and over, she says, the narratives refused to describe the writer's circumstances and feelings, hedging instead with sentences like, "Let us drop a veil over these proceedings too terrible to relate." Morrison thought that her job as a novelist was to "rip that veil" and to try to imagine her way into the thoughts and feelings of slaves, to "reconstruct the world, the atrocities experienced by blacks, that the narratives imply" (Morrison 1987, 110).

When we teach historical life stories in our schools, we need to ask: what are the stories being passed on, and what are the stories *not* being passed on? What is being covered up or lied about? What is important to teach? How can our children act in the world for others if they feel powerless and helpless and silenced themselves? How can they act on behalf of others if they don't know how others suffer? In the face of all that cultural not-knowing, how can children's writing about their lives not be automatically, profoundly political? Who is going to care about what they think as they walk down city streets on their way to school? Who will know how they make sense of the violent, racist, sexist, looks-obsessed messages our culture sends them via television, movies, magazines, and giant billboards?

We can begin to break these silences by giving children the space and time and freedom to write the stories of their lives. Maxine Greene says: "It would mean fresh and sometimes startling winds blowing through the classrooms of the nation. It would mean the granting of audibility to numerous voices seldom heard before" (1988, 126).

At an NCTE conference in Albuquerque several years ago, Maureen Barbieri (1998) told a story about Danling Fu, from the University of Florida, who consulted in a school in New York City's Chinatown. Danling told the teachers she worked with that in order to become more fluent in English, Chinese girls needed to speak in class more often. The teachers wondered how they could ask Chinese girls to speak out, when they were not encouraged to express their feelings and thoughts in their own culture. Danling understood that these teachers were attempting to respect their students' home culture and first language. However, she writes: "To respect their home culture doesn't mean we have to accept every belief that culture holds. Every culture has its beauty but also its faults. Some cultures believe girls are not as valuable as boys. . . . Do we have to encourage the children who come from that culture to hold onto these beliefs?" (Fu 1998, 5).

Maureen Barbieri also told a story about herself and a group of five girls from a Chinatown school who met on Fridays after school to write together, talk, go to museums. The girls felt close to Maureen, and they shared a number of personal stories with her. Three of the girls had grandparents who threw away girl babies, and these granddaughters carry that legacy around with them. Children are deeply affected by the decisions and actions of the adults who are responsible for them. Maureen hoped that by talking and writing their personal stories, these girls would begin to question the cultural imperatives inherent in both their cultures, Chinese and American, that threaten to destroy their spirits. This is very political work.

Maureen then read from the notebook of a Chinese girl, a seventh grader. How moving it was to be sitting in New Mexico, among an audience of people from all over the country, listening to page after page of the writing of this child from New York City's Chinatown, who attends school all day, but after school travels by subway deep into Brooklyn to work in her parents' Chinese restaurant until ten o'clock at night. She answers the phone, places orders, and deals with the public because she is the only one in the family who can speak English. People cried listening to her story, the story of a girl who would have been silenced had not Maureen worked with her in a writing workshop, had not Maureen copied her notebook onto transparencies to project on a screen and read aloud. This girl shared her life with the wider world and made all of us smarter, more humble.

Breaking silences. Ripping the veil covering proceedings too terrible to relate. Such violent images. But violent images are sometimes appropriate in this political work we do.

Fresh winds are blowing in writing workshops in classrooms all around the country. Children's voices are resounding in the world, at least in the world of their own classroom. Children are writing more honestly about what life is like for them, about what their relationships to family and friends involve and where these relationships break down, about what it feels like in the color, gender, and sexual-preference margins and cracks of our society. We are privileged to peek inside these worlds, to get closer to the interior space children occupy most of the time, even as we insist they "pay attention" to the lesson on semicolons or the procedures for lining up. Once a child has shared herself with me in the words from her notebook, it is as if a new child stands before me, a child who has particular fears, pain, and hopes. I cannot teach her the same way after that.

Together, Broken

Divorce is like a toy; once it's together, the next thing you know, it's broken, forever. I can really only remember one thing about the day my mom moved out of the house; my friend and I were running and laughing between pillows that were off the couch.

My mom still feels sad about the divorce, but she'll probably get over it. My dad feels sad also, but he said if we didn't do it, it would be much worse than now. I bet they both felt sadder seven years ago than now because they both had just experienced it. But it's been seven years, so we all feel better.

I feel sad like my parents. Maybe even sadder. Sometimes I feel sad, sometimes I don't. I think when I was little, I didn't feel anything. Like I didn't know what was happening. As I said, I was running and laughing between pillows that were off the couch. I'm always thinking, "Will they get back together?" But they won't, ever. (Jack, age 9)

Children's memoirs speak to Maxine Greene's idea of freedom: "a refusal of the fixed, a reaching for possibility, an engagement with obstacles and barriers and a resistant world. . . ." (Ayers 1998, 7). They speak honestly of very difficult subjects, of memories, often painful ones, that are still alive and breathing inside of them three, five, seven years later. These events do not belong only to a single child. Jack's experience of divorce is a social issue. This is not a matter of blaming parents. Randy and I have both been divorced, and we are raising children who deal daily with the effects of their parents' divorce. But scores of people are affected when parents divorce, and we are all responsible for helping Jack and the others through it. Sometimes children's memoirs deal with terrible obstacles; they try to make sense of the things that happen around, in front of, and to them. They reach for possibilities: of hope, of a love that lasts forever, of understanding, of forgiveness, of peace.

Memoir is my favorite genre because I love to know how other people view themselves and how they make sense of their lives. I want to know how life is for other people, especially people who have a different perspective to tell about because they are from different economic classes or ethnic backgrounds. I like to write memoir because I am still struggling to become, and memoir helps me get there. I learned to write memoir from the best teachers, the writers who publish it. I learned to teach it from the fine chapters about how to craft memoir in *The Art of Teaching Writing* by Lucy Calkins, in *Sounds from the Heart* by Maureen Barbieri, in *Write to Learn* by Donald Murray.

Memoir in the Socially Conscious Classroom

A few years ago, my class studied memoir from April to June, the culminating project of two years we spent together writing poetry, essays, and fiction. These students were ripe fruit, ready to drop from the vine. They were already in love with writing, comfortable with the process of crafting any genre that came their way. They were like artists choosing to express their ideas in collage instead of paint, musicians deciding to compose a symphony instead of a concerto. In minilessons, I concentrated on memory, on choosing an angle from which to view their lives, on noticing their relationships with others and their place in culture and society. I wanted them to look at the stream of their life experience, to find patterns in it, to organize and try to make sense of it by looking back and reflecting on what they saw there. I wanted them to understand that in the memoir they would write at this moment they were choosing only one angle, one incident and perspective among many, that there were still many untapped possibilities. A life is not a single fixed thing. John Dewey (1938) said that it isn't simply experience but the reflection on experience that enables individuals to understand that they must continue choosing themselves while they live.

We cannot help students produce reflective writing by giving rigid writing assignments. A writing workshop on memoir cannot be isolated from the stream of life experience in and out of the classroom. The depth, the history, the many-layeredness of a study like this happen in the context of *these* lives lived in *this* classroom. Tips I would give for writing memoir aren't limited to looking at old photographs or trying to describe your very first memory. Rather, they include:

- Create freedom.
- Create a critical consciousness.
- Honor all children's voices.

To encourage children to write from a place of honesty, no matter how difficult the subject, teachers have to *create freedom in the classroom*. The freedom to choose what to write about. The freedom of large amounts of time, at least thirty minutes every day, in which to write. The freedom to get real responses to their writing. The tangential freedom of parents who trust that their children are engaged in curriculum that matters, who support their children writing about their families.

Grownups—teachers and families—are responsible for creating safe spaces for children, for "laying out the blankets for them to stretch out their identities" (Fine 1998, 212). We must create spaces where children strive to become, where they invent the possible. Classrooms may be the last safe space for children before they are confronted with what Michelle Fine (1998) calls the "raced, gendered, and classed lettering on the stop signs of life" (213) that causes many teenagers to feel marginal, alienated, and unsafe. We must build trust in our classroom communities so that our students will feel safe enough to write about how life is for them, even if what they write alienates us.

Isaiah was an extremely wise and articulate boy who had excelled in school despite very serious difficulties at home. After three years of tragedies, one after another, he finally shut down emotionally. By fourth grade, he had begun to get in trouble in school and in my classroom. He stopped doing his homework, he left all his books in his cubby and school memos in his mailbox. One time he stole the class book-order money, and several children saw him do it. He wrote curse words on the closet wall. He took pens and pencils out of children's cubbies—again, in plain sight—and then claimed he had found them on the floor. He got into fights in the lunchroom or on the playground, and many afternoons found him in the principal's office. His former teachers stopped in to talk with him; everyone loved him dearly and was concerned. I felt that he was asking for help, and I asked him why he seemed to be falling apart. He cried but would not talk about what was going on. One day after school I found his writing notebook on the floor. I opened it and found this poem:

Hatred

Hatred burns inside my heart.
Hatred plays me like a harp.
Hatred builds after every hour.
Hatred controls me with very strong power.

After I found that poem in Isaiah's writing notebook, I felt as if I were seeing a new child in front of me. My relationship with Isaiah changed forever. His writing changed my thinking, my teaching, and my interactions with troubled children from then on. That is a political act.

Every pedagogical act or decision, from the greatest to the most mundane, is both personal and political. Every year I make personal/political decisions about curriculum—in my attempts to create freedom and a critical consciousness—decisions ranging from which genres to study to which books to read aloud to how much time I give to and take from each area of the curriculum. In a democratic classroom, where writing genres, curriculum content, and read-aloud selections are negotiated with children, the children can still resist those choices and decisions despite our most generous intentions. They resist learning from us, resist our attempts to create empathy for others less fortunate, resist our desire and need for them all to get along.

When Aaron so vigorously rejected my selection of read-aloud books and freedom-fighter curriculum, I explained that I made those choices because of my own values. I read to the class part of my memoir where I trace my liberal roots to the influence of my hippie, anti-Vietnam, pro-civil rights big sister. A sister I adored. A sister who was nine years old when I was born and who protected me from a world I experienced as very harsh and cold. Naturally, she is deeply inside of me, deeply an influence on my values. When I read them my memoir excerpt, I was helping to create a critical consciousness, showing them that the choices a person in power makes do not have to be the only or the right choices but that all choices rise out of value systems—that there are many angles. Perhaps I had not let Aaron find an identity as a freedom fighter by not providing enough models of white males like Thomas Paine and Benjamin Franklin in those read-aloud discussions.

Once we open our classroom to children's voices with their diverse perspectives, once we try to provide democratic discourse (which happens to include positions opposite our own), how can we ever again see teaching as simply a matter of telling fifth graders what every fifth grader should know? Who decides what every fifth grader should know, and why? We still need to look at the voices that are conspicuously absent from most prepackaged curricula. We need to create a curriculum that includes the stories of the politically oppressed, the stories that were absent in our own elementary education. We need to break the silence.

Tommy was a child I found hard to love. He was one of the three boys who very vocally expressed their disgust and anger at having to read the biographies of King and Wells. I took his behavior personally, as if he had consciously decided that he would not do any work in my class or at home, that he could get by on his great charm, his ability to dominate every conversation, to expound on any topic at length whether he knew anything about it or not. I finally figured out that beneath his confident, obnoxious veneer was a boy in a lot of pain, but I couldn't get to his true self. His writing, when he did any, was as silly as he acted in class, backing away from anything with teeth—until the day the class read excerpts from their memoirs aloud at the Sixth Avenue Barnes and Noble bookstore. In that vast, cavernous store, amid the hubbub of two classes of nine- and ten-year-olds and their parents with video cameras, amid the hustle and bustle of strangers shopping for books, Tommy read his excerpt. His little-boy voice projected through speakers all over the store:

I'm Not the Only One

Last summer, I was just getting back from Cape Cod when my mom was checking the messages. One message was from my father. He called to tell me that I had a new sister, Lily: 9 pounds, 2 ounces. Born June 12, 1996. When I heard, I was really happy. When I tried to call him, the operator said that number didn't exist, which meant my dad changed his number. Two days later, I saw him in the street. When I asked what happened, he said someone was playing phone pranks so he changed his number. But the new number they gave him was the same number of an office, so they had to change his number again. Then he said he would call me the next day with the new number, but silly me, I believed him. He didn't call, and a few days ago I found out he moved to New Jersey, so it's impossible to even see him now. I used to wish I could see him, but not now. If he doesn't want to see me, that's his problem. If I could see my dad once more, I would ask "why?" But I would not wait for an answer, I would walk away. I've lost many people in my life, but I'm not the only one who lost someone. I'm not the only one who has missed someone. Although I've sometimes felt that I am, I still know, I'm not the only one.

People froze in place, listening to this boy's pain. The store grew silent. After the reading, parents and shoppers stopped to tell Tommy that he was a brave boy for reading that. Tommy's mother, who had been crying, told me, "He has never talked about it in front of so many people before." Tommy had reached outside of himself to take in the pain of all other children who have experienced loss. He wrote to understand, forgive, and find peace for himself and his audience.

Maxine Greene calls for people to revisit their own inner geographies, to dwell in their own biographies in order to hit upon the themes that matter in education: imagination, art and spirit, possibility, freedom. When we wander into our own inner core, our own true selves, we usually encounter pain. Sharing that pain with others reawakens the interrelationship between others' pain and our suffering. It builds a community based not so much on our own suffering but on the suffering of all those we encounter. And that invites our compassion; it invites action. The poet Adrienne Rich (1993) writes about the importance of "naming and mourning damage, keeping pain vocal so it cannot become normalized and acceptable" (242). Once Tommy had named his pain, and mourned it publicly, he became a changed person in my classroom. He spent the last two months of school listening to others, writing a great deal in his notebook, speaking from a more true self, and discarding the veneer of having it all together. For he doesn't have it all together, and now everyone knows it.

Tommy worried at first that the particular details of his experience were so private that they would not only be painful to write about but also be boring to anyone else. He thought that memoir should be about winning the Indy 500 or scaling Mt. Everest or surviving the *Titanic*. What he discovered is what all writers know, that where the pain is hottest, where you feel you have to put down the pen because you cannot possibly write those hot, prickly words or you will start crying and maybe never stop, that's where the writing begins to feel alive. In her memoir *Two or Three Things I Know for Sure* (1995), Dorothy Allison writes: "Behind the story I tell is one I can't. Behind the story you hear is the one I wish I could make you hear. Behind my carefully buttoned collar is my nakedness, the struggle to find clean clothes, food, meaning, money. Behind this moment is silence, years of silence" (39). In *Writing Toward Home,* Georgia Heard (1995) has a chapter called "I Could Not Tell." She writes: "Hidden away in the wordless places of my heart are my deepest secrets, wrapped in silence, and sometimes shame." She suggests beginning a writing exercise with the words, "I could not tell" and seeing where those words lead. She knows what Tommy found out, that "what's hidden away, stored up, in all of us is our most honest, electric, and true power" (52).

Memoir writing is not "therapy." The point is not to gush out in daytime talk-show fashion all the dirty secrets of our lives. But what it can do is make public our own and our children's personal, private experience. Most teachers are afraid to touch pain, especially with the children for whom we're responsible. It's so messy. And we are not psychologists. Some teachers have family members object to their children writing about "private family matters." And children may fear their family's reaction to their writing about "secrets, wrapped in silence." But Mary Pipher, author of *Reviving Ophelia: Saving the Selves of Adolescent Girls* (1994), is a clinical psychologist, and she says it is critical for children to learn how to manage pain. "All mixed-up behavior comes from people trying to escape suffering," she writes.

> People drink, hit their mates and children, gamble, cut themselves with razors and even kill themselves in an attempt to escape pain. I teach girls to sit with their pain, to listen to it for messages from their lives, to acknowledge and describe it rather than to run from it. They learn to write about pain, to talk about it, to express it through exercise, art, dance, or music. (257)

Children telling their stories is not an end in itself. The sharing of personal stories should encourage social engagement with members of the community. The sharing of stories should move the audience to want to take action to help others. In my class, we had learned from studying the biographies of freedom fighters that life stories are situated in social contexts. Moving from a messy wallowing in pain to personal writing that reaches out to the world, from notebook entries to a crafted piece of literature that has the public in mind, comes about as a result of the questions we invite children to explore in their memoirs (see Figure 10–1). It lies in the angle they choose to take. It lies in reflecting on the experience, in beginning to see that the things that happen in their lives are not completely private and secular but are conditioned by present cultures, by the social world. I posed questions as my students composed their life-story that asked them to set it in a social/historical/political context, to look at their story with the eyes of an anthropologist writing about a culture that seems strange and new.

What have you been silent about before that you have now written about in your memoir?

What themes about fairness do you see in your memoir?

What customs and rituals do the people in your memoir observe?

Was money an issue?

How did your memoir help you think about the perspective of others?

If there were more justice in life, how would your memoir be different?

What connections can you see between your memoir material and your social action writing?

Are any themes in the biographies you've read similar to issues in your memoir?

If you projected your memoir into the future, how could you *act* to change the world?

Figure 10–1 *Some Questions Toward a Social Angle in Memoir Writing*

The projects my students originated in the social action study were located in personal agendas, although they may not have recognized it. For instance, Leah, who wrote frequently in her notebook about the difficulty of living with a father who has "old-fashioned ideas about being the man of the house," chose to form the Women's Rights Association. She looked critically at her home situation, and despite the intense pain of that, created a strong feminist voice and wanted to inform the world about it. Tommy, who still had not broken through to his true self during the time of our social action writing study, formed the Kids' Rights Group, arguing that no one ever listens to kids, adults just make all the rules, forgetting they were once kids. With my help, he was able to look back at his choice of political action and see that it had not been random or without personal meaning: "I guess I feel I have no rights, since my dad felt he could just leave without any explanation. I guess he couldn't remember how he felt about his dad when he was a kid. How would he have felt if his father left him?"

The notebooks ten-year-old Ruth kept in her two years in my class were full of her personal stories, her questions, and her attempts to deal with the homelessness that confronted her every time she left her Manhattan apartment.

> Another ride on the subway to Queens, another hour to dad's house. Times I think of the homeless and not see them. A day that was different. "Go Mets, you know it!" Was she crazy? "Stand clear of the closing doors." A man was trapped between them. Five seconds, a hand pushed out the doors. She wasn't crazy. Everything went through my mind. "Yes, I'm homeless," she started. "I live in the subway. Yes, I'm begging. Asking for any food, candy, vegetable, soda, juice, or water." I remembered the water bottle nearly full. Slowly, she walked around. Nothing was given. No thought. No smile. I extended my arm, with the water to her. "Thank you, baby," she said, quickly twisting open the cap. She drank a lot. "Mm, cold too. They're fighting for elevators, yet got no water fountains." She soon left. I got looks from other people that confused me. Next stop a man came on with a bag. Showed I.D. "I work for food for the homeless." He said his name. Pulled out a juice bottle and sandwich in a bag. Walked around offering them to the needy. To another homeless woman he found. She took the sealed drink. It was then, or several subway stops later, I realized, I.D. wasn't needed. Eyes were.

During our social action study, Ruth and Min became involved in an organization called Blankets With Love, which provides various life necessities not covered by welfare. They researched facts about the organization, and they got the idea of setting up boxes at P.S. 11 to collect blankets, clothes, and household items. They wrote a letter to our principal, asking her permission to use the school as a collection site. They designed a flyer and gave a copy to everyone in the school. They made special yellow boxes and placed them in the school entryway. They wrote ads for the school newspaper asking for donations. Hundreds of plastic bags full of items were collected for Blankets With Love. At the graduation ceremony, they both received a special award from the city for service to the community.

I used to think the essential question in memoir was, *What is my place in the universe?* I still think that is an essential question. But after living with my students year after year, after watching them construct their life stories in writing workshop surrounded by friends and children they struggled to tolerate, after hearing them discuss other people's life stories and the social action writing study, I realized a better question might be, *Who am I in the midst of all others?*

I decided to have a different kind of memoir celebration that year. I invited parents to listen in while children read their memoir in their writing response group. The children read first, then talked about the process of writing the piece and how the members of their response group had helped them. As I walked from group to group, I heard children jump in to help another child tell the story of his process. I heard them thank one another for good ideas. I heard parents ask sincere and interested questions of other children in the group. Galina said:

We should really thank the whole class for our memoirs. We went through things as individuals, groups, and the class. We learned so much about each other in our response groups—it's like all our memoirs connected to each other, like Tommy's is part of Ellen's and Ellen's part of Ruth's and like that all the way around. So it's like if we combined all four memoirs, we would have one big book.

Jack read his piece about divorce being like a broken toy. Both of his parents were there. They looked sad and proud at the same time. I told all three of them how brave they had been: Jack to write the piece and read it aloud in front of both parents, his parents to listen. That was a space of freedom—created by the classroom and by Jack's parents—that allowed him to engage with the obstacles and the barriers, that allowed his voice to be heard and gave him the support he needed to sit with his pain and not run from it.

Flannery O'Connor said that anyone who survives childhood has enough material to write for the rest of his or her life. I want my students to do more than "survive" childhood. I want them to create their childhood with the words they read and write. Poet Tess Gallagher survived a childhood that she said was "terrorized" by her father's drinking and the quarrels of her parents. She writes, "Even when you think you are only a child and have nothing, there are things you have . . . and one of these things is words. When I saw I had words and that these could affect what happened to me and those I loved, I felt less powerless" (1983, 116).

When graduation day came for that class of students I had lived with for two years, whose memoirs had changed my thinking, and whose social action writing had changed the world, I said goodbye to Min and Ruth, Tommy and Leah, and Jack. Teachers continually love and then lose their students. I loved these particular children very, very deeply. I sent them off to their summer vacations, to the next grade, to middle school, to their life experiences, and I can't stop wondering what kind of spaces they'll find out there. Will they hold on to their strengths and passions? Will they continue to write about their lives? Who will break their silence?

BIBLIOGRAPHY

Allison, D. 1995. *Two or Three Things I Know for Sure*. New York: Penguin.

Anderson, C. 2000. *How's It Going? A Practical Guide to Conferring with Student Writers*. Portsmouth, NH: Heinemann.

Applebee, A. N. 1974. *Tradition and Reform in the Teaching of English*. Urbana, IL: National Council of Teachers of English.

Arendt, H. 1958. *The Human Condition*. Chicago: University of Chicago Press.

Atwell, N. 1986. *In the Middle*. Portsmouth, NH: Boynton/Cook-Heinemann.

Ayers, W. 1998. "Doing Philosophy: Maxine Greene and the Pedagogy of Possibility." In *A Light in Dark Times: Maxine Greene and the Unfinished Conversation*, ed. W. C. Ayers and J. L. Miller, 3–10. New York: Teachers College Press.

———. 2000. "Urban Schools." Presentation at Indiana University School of Education, Bloomington, IN.

Bakhtin, M. M. 1981. *The Dialogic Imagination,* ed. M. Holquist. Trans. M. Holquist and C. Emerson. Austin, TX: University of Texas Press.

Barber, B. R. 1984. *Strong Democracy: Participatory Politics for a New Age*. Berkeley, CA: University of California Press.

Barbieri, M. 1995. *Sounds from the Heart: Learning to Listen to Girls*. Portsmouth, NH: Heinemann.

———. 1998. Keynote Address for the Conference on English Education. Presentation at National Council of Teachers of English Spring Conference, Albuquerque, NM.

Barnes, D., and F. Todd. 1995. *Communication and Learning Revisited: Making Meaning Through Talk*. Portsmouth, NH: Boynton/Cook-Heinemann.

Berlet, C., and M. N. Lyons, eds. 1995. *Eyes Right! Challenging the Right Wing Backlash*. Boston: South End Press.

Bernstein, B. 1990. *The Structuring of Pedagogic Discourse*. London: Routledge.

Bigelow, B. 1994. "Testing, Tracking, and Towing the Line: A Role Play on the Origins of the Modern High School." In *Rethinking Our Classrooms: Teaching for Equity and Justice*, ed. B. Bigelow et al., 117–125. Urbana, IL: National Council of Teachers of English.

Bomer, R. 1995. *Time for Meaning: Crafting Literate Lives in Middle and High School*. Portsmouth, NH: Heinemann.

———. 1998. "Transactional Heat and Light: More Explicit Literacy Learning." *Language Arts* 76 (1): 11–18.

———. 1999. "Conferring with Struggling Readers: The Test of Our Craft, Courage, and Hope." *The New Advocate* 12 (1): 21–38.

Burbules, N. C., and S. Rice. 1991. "Dialogue Across Differences: Continuing the Conversation." *Harvard Education Review* 61 (4): 393–416.

Calkins, L. M. 1994. *The Art of Teaching Writing,* 2d ed. Portsmouth, NH: Heinemann.

———. 2001. *The Art of Teaching Reading*. New York: Longman.

Calkins, L. M., with S. Harwayne. 1991. *Living Between the Lines*. Portsmouth, NH: Heinemann.

Carbo, M., R. S. Dunn, and K. J. Dunn. 1991. *Teaching Students to Read Through Their Individual Learning Styles*. Boston: Allyn and Bacon.

Christensen, L. 1995. "Whose Standard? Teaching Standard English in Our Schools." In *Rethinking Schools: An Agenda for Change*, ed. D. Levine, R. Lowe, B. Peterson, and R. Tenorio, 115–128. New York: The New Press.

———. 2000. *Reading, Writing, and Rising Up.* Milwaukee, WI: Rethinking Schools.

Christie, F. 1989. *Language Education.* Oxford, UK: Oxford University Press.

Cisneros, S. 1992. "Eleven." In *Woman Hollering Creek.* New York: Vintage.

Clay, M. M. 1991. *Becoming Literate : The Construction of Inner Control.* Portsmouth, NH: Heinemann.

———. 1994. *Reading Recovery : A Guidebook for Teachers in Training.* Portsmouth, NH: Heinemann.

Clayton, E. 1964. *Martin Luther King: The Peaceful Warrior.* Englewood Cliffs, NJ: Prentice-Hall.

Cole, M. 1996. *Cultural Psychology: A Once and Future Discipline.* Cambridge, MA: Harvard University Press.

Coles, R. 1995. *The Story of Ruby Bridges.* New York: Scholastic.

Cope, B., and M. Kalantzis. 1993. *The Powers of Literacy: A Genre Approach to Teaching Writing.* Pittsburgh, PA: University of Pittsburgh Press.

Counts, G. S. 1932. *Dare the Schools Build a New Social Order?* New York: The Stratford Press.

Curtis, C. P. 1995. *The Watsons Go to Birmingham, 1963.* New York: Delacorte.

———. 1999. *Bud, Not Buddy.* New York: Delacorte.

Dahl, R. 1988. *Matilda.* New York: Viking.

Dahl, R. A. 1956. *A Preface to Democratic Theory.* Chicago: University of Chicago Press.

———. 1998. *On Democracy.* New Haven, CT: Yale University Press.

Dash, J. 1998. *We Shall Not Be Moved: The Women's Factory Strike of 1909.* New York: Scholastic.

DeFord, D. E., C. A. Lyons, and G. S. Pinnell. 1991. *Bridges to Literacy: Learning from Reading Recovery.* Portsmouth, NH: Heinemann.

Dewey, J. 1916. *Democracy and Education: An Introduction to the Philosophy of Education.* New York: Macmillan.

———. 1927. *The Public and Its Problems.* Athens, OH: Ohio University Press.

———. 1938. *Experience and Education.* New York: Macmillan.

———. 1959. *Dewey on Education: Selections,* ed. M. S. Dworkin. New York: Teachers College Press.

Dixon, D. A. 1999. "Creating Community Democracy in Schools: Overlapping Memberships as Potentials for Public." Jamaica, NY: New York State Political Science Association.

Dudley-Marling, C., and D. Searle, eds. 1995. *Who Owns Learning?: Questions of Autonomy, Choice, and Control.* Portsmouth, NH: Heinemann.

Dyson, A. H. 1993. *Social Worlds of Children Learning to Write in an Urban Primary School.* New York: Teachers College Press.

Edelsky, C. 1986. *Writing in a Bilingual Program: Había una vez.* Norwood, NJ: Ablex.

———. 1992. *With Literacy and Justice for All.* London: Falmer Press.

———. 1999. "On Critical Whole Language Practice: Why, What, and a Bit of How." In *Making Justice Our Project: Teachers Working Toward Critical Whole Language Practice,* ed. C. Edelsky, 7–36. Urbana, IL: National Council of Teachers of English.

Edwards, D., and N. Mercer. 1987. *Common Knowledge: The Development of Understanding in the Classroom.* London: Methuen.

Fine, M. 1998. "Greener Pastures." In *A Light in Dark Times: Maxine Greene and the Unfinished Conversation,* ed. W. C. Ayers and J. L. Miller, 209–218. New York: Teachers College Press.

Flannery, K. T. 1990. "In Praise of the Local and Transitory." In *The Right to Literacy,* ed. A. A. Lunsford, H. Moglen, and J. Slevin, 208–214. New York: Modern Language Association.

Fleischer, C. 2000. *Teachers Organizing for Change: Making Literacy Learning Everybody's Business.* Urbana, IL: National Council of Teachers of English.

Fletcher, R. 1996a. *Breathing In, Breathing Out: Keeping a Writers Notebook.* Portsmouth, NH: Heinemann.

———. 1996b. *A Writers Notebook: Unlocking the Writer Within You.* New York: Avon.

Frantzich, S. E. 1999. *Citizen Democracy: Political Activists in a Cynical Age.* Lanham, MD: Rowman & Littlefield.

Freire, P. 1970. *Pedagogy of the Oppressed.* New York: Continuum.

Fritz, J. 1976. *Will You Sign Here, John Hancock?* New York: Coward McCann.

Fu, D. 1998. "Unlock Their Lonely Hearts." *Voices from the Middle* 6 (1): 3–10.

Gallagher, T. 1983. "My Father's Love Letters." In *In Praise of What Persists*, ed. S. Berg, 109–124. New York: Harper & Row.

Gardiner, J. R. 1980. *Stone Fox.* New York: Ty Crowell Company.

Gardner, H. 1991. *The Unschooled Mind: How Children Think and How Schools Should Teach.* New York: Basic Books.

Gee, J. 1990. *Social Linguistics and Literacies.* London: The Falmer Press.

Gibson, J. L. 1993. "Political Freedom: A Sociopsychological Analysis." In *Reconsidering the Democratic Public*, ed. G. Marcus and R. L. Hanson. University Park, PA: Pennsylvannia State University Press.

Gilbert, P. 1989. *Writing, Schooling, and Deconstruction: From Voice to Text in the Classroom.* London: Routledge.

———. 1994. "'And They Lived Happily Ever After': Cultural Storylines and the Construction of Gender." In *The Need for Story: Cultural Diversity in Classrooms and Community*, ed. A. H. Dyson and C. Genishi, 124–142. Urbana, IL: National Council of Teachers of English.

Gilligan, C. 1997. Virginia and Leonard Marx Lecture. New York: Teachers College, Columbia University.

Goodman, K. S. 1973. *Miscue Analysis: Applications to Reading Instruction.* Urbana, IL: ERIC Clearinghouse on Reading and Communication Skills.

Goodman, Y. M., and A. M. Marek. 1996. *Retrospective Miscue Analysis: Revaluing Readers and Reading.* Katonah, NY: Richard C. Owens.

Goodman, Y. M., D. J. Watson, and C. L. Burke. 1987. *Reading Miscue Inventory: Alternative Procedures.* Katonah, NY: Richard C. Owens.

Gramsci, A. 1991. *Selections from Cultural Writings*, ed. D. Forgacs, G. Nowell-Smith, and W. Q. Boelhower. Cambridge, MA: Harvard University Press.

Graves, D. 1982. *Writing: Teachers and Children at Work.* Portsmouth, NH: Heinemann.

Greene, M. 1988. *The Dialectic of Freedom.* New York: Teachers College Press.

———. 1995. *Releasing the Imagination: Essays on Education, the Arts, and Social Change.* San Francisco: Jossey-Bass.

———. 1998. "Teaching for Social Justice." In *Teaching for Social Justice*, ed. W. C. Ayers, J. A. Hunt, and T. Quinn, xxvi–xlvi. New York: Teachers College Press.

Gutmann, A. [1987] 1999. *Democratic Education.* Princeton, NJ: Princeton University Press.

Harste, J. C., and R. F. Carey. 1999. "Curriculum, Multiple Literacies, and Democracy: What If English/Language Arts Teachers Really Cared?" Presentation at National Council of Teachers of English Annual Conference, Denver, CO.

Heard, G. 1995. *Writing Toward Home.* Portsmouth, NH: Heinemann.

Heath, S. B. 1983. *Ways with Words: Language, Life, and Work in Communities and Classrooms.* Cambridge, UK: Cambridge University Press.

Henkin, R. 1998. *Who's Invited to Share?: Using Literacy to Teach for Equity and Social Justice.* Portsmouth, NH: Heinemann.

Hindley, J. 1996. *In the Company of Children*. York, ME: Stenhouse Publishers.

Horton, M., J. Kohl, and H. Kohl. 1998. *The Long Haul: An Autobiography*. New York: Teachers College Press.

Kamberelis, G. 1993. "Critical Reexaminations of Writing Process." Charlotte, NC: National Reading Conference.

Kerr, A., A. H. Makuluni, and M. Nieves. 2000. "The Research Process: Parents, Kids, and Teachers as Ethnographers." *Primary Voices* 8 (3): 14–23.

Kohn, A. 1993. *Punished by Rewards: The Trouble with Gold Stars, Incentive Plans, A's, Praise, and Other Bribes*. Boston: Houghton Mifflin.

Laminack, L. L. 1998. *Volunteers Working with Young Readers*. Urbana, IL: National Council of Teachers of English.

Leland, C. H., and J. C. Harste. 1994. "Multiple Ways of Knowing: Curriculum in a New Key." *Language Arts* 71: 337–345.

Lemke, J. 1995. *Textual Politics: Discourse and Social Dynamics*. London: Taylor & Francis.

Lensmire, T. 1994. *When Children Write: Critical Revisions of the Writing Workshop*. New York: Teachers College Press.

Lewis, B. A. 1998. *The Kid's Guide to Social Action*. Minneapolis, MN: Free Spirit.

Lorbiecki, M. 1996. *Just One Flick of the Finger*. New York: Dial.

Mahn, H., and V. John-Steiner. 1998. "Introduction to Special Issue: Scientific and Everyday Concepts Revisited." *Mind, Culture, and Activity* 5 (2): 81–88.

Mann, H. 1957. *The Republic and the School: Horace Mann on the Education of Free Man*, ed. L. A. Cremin. New York: Teachers College Press.

Mayher, J. 1990. *Uncommon Sense: Theoretical Practice in Language Education*. Portsmouth, NH: Boynton/Cook-Heinemann.

McCormick, K. 1994. *The Culture of Reading and the Teaching of English*. Manchester, UK: Manchester University Press.

McDermott, R. P. 1997. "Wisdom from the Periphery: Talk, Thought, and Politics in the Ethnographic Theater of John Millington Synge." In *Mind, Culture, and Activity*, ed. M. Cole, Y. Engeström, and O. Vasquez. Cambridge, UK: Cambridge University Press.

Medearis, A. S. 1997. *Princess of the Press: The Story of Ida B. Wells-Barnett*. New York: Lodestar.

Moll, L. C. 1997. "The Creation of Mediating Settings." *Mind, Culture, and Activity* 4 (3): 191–199.

Morrison, T. 1987. "The Site of Memory." In *Inventing the Truth: The Art and Craft of Memoir*, ed. W. Zinsser, 103–124. Boston: Houghton Mifflin.

Murray, D. M. 1985. *A Writer Teaches Writing*, 2d ed. Boston: Houghton Mifflin.

———. 1990. *Write to Learn*, 3d ed. New York: Holt, Rinehart, & Winston.

Nieto, S. 1999. *The Light in Their Eyes: Creating Multicultural Learning Communities*. New York: Teachers College Press.

Nystrand, M., A. Gamorand, R. Kachur, and C. Prendergrast. 1997. *Opening Dialogue: Understanding the Dynamics of Language and Learning in the English Classroom*. New York: Teachers College Press.

Paley, V. G. 1992. *You Can't Say You Can't Play*. Cambridge, MA: Harvard University Press.

Pateman, C. 1970. *Participation and Democratic Theory*. Cambridge, UK: Cambridge University Press.

Perry, T., and L. Delpit, eds. 1998. *The Real Ebonics Debate: Power, Language, and the Education of African-American Children*. Boston: Beacon Press.

Piercy, M. 1986. *The Moon Is Always Female*. New York: Alfred A. Knopf.

Pipher, M. 1994. *Reviving Ophelia: Saving the Selves of Adolescent Girls*. New York: Ballantine Books.

Power, B. 1995. "Bearing Walls and Writing Workshops." *Language Arts* 72 (7): 483–488.

Rich, A. 1993. *What Is Found There: Notebooks on Poetry and Politics*. New York: W. W. Norton.

Rorty, R. 1998. *Achieving Our Country*. Cambridge, MA: Harvard University Press.

———. 1999. *Philosophy and Social Hope*. London, UK: Penguin Books.

Sabin, F. 1990. *Elizabeth Blackwell: The First Woman Doctor*. New York: Troll.

Shannon, P. 1995. *Text, Lies & Videotape: Stories About Life, Literacy & Learning*. Portsmouth, NH: Heinemann.

Shaughnessy, M. P. 1977. *Errors & Expectations*. New York: Oxford University Press.

Short, K. G., and C. Burke. 1991. *Creating Curriculum: Teachers and Students as a Community of Learners*. Portsmouth, NH: Heinemann.

Short, K. G., J. C. Harste, and C. L. Burke. 1996. *Creating Classrooms for Authors and Inquirers*, 2d ed. Portsmouth, NH: Heinemann.

Smith, F. 1988. *Joining the Literacy Club: Further Essays into Education*. Portsmouth, NH: Heinemann.

Smitherman-Donaldson, G. 2000. *Talkin That Talk: Language, Culture, and Education in African America*. London and New York: Routledge.

Stock, P. L. 1995. *The Dialogic Curriculum: Teaching and Learning in a Multicultural Society*. Portsmouth, NH: Boynton/Cook-Heinemann.

Sweeney, M. 1999. "Critical Literacy in a Fourth-Grade Classroom." In *Making Justice Our Project: Teachers Working Toward Critical Whole Language Practice*, ed. C. Edelsky, 96–114. Urbana, IL: National Council of Teachers of English.

Tharp, R., and R. Gallimore. 1988. *Rousing Minds to Life: Teaching, Learning, and Schooling in Social Context*. Cambridge, UK: Cambridge University Press.

Truman, D. B. 1951. *The Governmental Process: Political Interests and Public Opinion*. New York: Alfred A. Knopf.

Turner, A. W. 1987. *Nettie's Trip South*. New York: Simon & Schuster.

Varenne, H., and R. McDermott. 1999. *Successful Failure: The School America Builds*. Boulder, CO: Westview Press.

Vygotsky, L. S. 1962. *Thought and Language*. Cambridge, MA: Massachusetts Institute of Technology Press.

Walton, C. 1996. *Critical Social Literacies*. Darwin, Australia: Northern Territories University Press.

Wells, G. 1999. *Dialogic Inquiry: Toward a Sociocultural Practice and Theory of Education*. Cambridge, UK: Cambridge University Press.

Wenger, E. 1998. *Communities of Practice: Learning, Meaning, and Identity*. Cambridge, UK: Cambridge University Press.

White, E. B. 1952. *Charlotte's Web*. New York: HarperCollins.

Whitmore, K. F., and L. A. Norton-Meier. 2000. "Welcome to PKTI." *Primary Voices* 8 (3): 3–11.

Wood, D., J. S. Bruner, and G. Ross. 1976. "The Role of Tutoring in Problem Solving." *Journal of Child Psychology and Child Psychiatry* 17: 89–100.

INDEX